BELIEVE!

In memory of Wallace Mercer, 1946–2006

BELIEVE!

HEARTS: FROM TURMOIL TO TRIUMPH AT TYNCASTLE

MARK DONALDSON WITH GARY MACKAY
FOREWORD BY STEVEN PRESSLEY

MAINSTREAM
PUBLISHING
EDINBURGH AND LONDON

First published in Great Britain in 2006 by
MAINSTREAM PUBLISHING COMPANY (EDINBURGH) LTD
7 Albany Street
Edinburgh EH1 3UG

ISBN 978 1 84596 230 2 (from January 2007)
ISBN 1 84596 230 3

A catalogue record for this book is available from the British Library

Typeset in Frutiger and Galliard

Printed in Great Britain by
William Clowes Ltd, Beccles, Suffolk

ACKNOWLEDGEMENTS

MARK DONALDSON WOULD LIKE TO THANK
Steven Pressley, John McGlynn, Stephane Adam, George Foulkes, Doug Smith and Charlie Mann, among many other valued contributors, for giving up some of your precious time to help us produce this publication.

Anne and Iain Mercer for providing an emotional tribute to Wallace.

David Southern and Lawrence Broadie from Hearts. Freelance photographer Eric McCowat for all the excellent pictures. Davy Allen from London Hearts – the best Hearts website for stats bar none (www.londonhearts.com). Paul Kiddie and Rob Robertson.

Adam Findlay, Luke McCullough, Scott Wilson, Paul Robertson and Luisa Cairns at Radio Forth for allowing me this opportunity and also for your help with putting this book together.

Donald Walker and Mike Aitken at *The Scotsman* plus Richard Bath and Jim Duffy at *Scotland on Sunday*.

My girlfriend Laina for putting up with regular mood swings throughout the writing of this book.

Also, my mother and father – Marion and Andrew – for introducing me to the unique life of a Hearts fan on 19 October 1985!

GARY MACKAY WOULD LIKE TO THANK
Alex MacDonald and Sandy Jardine plus George McNeil and Bert Logan for allowing me to live the dream of playing for the club I supported.

Gilles Rousset and Ken Stott for being top blokes.

Ian McLeod, John Borthwick, Colin Sime, Wee Fergie, Jimmy Dunn, Stevie Anderson, Bread and Big Al for being great Jambos and good friends.

Also, to my granddad Jimmy for leading me along the right road as far as football allegiance goes.

Both authors would also like to sincerely thank Bill, Lindsay, Sharon, Graeme, Paul and all the team behind the scenes at Mainstream, plus all the other contributors to this book.

CONTENTS

FOREWORD

WHEN MARK AND GARY INFORMED ME THEY WERE WRITING a book about the incredible events of the 2005–06 season, I wondered if one publication would be sufficient to encapsulate everything that has happened to this football club in recent times. It's not been dull – I'll say that!

I was delighted when I was asked to pen the foreword. I know both Mark and Gary are extremely passionate about Heart of Midlothian, just like myself, and it pleases me greatly that they have taken time to produce a lasting record of our memorable campaign.

I will never forget the occasion when I finally got my hands on silverware while wearing a maroon jersey, but maybe I should have realised back in July 2005 that it wasn't going to be a normal season – an ongoing contractual wrangle meant I had to be listed on the teamsheet as a trialist for the pre-season friendly at East Fife! I signed a new contract in March 2005 to extend my stay at Tynecastle, but the introduction of new paperwork that summer caused some confusion. I refused to transfer my signature over to the new Scottish Premier League (SPL) contracts unless certain optional clauses were either removed or amended.

Clause two in the new paperwork stipulates that clubs can rip up a player's contract after six months if he is out injured and has not played a match during that time. I understand that clubs need to protect themselves, but there has to be an element of protection for the player, too. And there were other clauses in the contract I was not happy with, in particular one which gives clubs the ability to sack players when they don't adhere to certain rules. This, again, is very much in favour of the football club.

Despite all this, I was very confident we would reach a compromise – I was desperate for that to be the case. I have spent eight years at this football club, and they have been the happiest eight years of my career. There was no way I wanted to move elsewhere; it was just a matter of both parties getting round the table and coming to an agreement. In the end, we found a happy medium.

Pre-season was certainly an eye-opener, following the departure of so many of the squad during the summer, but we managed to make a fair bit of progress considering only four players who featured in the opening match against St Pat's in Dublin also played in the final friendly at Hull thirteen days later. During training sessions, I could see the quality of the players we were about to sign, and the supporters got to witness their ability when we played Middlesbrough at Tynecastle.

Prior to the first league game of the season, we had a meeting and were asked for our thoughts and expectations for the upcoming campaign. I said I believed we could win the title. I fully believe if you aim to finish first and end up second, then it's been a pretty successful season, rather than us aiming to finish third and perhaps coming fifth. You must aim as high as possible. If you set your goals high, then standards have to be met. They almost were . . .

There had been rumours and reports in the media that there was unrest between George Burley and Mr Romanov, but as a squad we never believed it would come to what happened. George had a great rapport with the players; we had grown to trust and believe in him, and we were extremely disappointed at what occurred. I did not agree with the decision, but, on the other hand, I accepted it because Mr Romanov is the man who is taking us forward. There have been other decisions made in the past that I have disagreed with, but this club would not be where it is without Mr Romanov's backing and influence.

I think the players should take enormous credit for their performance against Dunfermline on the day we were informed that George had gone. In the dressing-room beforehand, we simply wanted to get the game over and done with, give our best, and hope it would be good enough to get all three points; the time for reflection was afterwards. We went out and gave a very professional performance that day and managed to continue our excellent start to the season.

In the weeks that followed, though, I believe George's departure did affect the dressing-room. Many players that he brought in felt unsettled during that period – quite understandably, in my opinion – but after a short time, we kicked on again.

When Graham Rix was appointed, I honestly felt he was the type of guy we needed at the club. He was very much a players' manager who liked to coach and had a good rapport with his squad. He obviously arrived with 'baggage', and there was a mixed response from our supporters to his appointment, but as captain I was behind him from the start.

On the day Graham arrived, I had a long conversation with him over dinner at the Radisson SAS Hotel on the High Street in Edinburgh. I said to him we were very much a high-tempo team, we played an aggressive and positive style of football, and that was the main reason for our excellent start to the season. However, if you are going to be a manager, you don't want to be hung by someone else's rope. You have to do it the way *you* believe the team should play and the way *you* want the team to function. If that means change, then so be it; the players will try and adapt. Mr Romanov had obviously spoken to Graham prior to his appointment and had gauged the new coach's thoughts about how he believed football should be played. If that was why he brought Graham to the club, then the head coach *had* to put those thoughts into practice.

Footballers, in general, like to feel comfortable and enjoy being in a positive environment – one in which they can feel safe and wanted. But it was a very unsettling period – we had lost a manager with whom we had a great relationship. The club employed a new boss, and we had to try and build a similar understanding with him and develop that same trust and belief. That is unsettling for any player midway through a season.

The main problem we had when Graham initially came in was that our training changed and it affected us – it became more technical than intense. We were not that type of team, but, with time, I am sure we could have adapted. Full credit to Graham, though: after a few weeks, he recognised this and got us back to playing the way we felt most comfortable with. I would not criticise him in any way because I think when you arrive at a football club you have to try and get your team playing the way you believe football should be played. Graham Rix came in at a difficult time, and there was a settling-in period – perhaps he was the right guy but just at the wrong time . . .

I felt the situation following the match at Tannadice in February – when Graham announced that he had not picked the team – had to be addressed, but there was no way I was going to seek a meeting with Mr Romanov without the full backing of our dressing-room. Yes, I am the captain, but, ultimately, I have to have the support of the players I represent. It was important, therefore, that we spoke about the issue as a squad and discussed it at some length before voting on the best way forward.

It was a unanimous decision. We felt we had to address the problem of team selection with Mr Romanov and were given the opportunity to meet him. We had a good discussion; he is a very approachable man. He took on board what the players had to say, we spoke about it and the whole meeting was very productive.

People need to understand that we are faced with a situation that is very common on the Continent, just not here. It is almost seen as unacceptable in Scotland, but guys like Mr Romanov are putting serious money into football clubs – I don't think it's been fully highlighted just how much he has invested – and they want to have an influence on decision making. It can work, although it has to be managed properly. However, I should emphasise that the coach *must always* have the final say on team selection . . .

When Graham was sacked, I privately felt that Mr Romanov had made the wrong decision, because I thought the last thing we needed was more instability at that time. However, Valdas Ivanauskas was appointed quickly, and I thought he handled the situation extremely well. He quickly put his stamp on things, and the transition was extremely smooth – it did not affect the team in the manner it could have.

It is difficult to know if we would have had the same success if Graham Rix had stayed – we may have done, but we'll never know. I don't think, however, that Graham's departure affected us the way George's did.

There was no way I was ever going to end this foreword with any topic other than the Scottish Cup final! I didn't train much during the second half of the season because of illness and injury, and I spent a lot of time in the treatment room with Neil McCann, who was recovering from a knee injury. He constantly spoke about the 1998 cup final, saying it was the most enjoyable experience of his career. Neil is no stranger to winning silverware, but he still ranks that weekend as the best of his footballing life and was always going on about how great it was. He was correct in everything he said . . .

Saturday, 13 May 2006 was a day I don't think any of the players will ever forget. We endured a lot of upheaval during the season, and for it to end like that was fantastic. I think that day showed the true potential of Hearts.

The supporters were phenomenal at Hampden, and they were also outstanding the following day when we paraded the Scottish Cup on the open-top bus through the streets of the capital on our way to Tynecastle. It was simply exceptional. It made the players very proud and brought tears to the eyes of many Hearts fans. People forget it's not only the players who are affected during the season, the supporters are too. They are the ones who eat, sleep and breathe Heart of Midlothian Football Club, and they live for days like that at Hampden – it was the perfect way to end an incredible season.

Steven Pressley
Heart of Midlothian Football Club captain
September 2006

PROLOGUE

3 MAY 2006

THE TENSION WAS INSUFFERABLE. JUST MINUTES REMAINED. Fingernails were practically gnawed down to the knuckles. Tynecastle Stadium had never before seen scenes like it . . .

Hearts supporters were regularly checking their watches, willing the second hand to move quicker. The dream would soon become reality if only their beloved team could hold on to their precious one-goal lead against Aberdeen. The possibility of Champions League football for the first time was just around the corner.

Meanwhile, on the pitch, match referee Stuart Dougal – the man who would ultimately determine when the celebrations could begin – was being incessantly pestered by a frantic midfielder desperate for him to blow the full-time whistle. Goal-scorer Paul Hartley, along with nearly everyone else inside the stadium, was getting very anxious and impatient as the game entered stoppage time:

Paul Hartley: Oi, ref, how long to go? That must be about time up.

Stuart Dougal: One minute remaining, Paul.

PH: C'mon, ref – how long now?

SD: 30 seconds left.

PH: That must be time now, ref.

SD: Nope, 15 seconds to go.

PH: You are having a laugh. That's time up, surely.

SD: Five minutes extra, Paul.

PH: WHAT? Are you taking the p*ss?

'At that point,' says Dougal, 'I winked at Takis Fyssas and let him know I was about to blow the whistle. I just didn't let Paul see me!'

ONE

SAVED OUR HEARTS

TURMOIL AND TRIUMPH: TWO WORDS LOCATED AT OPPOSITE ends of the emotional spectrum but very much associated with life as a football fan, especially at Tynecastle. Being a Hearts supporter is never dull. Anyone seeking normality would be well advised to avoid EH11 – it's usually one extreme or the other for followers of the team. Heart of Midlothian just don't seem to do things the easy way!

Disappointment, unfortunately, has been more prevalent at the football club than success in recent times. Those old enough to remember the 1964–65 campaign will recall the heartache on the last day of the season as Kilmarnock beat Hearts 2–0 at Tynecastle to clinch the league on goal average. Fast-forward 21 years for more last-day drama as the Gorgie Boys lost the title at Dens Park on goal difference and were then beaten in the cup final seven days later by Aberdeen. In between, the club endured a Scottish Cup-final loss to Dunfermline in 1968, a 3–1 defeat by Rangers at Hampden in 1976 and relegation to the second tier of Scottish football in

1976–77, 1978–79 and 1980–81. The double whammy in 1996 was hard to take as Rangers lifted both the League Cup and Scottish Cup at Hearts' expense, but, thankfully, the good times returned in 1998 with victory against the Gers at Parkhead when the oldest trophy in world football still in existence – the Scottish Football Association Cup – returned to Tynecastle after a 42-year absence: at last, a triumph to celebrate.

Fresh from his Buckfast-swigging exploits on Gorgie Road in celebration of his favourite team bringing the Scottish Cup back to Gorgie the previous night, Edinburgh's Lord Provost (thankfully) changed into his best clobber to host a civic reception for the team at the City Chambers on the Sunday. This was followed by the trophy being paraded on an open-top bus through the capital. Lothian and Borders police estimated that more than 250,000 people lined the streets of Edinburgh city centre to salute the achievements of the players, while more than 16,000 supporters were inside Tynecastle as the team went on a lap of honour with the newly obtained silverware.

Two days after winning the cup, Hearts chairman Leslie Deans told the *Edinburgh Evening News* that the club was prepared to spend millions in an attempt to compete with the Old Firm on a regular basis. Hearts were prepared to speculate to accumulate, but there was one main problem: the funds required were simply not available. Ultimately, chasing this dream cost Hearts dearly and nearly led to financial ruin.

'Leslie Deans was criticised for promising to spend a lot of money,' said former club chairman Doug Smith, 'but I completely understand why he said it. Les is a fan just like the rest of us and perhaps got caught up in the moment. However, as chairman of a publicly quoted company, he should not have made those kind of comments, in keeping with Stock Exchange rules and regulations. Even though we won the cup, there was still not a lot of money to play with. We sold Neil McCann and only just made a profit. To keep the players together and pay them the wages that the market dictated at that time without putting season-ticket prices up was very, very difficult. The loss of David Weir, Paul Ritchie, Colin Cameron, Gary Naysmith and McCann over a three-year period was a blow to the club, but we simply could not compete with the wages the players were being offered in the English Premiership.'

The big-money signings promised by the board following the cup final did not materialise over the summer of 1998. Steven Pressley and Rob McKinnon, the only new faces at the club, both arrived on free transfers.

Despite this, supporters had a spring in their step as they left Tynecastle following the opening match of the 1998–99 season – Rangers had once again been put to the sword, this time in Dick Advocaat's first match in charge of the Ibrox side. The season continued to start brightly, including victory against Estonian opponents Lantana in the European Cup-Winner's Cup, until a hat-trick from Kilmarnock striker Ally McCoist condemned Hearts to their first defeat at the end of August. Over the next two months, the team won just once in normal time – 3–0 against Motherwell at Tynecastle. Even the arrival of Spanish winger Juanjo, French midfielder Vincent Guérin and striker Gary McSwegan from Dundee United – all on free transfers – failed to halt the slide.

As the team haemorrhaged points, dissent amongst the supporters was almost inevitable and the main target for their anger was chief executive Chris Robinson. He and the board were first jeered at a match against Kilmarnock in November 1998, despite Killie being beaten 2–1 that day, and it became clear that the fans were not happy with the direction the club was taking.

The situation had also proved frustrating for Jim Jefferies, but when he attempted to force Robinson's hand at a board meeting towards the end of 1998, he was told that the money was just not available. It was around this time that the chief executive tried to get rid of Jim Jefferies as manager after the team had won just twice in three months, but Robinson failed to get enough support from his fellow board members.

Hearts finished a disappointing season in sixth position behind the likes of St Johnstone, Kilmarnock and Dundee. It was not exactly the sort of campaign supporters had expected following the Scottish Cup win only 12 months previously. The decision by the board to reject a bid of £850,000 from Rangers for defender Paul Ritchie – who would subsequently leave on a free transfer 12 months later – epitomised the kind of year it was. All was not well at Tynecastle . . .

The increasingly strained relationship between the chairman and the chief executive finally fell apart during the summer of 1999, and it was no real surprise when Leslie Deans resigned as chairman in June of that year. Robinson had been awarded a new one-year contract in March, but Deans was deeply concerned about the club's financial plight and the rapidly rising debt. Deans was replaced as chairman by Newcastle-born businessman, and Hearts supporter, Doug Smith but retained his seat on the board.

The injection of cash that the club was so desperately in need of finally arrived in September 1999 when broadcasting company Scottish Media Group (SMG) invested £3.5 million in Hearts, accompanied by a £4.5 million loan. It was a familiar scenario, with media organisations keen to invest in football at a time when it was believed that clubs would soon be in a position to negotiate their own television rights. Sky were willing to pay £624 million for Manchester United until the Government's Monopolies and Mergers Commission vetoed their bid, cable giant NTL were in talks with Newcastle United,

Arsenal were courted by London-based ITV company Carlton Communications while Tottenham Hotspur had been approached by football investment trust ENIC.

The deal agreed with Hearts meant that SMG held a 19.9 per cent stake in the club with an option to increase this to 37 per cent over five years. They also had the option of converting their £4.5 million loan into shares if it meant making money on their initial investment.

Naturally, the news of the SMG investment was greeted with real enthusiasm by the supporters. The injection of a substantial amount of cash from a reputable media organisation was perceived to be an opportunity for Hearts to make the step up and perhaps even challenge the Old Firm more consistently. However, the full ramifications of the deal were not fully grasped by most observers. Leslie Deans, on the other hand, was sceptical about the SMG agreement from the outset, especially as a substantial part of the £8 million was in the form of a loan. He feared that an extra £4.5 million worth of debt could prove to be problematic for Hearts if the media company requested repayment after the money had been spent.

Of the initial investment, £1.2 million was given to Jefferies to strengthen his squad. Gordan Petric (£500,000), Antti Niemi (£400,000) and Robert Tomaschek (£300,000) were signed, a further £1 million was paid out for signing-on fees, £300,000 went on agents' commissions and a significant figure was spent on securing existing players on improved contracts. A bid of £850,000 for Motherwell striker Lee McCulloch was also turned down. As a result, the wage bill at Tynecastle rocketed. With a real lack of foresight, it seems that nobody at the club regarded this as a problem at the time, but the resulting debt would soon get out of hand.

The higher wage bill as a consequence of the new signings and improved player contracts put a heavy burden on the club.

Although the SMG money had allowed Hearts to make what seemed like progress, the club's revenues were insufficient to support an annual wage bill in the region of £5 million. With £250,000 being lost every month, the club found itself in a financially precarious position, one which needed to be addressed immediately. The only answer was to reduce the club's outgoings, so every first-team player was made available to the market at the right price.

Of course, this course of action deeply upset the fans, many of whom could not understand why the club was facing such difficulty so soon after receiving a huge financial boost. The supporters were rightly angered by the asset-stripping of their club and felt that something had to be done. Demonstrations became a regular occurrence at Tynecastle as the fans vented their frustration at the apparent mismanagement of their club.

The mood of the supporters was not helped when Jim Jefferies resigned. Jefferies was a Hearts legend, having secured the club its first silverware since the '60s, and the fans felt he had been forced out by Robinson. 'I never had a stand-up fight with Chris,' Jefferies told *The Scotsman* in April 2006, 'but he said things about me which were not true and wanted to take the club in a different direction, which meant it was best that I resigned.'

The search for a new boss took just over a month, culminating in the appointment of former Hearts player Craig Levein. The former Scotland international defender, who made 401 appearances in the maroon jersey before being forced to retire in 1997 after failing to recover from a knee injury, was selected by the Tynecastle board to replace Jim Jefferies after beating off the challenge of several other strong candidates. 'When a job as sought-after as Hearts comes along, you get a whole lot of applicants – big names mixed with computer-addicts who believe they deserve the position after guiding

Northampton Town through three divisions on *Championship Manager* and securing the Premiership title,' said Doug Smith. 'Well-known people in the game also applied, such as Bernd Schuster, but that was a non-starter. We had 20 serious applications. We then narrowed the field down to six and met three of them before deciding to offer the job to Craig.'

The three candidates who reached the interview stage were Eric Black, Stuart Baxter and Craig Levein. Neil Warnock, Steve Bruce and Peter Beardsley made up the longer list of six, and the board planned to speak to them if Black, Baxter and Levein failed to impress. 'As well as being chairman of Hearts,' explained Smith, 'I also had strong connections with Newcastle – the team I supported as a boy – and knew Freddie Fletcher well. I was also on good terms with a number of others at St James' Park, and as a result of that Peter Beardsley phoned me to express an interest in the Hearts job. I think initially Peter was keen on becoming a coach, but he impressed me during our telephone conversations, and I recommended to the board that he be considered as one of the final six.'

The interviews with Stuart Baxter, Eric Black and Craig Levein were held at the Clydesdale Bank Plaza, just off Lothian Road in Edinburgh, with Doug and four other board members doing the interrogating. 'Until that meeting, I had never really spoken to Craig before, and I had never previously met either Stuart or Eric,' said Smith. 'Stuart Baxter showed a lot of enthusiasm in wanting to move to Hearts. He'd spent a few years in Japan coaching Sanfrecce Hiroshima and Vissel Kobe – at the same time as Arsène Wenger was out there – and we were impressed when checking out his credentials. I spoke to Freddie at Newcastle, as well as Gordon Milne, who had also coached in Japan, and they both said that Baxter had consistently produced a team that performed extremely well, despite the financial restraints he was forced to work under.

'When we interviewed Stuart, he said he would love to come to Hearts, but his long-term ambition was either to coach at international level or to manage Aston Villa, and if either opportunity came along, he would ask us to break the contract. He was very honest about that, which we appreciated, but after the departure of Jim Jefferies, we felt we needed a period of stability.

'Craig Levein had a lot going for him. He had done very well at Cowdenbeath with limited resources, he was a former Hearts player who was well respected by people in the game and the supporters, and he was also very committed and intelligent. He also interviewed extremely well.'

The other person on the shortlist was Eric Black, but the board were annoyed when he went public and claimed he had been offered the job. 'I can categorically state that at no time did the board sanction an offer of employment be made to him,' said Smith. 'He may have met other directors at different times and been given a feeling that he was in the running. However, during those days at Hearts, it would have required a full board meeting to make any major decision, and at no point in time did that happen.

'Stuart Baxter and Craig Levein both impressed us. I thought at one stage during the proceedings that Baxter would have given us more international experience, but that was not what we needed at that time. We required someone like Craig, who would be initially accepted by the fans due to the time he'd spent at Tynecastle as a player. He was someone whom we all felt could do an excellent job for us.

'We sent people across to see the set-up at Cowdenbeath under Craig Levein, how he went about the whole approach of preparing for a game, but without him knowing that they were there. We spoke to a few influential people in the game, and within a few days we brought in his agent John Colquhoun and agreed terms. It has often been said that we chose the most inexpensive option, but we did not get him cheap. Craig was on a performance-related contract, and he ended up being a highly paid manager at Hearts.'

After taking over the hot seat from Jim Jefferies near the end of 2000, Craig Levein recorded nine wins and eight draws in the twenty-five games between December and May – the 7–1 victory over Dunfermline at Tynecastle in February was the highlight of his first season in charge.

Things were progressing adequately on the park, but that was not the case behind the scenes as the split between Chris Robinson and Leslie Deans intensified. Shortly after Levein's appointment, the chief executive unveiled plans for an alternative to Tynecastle, a project entitled the 'Towards 2005 Initiative', which consisted of the creation of a 30,000 all-seater stadium in the west of Edinburgh. Nothing, ultimately, came of the idea, but the proposal to quit Gorgie provided Deans with another reason, if one was required, to dislike Robinson, and the former chairman stepped up his bid to try and oust the chief executive from power. A consortium, led by Deans, was formed, and plans were drawn up to invest £8 million in Hearts over three years. However, there was one condition attached: Robinson would be removed as chief executive. The offer was made to the Hearts board in June 2001 but was rejected. When Deans went public two months later to inform supporters that the cash-strapped club had rejected the substantial investment from his consortium, the news went down like a lead balloon among Hearts supporters. They were becoming increasingly annoyed and frustrated that the man they loved to hate continued to hold the balance of power in the boardroom.

The fans felt something had to be done, and in November 2002 John Borthwick, the secretary of the Federation of Hearts Supporters Clubs, was approached by three members of the

Supporters Trust and asked to attend a meeting at the Grosvenor Hotel in Edinburgh; John asked Gary Mackay to accompany him. 'The purpose of the meeting was to see if it was viable for various fans' groups to come together and form one organisation in a bid to purchase a shareholding in the club, giving us some kind of say in the way it was run,' explained Gary. 'We felt aggrieved about many things at the football club at that time: mainly the precarious financial state that Hearts were in but also the change of name from Heart of Midlothian to Hearts Football Club and the alterations to the badge. Both had been done without any consultation with the fans and with no thought to our feelings. We believed it was time to have some sort of say in the way the club was run, and this was our bid to stimulate change.'

Hearts' debt continued to rise, prompting the board to examine the possibility of selling Tynecastle to raise much-needed funds. Alternative venues were looked at, and the prospect of Hearts and Hibs sharing a stadium at Straiton on the outskirts of Edinburgh was discussed with Midlothian Council, but both clubs eventually threw in the towel when it became abundantly clear that neither set of supporters was going to welcome the move.

Murrayfield Stadium was also mentioned as a possibility, and the venue was road-tested in October 2003 when Hearts faced Dundee in a bounce game at the home of Scottish rugby. The Supporters Trust informed Chris Robinson that it would continue to oppose leaving Tynecastle unless he proved that moving was the only option available. The chief executive maintained that there was no alternative and pressed for a move to Murrayfield, alienating himself even further from the supporters.

Stability may not have been evident off the park, but Craig Levein was proving a success as manager: his team finished third

in 2002–03, despite limited funds, and in the process secured a
UEFA Cup spot for the first time in three years. A tricky tie
against Bosnian side Željezničar was safely negotiated to set up
a second-round tie against Bordeaux. Three thousand Hearts
fans made the trip to France and watched their side record a
memorable 1–0 victory. Unfortunately, the French side won
2–0 at Tynecastle in the return leg to go through.

A couple of trips overseas meant supporters were able to
forget about the off-field turmoil back home for a few days, but
it was business as usual on their return to Scotland as fans once
again felt the need to make their feelings about Chris Robinson
known in public. By this time, the chief executive was adamant
that Hearts had to sell Tynecastle. To Robinson's credit,
however, he agreed to attend a public meeting at the Orwell
Lodge hotel in January 2004 at which he and Deans were given
the chance to put their points of view across. It was the first
time they had shared a platform since their acrimonious split.

I was MC for the evening. Standing in the middle of the
podium, with Robinson to my left and Deans and Robert
McGrail to my right, I tried to maintain some sort of order – it
was reminiscent of referee Zack Clayton telling Ali and
Foreman to behave themselves in Zaire in 1974!

Both Robinson and Deans were given the opportunity to
speak to the audience for ten minutes. Deans made an
impassioned speech, claiming a move to Murrayfield would
signal the death knell for the football club, while Robinson,
trying to make himself heard above all the insults aimed in his
direction, admitted for the first time that the club was on the
brink of administration unless Tynecastle was sold.

The pair verbally slugged it out, and the intended question-
and-answer session descended into chaos as Robinson was
constantly shouted down. The room was packed so full that it
wasn't until I called the meeting to a halt that I realised the bar

had remained open throughout the evening – at least that explained some of the behaviour from the floor!

A few days later, Chris Robinson announced the news that all supporters had been dreading: he had secured an agreement in principle with the Scottish Rugby Union for Hearts to play at Murrayfield from the start of the 2004–05 season, and Tynecastle was to be put on the market. This was a dagger through the heart of those who were determined to keep Hearts in Gorgie.

In one last attempt to try and halt the sale, three prominent members of the Supporters Trust – John Borthwick, Martin Laidlaw and Derek Watson – met representatives of SMG in Glasgow to discuss the purchase of the media organisation's 19.9 per cent stake in the club, but that plan, like so many others around that time, did not come to fruition. However, the fight continued and representatives of the Federation of Hearts Supporters Clubs and the Supporters Trust ensured that thousands of placards were printed with the words 'Robinson Must Go' on them for fans to hold aloft at games.

Gary Mackay, Freddie Glidden and Bobby Kirk were all guests of the federation at the Scottish Cup fixture against Celtic on Saturday, 7 February 2004. As well as enjoying the hospitality and company of two footballing greats – both Scottish Cup winners in 1956 – Gary was also asked to make the half-time draw on the pitch during the interval. 'I had been handed my placard outside on my way to the game, and it was neatly folded in my jacket pocket as I entered the stadium,' he said. 'I had been thinking about ways to try and highlight our campaign – what better way to do so than in front of a Europe-wide audience live on Sky Sports, who were broadcasting the game!

'In a moment planned with military precision, I strode onto the pitch at half-time and shook hands with Scott Wilson. I then took it upon myself to unfurl the placard with the words "Robinson Must Go" on it in front of a capacity stadium and thousands watching on live television.

'This abruptly ended my involvement with the half-time draw. Scott immediately cancelled our planned chat, perhaps saving me from a night in the company of Lothian and Borders' finest if my views had been broadcast! Needless to say, my presence on the park was no longer welcomed for the remainder of Robinson's reign . . .'

Following countless meetings over a period of 16 months, the supporters were finally in a position to launch their brand-new organisation at the start of March 2004. A huge question mark hung over the future of both the club and Tynecastle, so the federation and the trust agreed to team up under the banner of 'Save Our Hearts'. The campaign was designed to raise funds to purchase shares in Heart of Midlothian Football Club, and the newly formed group received support from people such as Robert McGrail, Leslie Deans and Peter McGrail as it set about galvanising a working group to somehow try and stop the impending sale of Tynecastle.

In a press statement at the launch of Save Our Hearts, John Borthwick outlined why he felt it was necessary to take that step and why he had become involved:

> The federation and the trust believe that the proposed move to Murrayfield will signal the death of the club. The figures released by the present board predict income of £7.5 million at Murrayfield for 2004–05. This is not credible given the present income of around £6 million at Tynecastle. According to our recent survey, two thirds of existing season-ticket holders polled said that they would not buy season tickets for Murrayfield. This in itself will cause profound cash-flow problems for Hearts.

'We worked tirelessly with several people to set up various fundraising events,' explained Gary, 'but I have to admit the wind was taken out of my sails slightly following a discussion I had with Robin Beith [former vice chairman of the Federation of Hearts Supporters Clubs]. We had a heated exchange in the Orwell Lodge in Edinburgh one Friday evening, and he suggested it didn't matter what Save Our Hearts did because it would probably be a waste of time. I suggested there was no chance of winning if people like him were not up for the fight. John Borthwick tried to cajole me afterwards, but Robin's views remained in the back of my mind throughout the campaign. I was desperate for Hearts to remain at Tynecastle and was prepared to do anything I could for those people who had ashes of family and friends scattered on the hallowed turf. Whenever we were faced with tough times, that drove me on, as did the words of Robin Beith that we wouldn't be able to succeed.'

Marches through Gorgie took place, more money-raising events were organised and the campaign received a huge boost when Peter McGrail agreed to donate an extra £50,000 every time the group mustered another £250,000. Nearly £700,000 was eventually raised courtesy of charitable donations (some anonymous), plentiful fundraising and even children giving their weekly pocket money. Gary Mackay put in £10,000. 'I felt it was the least I could have done, having never achieved anything tangible with Hearts,' said the Jambos legend. 'I had an unfailing belief that what that board was doing was wrong and would eventually have been hugely damaging – maybe even fatal – to our club. I wanted to put my heart and soul into the campaign to stop them, but what I put in was nothing compared to what so many other individuals contributed who didn't have a background of having played for the club. They became an inspiration to me with their devoted support to the football team on the pitch and to our cause off it.

'Some people disagreed with certain aspects of the Save Our Hearts campaign. I agree that a lot of the things we did were wrong, but they were a means to an end, including around 100 vociferous supporters standing outside [Hearts director] Brian Duffin's office in St Andrew's Square during a lunch hour calling for his resignation. Duffin seemed to be the main ally of the tyrant – we had to try and get to him and apply pressure on him to resign, but on that occasion we were unsuccessful.'

Doug Smith joined the Hearts board at the time of the club's flotation in May 1997 and was an independent director for two years before succeeding Leslie Deans as chairman in June 1999. Where Hearts played their football was by far the most contentious issue during his time as chairman. So many supporters were against selling Tynecastle and moving to Murrayfield, and that persuaded Smith to concede to *The Scotsman* in March 2004 that the board had yet to win the argument for both hearts and minds:

> There is a lot going on and plenty of dialogue about Murrayfield. What I appreciate, as we found at the AGM, is we have a 51–49 majority for the move. Now, for such a momentous decision, do you want to go to Murrayfield based on that narrow a majority? A lot of ordinary football supporters that I know from business are saying to me, 'Doug, I'm worried about Murrayfield.' You could argue that Fergus McCann had a similar concept [about the stadium] at Celtic Park that provoked a lot of criticism and opposition at the time. Ten years later and he's been proven right. I am spending a lot of time talking to people, and if we go forward with Murrayfield, the issue will have to be

decided at an EGM. When that happens, I think it must
be something that the vast majority of shareholders and
fans embrace. Right now, I don't think we're at that
stage.

A decision by SPL bosses at the end of March to grant Hearts
permission to play their football at Murrayfield the following
season effectively ended Doug Smith's hopes of remaining as
Hearts chairman in the long term. Furious supporters vented
their frustration at the decision outside Tynecastle; discontent
turned to anger when Chris Robinson arrived back at the
stadium following the meeting at Hampden Park, and the chief
executive was the subject of both verbal and, in one case,
physical abuse, although he did not press charges.

Hearts had now been given permission by the SPL to make
the short move to the home of Scottish rugby. The only thing
delaying the switch was the creation of a legally binding
document with the Scottish Rugby Union – both parties had
until the end of May to get it drawn up and signed.

There appeared to be no evident solution to the stadium
situation as far as Hearts supporters were concerned, but a
meeting in April 2004 between former chairman Leslie Deans
and Russian-born Lithuanian multimillionaire Vladimir
Romanov would have huge consequences for the future of the
football club. Edinburgh's Deputy Lord Provost Steve
Cardownie brokered the meeting, having been convinced that
the businessman he first met socially at a Scotland game in
Kaunas was a man of financial substance and, just as importantly,
was genuine. 'The best thing I could do was encourage him to
get involved with Hearts and then talk to the major shareholders
to see if they would be able to deal with him. Having established
both, I set up meetings,' said Cardownie.

Doug Smith's comments about Murrayfield in *The Scotsman*

in March meant it wasn't too much of a surprise when he tendered his resignation on 5 April 2004, admitting he had done as much as he could at Hearts. 'I was chairman of the board which unanimously decided to proceed with plans to move to Murrayfield,' said Smith. 'However, the success of the move will ultimately hinge upon the board's ability to build broad support among Hearts fans, and I am disappointed that we have not yet been able to achieve this. Accordingly, I think it is in the best interests of the company if I make way for a new chairman who will bring a fresh approach to the issue and offers the prospect of building a solid consensus for the stadium and financial challenges we face.'

A very astute man, Doug was always willing to take on board the views of the supporters; however, he realised that, as chairman, pushing through a course of action that would have dire consequences for the club was not for him, and he admirably fell on his sword. His resignation was one of the key moments in the Save Our Hearts campaign – Chris Robinson had lost a trusted ally. 'I certainly do not have any regrets about stepping down as chairman when I did,' said Smith. 'I felt it was the right decision to make at the right time, but I do miss being involved.'

Unlike Smith's decision to resign, the appointment of Labour MP George Foulkes as his replacement caught most people by surprise, not least Gary Mackay. 'Having never really come across many politicians in my life, I was probably as shocked as anyone when the announcement was made on Tuesday, 7 April that George Foulkes had been appointed chairman,' said Gary. 'Only 48 hours previously, Ian McLeod, John Borthwick and I had attended a meeting with George in the centre of Edinburgh to ask him to lend his support to the Save Our Hearts campaign.

'As we walked from the meeting, I said to Ian that it would

be great if George came on board and suggested flippantly that he would also make a great chairman for the football club. My throwaway comment became reality, and I'm not sure whether his appointment or the fact he said absolutely nothing during our meeting to suggest that he was on the verge of a switch to the boardroom at Tynecastle shocked me more!'

The appointment of George Foulkes as chairman was probably the best choice that the Save Our Hearts group could have wished for – within the boardroom, he worked diligently to help the group achieve their two final goals: first, to remain at Tynecastle; and second, to remove Robinson from office.

There is no doubting George Foulkes' loyalty to Hearts: he has been an active supporter for more than two decades and is a shareholder and Supporters Trust member. When he was appointed chairman, he posed for pictures with Chris Robinson on the roof of the tunnel at Tynecastle. In the photo, both men can be seen smiling as they hold a maroon scarf aloft. That was about as close as they ever got!

When addressing the media moments after taking over as chairman, George immediately contradicted Chris Robinson's long-held position by advocating a year's delay in the move to Murrayfield. That was to be the first of many differences of opinion between the pair. 'Chris Robinson would have nothing to do with a scheme put forward by Leslie Deans and Robert McGrail in which they proposed to buy Tynecastle and lease it back to Hearts – he refused even to talk to them,' said Foulkes. 'I spoke to both Deans and McGrail individually and together to try and find some way that they could come on board, but I came to the fairly inevitable conclusion that they would have liked to have done it but didn't have the resources. They might have been able to put something together to get a way in, but it's unlikely they would have had enough money to keep the whole thing going. The truth was, with the kind of wage bill and expenditure we had, we were just losing money every year.

'I ended up speaking to all sorts of people in a bid to find some sort of investment – even uncertain Nigerian businessmen. Thank goodness they never came up with the goods as I hate to imagine what might have happened!'

While investment from Nigeria did not materialise, it looked like the interest from Lithuania was on the wane as well. Following discussions with Leslie Deans in April, Vladimir Romanov had disappeared off the radar. It appeared his initial enthusiasm had diminished but perseverance from George Foulkes and Leslie Deans resurrected the investment. 'Les said to me one day, "Why don't you see if Romanov will come back in – I'd be willing to deal with him,"' said Foulkes. 'I managed to fix up a meeting in the House of Commons with Vladimir Romanov and persuaded him to come back. Thankfully, that was the catalyst for discussions with Chris and Leslie.

'It needed a lot of money to buy the shares and stabilise the position [of the club]. Eventually, I was able to persuade the board how desperate the situation was and that a move to Murrayfield simply would not work. The only person who had shown any degree of real interest in investing in Hearts had been Vladimir Romanov. Persuading Romanov to get back around the table was a crucial part of the whole plan. I do not like his management style, but if he had not come in, we would have been in dire straits. The pressure from Save Our Hearts played a major part in making it all possible.'

It didn't take George Foulkes long to make his mark: he confirmed before the end of the 2003–04 season that the club was to play domestic home matches at Tynecastle during the following campaign and would play their UEFA Cup ties at Murrayfield, pending approval from the Scottish Football Association (SFA) and UEFA (European football had been secured with another third-place finish). Foulkes had been in the post for less than a month but had already managed to buy additional time for Tynecastle – suddenly, there was a glimmer of light at the end of the tunnel.

Unfortunately for Hearts fans desperate for the club to remain in Gorgie, and just when it seemed that Foulkes had waved his magic wand to great effect, an announcement on 18 August 2004 provided a bolt from the blue. The statement confirmed that an agreement had been reached with CALA Management Group for the sale of Tynecastle for £22 million. Shareholders would get the chance to vote on the proposal at a specially convened EGM on 13 September. There were many occasions when the Save Our Hearts campaign seemed to take a step forward with their aims and objectives, but they were practically forced back to square one ahead of the EGM.

In front of the most volatile and raucous audience you would ever be likely to witness at such an event – three Hearts security officers were positioned in front of the top table as Robinson and his colleagues sat down, while police were stationed at either end of the hall and outside – the sale of the stadium was passed by a narrow majority. However, it was agreed that the deal would not be concluded before 31 January 2005, after George Foulkes insisted on a five-month get-out period to allow people to come up with alternatives.

George's wasn't the only contribution made that night, as Gary Mackay explained: 'Leading up to the event, George confirmed to us that Ian McLeod would be given the use of a projector screen to address the shareholders present with his response to the *Tynecastle: Not Fit for Purpose* document that had appeared on the official club website the previous December, but this was withdrawn just hours before the meeting. Ultimately, Ian was allowed to speak but could only address the audience verbally with no props – all his hard work seemed like it was being sabotaged. At times like that, you need strong characters, and Ian used all his experience to deliver a magnificently emotive speech on behalf of himself and thousands of other Hearts fans, all the time attempting to engage Chris Robinson in eye contact, which was not reciprocated, of course.'

As the evening wore on, emotions ran to a level not in keeping with such an event. With the validity of the *Tynecastle: Not Fit for Purpose* publication having already been questioned on more than one occasion by Ian McLeod, the final nail in its coffin was supplied by the man who was responsible for the design and redevelopment of Tynecastle in the '90s. Architect Jim Clydesdale confirmed to everyone present at the EGM that the pitch would be, in fact, compliant with forthcoming UEFA regulations if there was a will on behalf of the football club to implement minor changes at a cost of just £100,000, including the removal of a few rows of seats in the Roseburn Stand resulting in a reduction of capacity of less than 500.

'On leaving the meeting that night, I felt a warm glow,' said Gary. 'That was the catalyst for us to push on and give the chairman as much support as we could in his attempts to attract new investment into the football club while continuing to fend off the imminent sale to property giants CALA.'

Less than a week after the stormy EGM at Tynecastle, Vladimir Romanov sent two representatives – including Sergejus Fedotovas, one of his key aides – to East End Park to watch Hearts lose 1–0 to Dunfermline. The foreign pair were in Scotland for discussions with Hearts' major shareholders – Chris Robinson, Leslie Deans, Robert McGrail and SMG – as Romanov stepped up his bid to invest in the club.

The month ended on a high on two counts for Save Our Hearts campaigners and supporters: a magnificent 2–2 draw in Braga ensured Hearts' progression to the inaugural group stage of the UEFA Cup, and while the team was in the northern Portuguese city it was revealed that Robinson had finally agreed to sell his 19.6 per cent stake in the club to Vladimir Romanov (although the deal was not concluded for another four months). There was finally more than just light at the end of the tunnel for Save Our Hearts after a long and arduous campaign – the end was in sight!

The draw for the inaugural group stage of the UEFA Cup could not really have been much harder for Hearts with Feyenoord, Schalke, FC Basel and Ferencváros providing the opposition. Two days prior to the match against Feyenoord in Rotterdam, Vladimir Romanov increased his shareholding in the club to 29.9 per cent after purchasing a 10.3 per cent stake from former chairman Leslie Deans. That left the club on the verge of a takeover by Romanov. On the field, the Jambos slumped to a 3–0 defeat in Holland in what turned out to be Craig Levein's last European match in charge of Hearts. A 1–1 draw against Dundee United at Tannadice the following week – with Hearts watched by Romanov in the flesh for the first time – proved to be Levein's swansong as he headed south to join Leicester City.

Levein did not even have a chance to warm the managerial hot seat at the Walkers Stadium before Caley Thistle boss – and Hearts hero – John Robertson was made the favourite by the bookies to replace his former teammate at Tynecastle. It was no surprise, therefore, when Robbo was appointed the day before the second UEFA Cup Group A match against Schalke at Murrayfield on 4 November, although team selection for the game against the Germans was made by coach John McGlynn.

Vladimir Romanov swiftly announced his approval of the appointment through one of his Lithuanian spokesmen. It was to be the last time Romanov would need an Eastern European colleague to put his point across to the media north of the border because a Scottish-based public-relations agency was chosen to represent him in the UK. The company assigned to handle the account was Weber Shandwick, and the man assigned the task of becoming Romanov's UK spokesman was associate director Charlie Mann, better known for his involvement most Saturdays on BBC Radio Scotland's *Sportsound* football show. 'The Lithuanians wanted an agency in Scotland that had a business connection, a news connection and a football connection,' said Mann. 'After winning the contract, it was important for me to meet Vladimir Romanov in his territory. I would never have taken on the project unless I had cast-iron guarantees that this man had the best interests of the club at heart. I flew over to Lithuania with a bit of trepidation, having never previously visited an Eastern Bloc nation. I took a taxi from my hotel in central Vilnius to the office of the agency that Romanov uses over there. That was followed by another cab to a Ūkio Bankas building in another part of the Lithuanian capital. I got out the taxi believing I had reached his office . . . How wrong I was!

'A huge Mercedes with blacked-out windows swiftly arrived, and I was told that we had to make our way to Kaunas, a drive of about an hour. When we arrived, we negotiated our way down some back streets and then a dirt track behind a very imposing building before eventually reaching a basement. Three burly-looking chaps blocked the doorway. They grunted and eventually let us through and into the lift. We reached the 15th floor, and I could not believe my eyes – I was led into a palatial office and was met by Liutauras Varanavičius, who introduced himself in perfect English. We were called into Mr Romanov's office. Liutauras, Sergejus Fedotovas, Mindaugas Majauskas [Lithuanian PR] and myself sat opposite each other at a grand old table. Vladimir sat in a big chair at a huge desk before deciding to come and join us. He then sat imposingly at the top of this huge table, as if he was chairing proceedings. There were piles of papers around a room that contained good-quality older furniture. There were also lots of pictures on the walls – including one of Tynecastle.

'When I was given the chance to speak to Mr Romanov, I outlined our plans, and it was translated for his benefit. The Lithuanians then chatted amongst themselves, in front of me, and I knew – despite not understanding a word of what they were saying – this was not a good conversation because of the look on their faces. We all shook hands and left the room. I immediately asked Mindaugas what on earth was going on. He said Romanov was asking his fellow countrymen why he needed PR and why he needed me – what would I deliver to him? Mindaugas moved to quickly allay my fears, explaining that Vladimir was on board even although it seemed to me he was not at all happy. I had asked him some fairly hard questions regarding his involvement in Hearts and how sincere he was. Eventually, I received the answers I was looking for, but my initial involvement with Vladimir Romanov showed me that he was not a person with whom you would want to mess!'

Meanwhile, it didn't take John Robertson long to taste success as Hearts manager – Robbie Neilson's late winner secured a magnificent 2–1 win away to FC Basel to keep hopes of progress in the UEFA Cup alive (although this was ultimately dashed by a 1–0 defeat at Murrayfield by Hungarian champions Ferencváros the following month). Robbo joined in with the celebrations in the dressing-room after the match but experienced the first sign of the new regime having a direct input at the club when Anatoly Byshovets – one of Vladimir Romanov's lieutenants who had been lingering around Tynecastle at that time – instructed the celebratory music to be turned down and the players to start focusing on the next game against Rangers three days later. It wasn't the last time there was to be interference from above . . .

There have been many important dates in the recent history of Heart of Midlothian Football Club but perhaps none more so than 21 December 2004. Vladimir Romanov called an EGM to stop the sale of Tynecastle. The club was not out of the woods at that time, despite Romanov's financial input, and was thrown into fresh turmoil when the EGM to block the sale of the stadium was postponed for three weeks on the orders of the Hearts board – they wanted additional time to check the validity of Romanov's business plan. An official statement was released to the press:

> Further clarification and formalisation of the proposals is required. The Hearts board recognises this cannot be done prior to the EGM on Monday and, therefore, the EGM should be adjourned to give the Hearts board an opportunity to give due consideration to the proposals. The directors intend that the chairman seeks the consent of shareholders at the EGM to adjourn the meeting until 27 January.

In a stunning twist, however, Romanov arrived at Tynecastle on the morning of Monday, 10 January 2005 unannounced and insisted to the board that the meeting should go ahead as planned, instead of being adjourned for another three weeks. He eventually got his way courtesy of the fact that he owned more than 10 per cent of the shares in the club, and a vote was taken in the Gorgie Suite at Tynecastle that day to annul the sale of the stadium to CALA Management Group. The prospective owner had promised Hearts several million pounds of investment if shareholders voted to scrap the controversial proposal to sell the stadium.

At the meeting, 70.2 per cent of the votes were cast in favour of the proposal – ironically, Chris Robinson was obliged to vote with the Baltic banker under the terms of the initial agreement to sell his shares. Vladimir Romanov, subject to getting board approval at the end of the month, was the fans' new saviour.

'It was a historic day for Heart of Midlothian and all its supporters for two reasons,' said Gary Mackay. 'The first and most crucial decision for the future of the club was the agreement reached to withdraw from the deal with CALA for the sale of the stadium. Second, but every bit as important, was the stage-managed arrival at the EGM of our new owner-to-be.

'The atmosphere in the Gorgie Suite was in total contrast to the previous EGM in September. Vladimir Romanov – following a speech read out on his behalf by Sergejus Fedotovas – was given a standing ovation as he departed the venue. Only four months beforehand, I had attended the previous meeting when the presence of police was required to ensure the safety of certain individuals. This was undoubtedly a huge step forward in the progression of our famous club.'

Hearts fans celebrated as if they had won the Scottish Cup again; shareholder and supporter Ian Dickson from Penicuik was full of praise for the man who he believed had helped save the club from oblivion. 'He stage-managed his entrance to the Gorgie Suite that day to perfection, and the fans and shareholders in attendance immediately felt they were in the presence of somebody rather special. I happened to be sitting just three rows behind him when he eventually took his seat. If first impressions count, then he certainly made an impact on me.'

However, Vladimir Romanov nearly did not attend that vital meeting at all. 'The EGM in the Gorgie Suite on 10 January 2005 was arranged so that Vladimir Romanov came in slightly after everybody else, but, in fact, that morning he was not even going to attend,' said Charlie Mann. 'I was called to a meeting at the Balmoral Hotel with him, Liutauras and Sergejus – he said he did not want to go to the EGM. He was incandescent with rage because some of the coverage in the weekend newspapers had been very negative and was not very complimentary about either his character or his plans for Hearts.

'I insisted that he attend the meeting. Had I not done so, and had he subsequently not attended, then I don't know what would have happened. I am not claiming the takeover would not have happened, but I was very forceful in those talks and told him he *must* attend after calling the EGM. The rest is history – sometimes he does listen to advice and sometimes he does not!'

The mood among supporters was buoyant following the meeting in the Gorgie Suite, yet the fans were unaware that the atmosphere behind the scenes was not quite as positive. Vladimir Romanov's decision to send 20 footballers from Eastern Europe to Scotland for a trial match – arranged by Anatoly Byshovets – did not go down too well with John Robertson. The head coach was kept in the dark throughout the planning stage, although he was given the opportunity to sign any of the players if he felt they were good enough. Robbo decided that four of the twenty were worth short-term contracts – Lithuania's Player of the Year Andrius Gedgaudas, Saulius Mikoliūnas, Gediminas Vičius and Marius Kizys – but only Mikoliūnas and Kizys eventually signed. It was reported at the time that Gedgaudas and Vičius were not fit enough to sign immediately, but the pair decided against moving to Scotland after expressing concerns to FBK Kaunas coach Valdas Ivanauskas that they would only be fringe players at Tynecastle and would not get a regular game.

January 2005 had been full of cheer for Hearts supporters

following the decision to stay at Tynecastle, but the first day of February produced the news that everyone connected with Save Our Hearts had been waiting for – the resignation of the chief executive after Vladimir Romanov finally completed a deal to purchase Robinson's 19.6 per cent shareholding. 'It was difficult to contain our celebrations that day after finally getting rid of the man we loved to hate,' said Gary Mackay.

Just a few days after the formal withdrawal from the agreement to sell Tynecastle to CALA was confirmed in a statement to the Stock Exchange, the club announced another significant piece of news: Hearts switched their main banking facilities from Halifax Bank of Scotland (HBOS) to Ūkio Bankas, the Lithuanian bank in which Romanov has a significant interest. While HBOS still held the account used by the club for their day-to-day business, Ūkio Bankas became the main debt provider.

It had been a long hard struggle, but finally the threat of a permanent flit to Murrayfield had been extinguished, while the first steps had been taken towards a complete restructuring of the club's finances. After months of negativity, Hearts chairman George Foulkes was delighted to get the chance to finally accentuate the positives. 'It is a very exciting time for Hearts,' he said. 'It means that, financially, we are on a sound basis and are no longer being forced or required to sell Tynecastle. The new board of directors can now sit down in an unhurried way and plan for the future of the club.

'The first option, our preferred option if it is possible, is the redevelopment of Tynecastle, and I'm more optimistic that we can find a way to achieve that. If not, then we will look at our second option of finding a suitable site for a new stadium.

'We now have a bank which is giving us better terms and not putting pressure on us to sell. We are getting funding to strengthen the playing squad, and we have the opportunity of sitting down and seeing how we can develop the club. It is a massive turnaround from the position we were in several months ago.'

It was all change, then, at Tynecastle at the start of February, especially in the boardroom. Sergejus Fedotovas replaced Robinson as chief executive while Romanov's son Roman became a non-executive director. Lithuanian Football Association president – and one of Romanov's closest business advisers – Liutauras Varanavičius was also brought onto the board to replace former director Brian Duffin, who resigned.

The appointment of Varanavičius raised a few eyebrows at the SFA offices at Hampden – the president of a national association becoming a director of a club from another country was certainly not the norm. Even FIFA vice-president David Will found it strange. 'It's somewhat unusual, to say the least, to have a president of a national association seeking to be a director of a Scottish club,' said Will, who is from Brechin. 'However, I've had a look and haven't seen anything in the FIFA or UEFA statutes that says he can't be a director. It comes down to the SFA's own rules and criteria for whether a person is acceptable or not.'

SFA bosses quickly consulted their rulebook to see if the appointment could be challenged but were unable to come up with any argument against either Hearts or Varanavičius. When asked, a spokesman for the association said, 'The general principle is unusual and hasn't been foreseen. There's nothing specific mentioned in our articles about this eventuality, but you can understand there are concerns about the principle and whether this is an acceptable move. The difficulty is the cross-border aspect of having people involved in two different countries. It's not something we would particularly welcome.'

Whether they welcomed it or not, there was nothing the SFA could do about it, and for the next 371 days, Liutauras

Varanavičius served as a non-executive director on the Hearts board.

On the park, the rest of the season was average by Hearts' standards – reaching the semi-finals of the League Cup and the Scottish Cup was about as good as it got, and the team eventually finished fifth in the SPL. This was not acceptable as far as Vladimir Romanov was concerned, and he got rid of his first Hearts manager following a review of the entire football club.

John Robertson had only been head coach at Tynecastle for seven months but parted company with the club after rejecting a lesser role. The former Hearts striker spent several hours discussing his future with the recently appointed chief executive Phil Anderton the day after the 2–1 defeat by Rangers at the beginning of May 2005 but turned down the role of assistant head coach. The search was on for his replacement . . .

TWO

THE BURLEY ERA

JUNE 2005

THE LIST OF NAMES INITIALLY CONSIDERED TO REPLACE JOHN Robertson as head coach of Hearts was like a *Who's Who* of top football managers. From Gérard Houllier to George Graham, Kevin Keegan to Sir Bobby Robson – the club was certainly aiming for the best. Chief executive Phil Anderton drew up two strategies in a bid to find the right man:

> Strategy A: Proven UK track record at the highest level with 'star' name to excite and attract supporters. High cost – high expected return on and off the field.

> Strategy B: Proven track record of step-changing performance of UK club(s) at a high level without 'star' name attraction. Lower cost – expected to deliver on the field.

Nine star names who matched the Strategy A criteria were selected for consideration; a further ten names were considered when the list for Strategy B was drawn up:

A: Sir Bobby Robson, Gérard Houllier, Graeme Souness, Ron Atkinson, Kevin Keegan, Gordon Strachan, George Graham, Co Adriaanse and David Platt.

B: George Burley, Billy Davies, Neale Cooper, Steve Cotterill, Gary Johnson, Dave Jones (also applied), Gary Megson, Joe Royle, Paul Sturrock and Peter Taylor.

The new man did not necessarily have to come from the Strategy A list; it was a case of finding the best person available and the right man for Hearts.

The club also received several applications from, and on behalf of, a wide variety of people. The hierarchy initially considered the following 16 names from 13 different nations before drawing up a shortlist:

Gilbert Bodart (Belgian) – The former Belgian international keeper, who won 12 caps for his country, spent 15 years with Standard Liège between 1982 and 1997 and played against Hearts in both legs of the UEFA Cup second-round tie in 1992. Bodart took over as manager of Belgian side La Louvière when he finished playing but resigned in February 2006 amid allegations that he was involved in a gambling scandal that rocked Belgian football.

Craig Brown (Scottish) – Brown was appointed manager of Scotland in 1993 after coaching the national Under-

16 side to the final of the FIFA Under-16 World Cup, held in Scotland in 1989. The former Falkirk and Dundee player also led the Under-21s to the semi-finals of the European Championships in 1992. During his time in charge of the senior squad, Brown led the country to qualification for Euro 96 and the 1998 World Cup but resigned in 2001 after failing to qualify for Euro 2000 and the 2002 World Cup. He went on to manage Preston North End between 2002 and 2004 before taking up the role of international representative at Premiership side Fulham.

Nigel Clough (English) – Most famous as a skilful attacking midfielder with Nottingham Forest, where his father, Brian Clough, coached him. Clough junior, who won 14 caps for England, moved into management in October 1998 when he took over as player–manager of non-league Burton Albion – he is still plying his trade at the Pirelli Stadium.

Dave Jones (English) – Jones began his managerial career with Stockport in 1995, and his success at Edgeley Park earned him a move to Southampton ahead of the 1997–98 season. During the 1999–2000 season, he was arrested on charges of alleged child abuse during his employment as a care worker in the late 1980s. Southampton suspended their manager on full pay in January 2000 until the case was resolved. When the case eventually came to court, it was thrown out in its first week. The judge recorded a not-guilty verdict and commented that proceedings should never have reached the trial stage.

Dariusz Kubicki (Polish) – A former Legia Warsaw player who also had spells at Aston Villa, Wolves, Sunderland, Tranmere, Carlisle and Darlington before moving back to Legia Warsaw as boss, Kubicki took over as manager of Polonia Warsaw in the summer of 2005 after failing to land the Hearts job.

Stefano Impagliazzo (Brazilian) – Impagliazzo, a little-known Italian-born Brazilian, qualified as a professional coach in Italy and was employed by Al-Ansar in Saudi Arabia. He subsequently worked with teams in Bahrain and Brazil.

Augusto Inácio (Portuguese) – Inácio took over as the coach of Beira-Mar in Portugal in the summer of 2004 and led the team to the 2006 *Liga de Horna* (second division) title, securing the club's return to the top flight of Portuguese football. He previously had spells with Vitória de Guimarães, Sporting, Marítimo and Felgueiras, as well as being involved with Al-Ahli in Qatar and Belenenses from Lisbon.

Lothar Matthäus (German) – A World Cup winner with West Germany as a player and the European Footballer of the Year in 1990, Matthäus left Bayern Munich in the summer of 1988, denying him the chance to face Hearts in the UEFA Cup quarter-final! Matthäus first tasted managerial success in 2003 when he won the Serbian title with Partizan Belgrade. The German legend started his coaching career with SK Rapid Vienna in 2001 and has now returned to Austria with SV Salzburg, working alongside Giovanni Trapattoni, following a two-year stint as national coach of Hungary and an ill-fated spell in charge of Brazilian side Clube Atlético Paranaense.

Ivica Osim (Bosnian) – Began life as a coach with Željezničar in 1978 then took over as coach of Yugoslavia, holding the post between 1986 and 1992. Osim spent nine seasons in charge of Austrian side Sturm Graz before becoming boss of Japanese side JEF United in 2003. In July 2006, Osim was appointed the manager of the Japanese national team.

Graham Rix (English) – Rix won 17 caps for England during his 11 years as a player with Arsenal, winning the FA Cup in 1979. He joined Brentford on loan in 1987 before heading to France for spells with Caen and Le Havre. Rix came back to the UK in 1992 to join Dundee before beginning his coaching career with Chelsea the following year. In March 1999, Rix was sentenced to 12 months in prison for having unlawful sex with a 15-year-old girl. The former England international took over as manager of Portsmouth in 2001 and was then in charge at Oxford United for eight months between March and November 2004, winning just six of his twenty-nine games. He was successful with his second application for the Hearts job and moved to Tynecastle in November 2005.

José Romão (Portuguese) – Romão is little known outside his homeland following a journeyman career as both a player and manager. He took over as head coach of the Portuguese Olympic team following spells in charge at Vizela, Penafiel, Chaves, Vitória de Setúbal, Famalicão, Belenenses, Tirsense, Académica and Alverca.

Ivo Sajh-Scheich (Slovenian) – Sajh-Scheich began his coaching career with FC Beltinci in Slovenia before moving on to FC Tahhadi in Libya. The Slovenian took over as technical director of the Indian national team and held the post until June 1998, during which time he wrote a book on youth coaching. His travelling continued in 2000 when he was appointed as the director of coaching and football development in Myanmar!

Jacques Santini (French) – The veteran coach has been involved with many French clubs, including Toulouse, Lille and Lyon (where he won *Le Championnat*), as well as coaching the French national team between 2002 and 2004. Santini had a short, unsuccessful spell as coach of Tottenham Hotspur that resulted in his resignation after just 13 matches – it's claimed a series of disputes with sporting director Frank Arnesen led to his departure. Santini replaced the legendary Guy Roux at Auxerre after failing with his application for the Hearts job but was sacked in May 2006 because of his failure to secure European qualification for the French side.

Frank Stapleton (Irish) – Stapleton won 71 caps for the Republic of Ireland during a playing career with Arsenal, Manchester United, Ajax, Derby and Blackburn Rovers. He took over as player–manager of Bradford City in 1991 and spent three years at Valley Parade before heading to the United States to coach New England Revolution. Stapleton briefly returned to English football in 2003 as a specialist strikers' coach with Bolton Wanderers.

František Straka (Czech) – Quite a character . . . Straka spent nine years as a player with Sparta Prague (1979–88) before moving to Germany with Borussia Mönchengladbach and taking German citizenship in 1988, renaming himself 'Franz'! He began his coaching career in 1996 with Wuppertaler and registered as a licensed FIFA agent in 1998 before moving back into management with Wuppertaler (again), Teplice and Sparta Prague, whom he led into the Champions League in 2004. Straka applied for the Hearts job but failed to secure a move to Tynecastle so decided to move into politics with the Czech Christian Democrats in September 2005. He attempted to stand as a candidate in the Czech parliamentary elections but withdrew from the list of candidates after alleged problems over his citizenship. Straka moved back into football management in the summer of 2006 when he joined Austrian side FC Wacker Tirol.

Walter Zenga (Italian) – Formerly one of the world's top goalkeepers, Zenga won 58 caps for his country before moving into management. He started off life as a coach in 2001 with FC Brera in Italy before heading to Romania for three years, where he took charge of both National and Steaua Bucharest. Zenga joined Red Star Belgrade for the 2005–06 season and led Hearts' former European Cup-Winner's Cup opponents to the Serbo-Montenegrin league and cup Double. Zenga, however, left Red Star in the summer of 2006 amid speculation about lucrative offers from abroad – eventually ending up at Turkish side Gaziantepspor.

Gérard Houllier soon had to be discounted from consideration by Hearts when French champions Lyon appointed him as Paul le Guen's replacement. Sir Bobby Robson, though, was very much a live candidate. Tynecastle chief executive Phil Anderton held talks with Robson in Newcastle on Wednesday, 1 June 2005. Things went well, and the pair met again for further discussions two days later when an offer was made for the former England boss to take over as Hearts' new director of football. The 72 year old requested time over the weekend to make up his mind.

After a lengthy chat with his wife, Sir Bobby phoned Anderton the following Tuesday to inform the chief executive that, unfortunately, he had decided he would not be coming to Hearts due to 'family reasons'. Robson, though, would still have a big part to play in deciding who would eventually replace John Robertson and become the 23rd manager of Hearts since 1901 . . .

Although not one of the main names initially considered by the Hearts board, Nevio Scala declared his interest in the job after being approached by agent George Wright, one of the club's former players who had a mandate from the Tynecastle board to recruit a 'high-profile' candidate. Over a short period of time, Scala, who was interviewed for the Scotland job in 2001, became a regular name in the Scottish press because of the interest from Hearts, with any quotes attributed to the Italian usually being preceded by 'Speaking from his farm in Padova . . .'

At the same time, Hearts were also seriously considering a move for George Burley, who was out of work after leaving Derby County on Tuesday, 7 June. Although Burley appeared on the club's Strategy B list, and was not as big a name as some of the others being considered, the Cumnock-born 48 year old had made a decent name for himself as a manager after success at Colchester, Ipswich and Derby.

As the month wore on, discussions took place with various

candidates, but eventually the race to become the new Hearts boss was narrowed down to two candidates – George Burley and Nevio Scala. Burley soon became hot favourite after he and his agent Athole Still met Phil Anderton and George Wright.

Talks went very well, and Burley confirmed he was extremely interested in the position, subject to speaking to Vladimir Romanov. A meeting was set up between the pair in Lithuania on 28 June, and that sealed the deal, although a telephone conversation between Burley and a former front-runner for the job also helped. 'I had a chat with Sir Bobby Robson,' said Burley. 'It's no secret he was in talks with Hearts, and he spoke volumes about the club. He said it would be a very good job for anybody. I had to be persuaded, as I have had a successful time in England. I had to be convinced that it was right for me to move to Scotland.'

The appointment of George Burley as Hearts' new head coach was officially announced on Thursday, 30 June, bringing to an end a thorough search that had begun on 10 May, the day after John Robertson had left the club. Burley faced the press for the first time and outlined his plans for the club: 'Last season we finished eleven points off fourth position – there was a massive gap between Hearts and the top two. There is a lot of work to be done, but hopefully we can bridge it this season. To challenge the Old Firm would be dreamland, but I like to dream. And both my and Phil's dream is to take the club back towards its heights.

'They [the Romanovs] want to develop the club by bringing in players with quality, which will actually give us the chance to challenge the Old Firm. The players I have targeted will definitely excite the fans. I think we need around 20 in the squad; at present we have 14.

'This is not going to be easy, but within the next two seasons I want the club to be playing in Europe again. We have to try and keep improving, and that's what I'll be telling the players. The standards need to be lifted by everyone. I wouldn't have come here if I thought I wouldn't be able to push Hearts up the league and improve those standards. It was a decision I had to make, and I'm really looking forward to it.'

JULY 2005

The Hearts squad embarked on a two-match tour of Ireland to play St Patrick's and Bray, a schedule pre-arranged by former boss John Robertson. Andy Webster was notable by his absence from the travelling party. Rangers chairman David Murray had been in touch with George Foulkes on three separate occasions over the summer in an attempt to prise the Scotland international defender away from Hearts; Murray held direct talks with his Tynecastle counterpart after deciding not to involve Webster's representative Charles Duddy in proceedings. The discussions between the pair culminated in a verbal bid by Murray of £1 million plus Maurice Ross in exchange for Webster, but Foulkes – on behalf of the board – rebuffed the approach. Hearts decided Webster was an integral part of their squad and chose to keep him at Tynecastle.

The interest from Rangers unsettled Webster, and a decision was taken to leave the player in Scotland while the rest of the squad embarked on their pre-season tour. 'There was nothing sinister about Andy Webster's non-appearance in Ireland in July – it was quite simple,' explained John McGlynn. 'Rangers made a verbal offer for Andy that was rejected by the board, but this unsettled the player. George spoke with Andy and explained that the club wanted to hold on to their best players. It was suggested he spend a few days with his family and report back for training when we returned to action – both parties agreed on this course of action.

'George wanted Andy to take a few days off, clear his head

and realise the club was not prepared to let him go at that time for that amount of money. There was not much point in Webster being with the rest of the squad in Dublin if he was not fully focused.'

The new management team – George Burley, chief scout Simon Hunt and goalkeeping coach Malcolm Webster – were staying at the Marriott Dalmahoy Hotel and Country Club, so the trip to Ireland was the first time they were able to really get to know the rest of the coaching staff already at Hearts, although integrating with them fully took a while, as John McGlynn explained: 'George Burley, Simon Hunt and Malcolm Webster arrived as a package, and it was initially difficult to be part of their group. I would go home at night, while they would all be together at the Dalmahoy. They would socialise and talk about their plans for training the following day, as well as discussing which players they wanted to sign. They came as a team, and I appreciated that – it wasn't too much of a problem, but at times it was difficult. The trip to Ireland, though, was just what we needed for bonding purposes.

'The training camp in Dublin was certainly an eye-opener! The squad was down to the bare bones after Michael Stewart, Lee Miller, Kevin McKenna, Mark Burchill and Tepi Moilanen all departed for pastures new at the end of the previous season. I don't think George could quite believe the position he found himself in with such a dearth of players.

'There were no new signings for our opening match against St Pat's on 10 July – there was no point bringing anyone in before the arrival of the new manager, and George did not have enough time prior to heading to Dublin to get anyone on board. As a result, we were left with a very young and inexperienced squad playing against Irish teams in the middle of their season.'

Burley did not say much to the players after the matches against St Pat's and Bray but privately was not particularly impressed, to say the least, with what he had to work with. 'I think he knew there and then that he had a big job on his hands – much bigger than he had initially thought,' confirmed McGlynn. 'Having worked with the squad since the start of pre-season training, this was no surprise to me – I felt we needed at least six or seven new players.'

The first match against St Pat's finished goalless. The new management team were not too bothered about the result but were concerned about Graham Weir, who suffered a broken leg. The squad was already stretched to the limit, and this was the last thing either the player or the club needed. Burley was a little happier following the second match – a 5–1 victory against Bray – but the new boss knew he still had to sign several players to ensure competition for places in the squad.

'I remember a conversation on the bus coming back from Bray between George, Simon Hunt, Malcolm Webster and Valdas Ivanauskas,' said McGlynn. 'Valdas was on the trip as he was the only one who could speak Lithuanian and relay messages back to Mr Romanov about which players the manager wanted to sign, which positions needed strengthening and how urgent the situation was. That was the first occasion when the wheels were really put in motion to bring in new faces, although it wasn't until the Middlesbrough game that we saw real signs of progress.'

The busy pre-season schedule kept the players occupied and really ought to have kept George Burley busy as well. It did most of the time, but a friendly at Berwick Rangers, pre-arranged before his arrival, was a step too far for the new gaffer. With a summer heatwave enveloping the UK and the mercury hitting the high 80s in the northernmost town in England, Burley decided to engage in a spot of sunbathing behind one of the goals on arrival at Shielfield Park!

As this was the second friendly for Hearts in the space of 24 hours, wholesale changes were made to the team, with only Christophe Berra, Joe Hamill, Julien Brellier and Hjálmar Thórarinsson keeping their places in the starting line-up from the game against Stirling Albion at Forthbank the day before. A very young Hearts side took to the field under the guidance of John McGlynn and Stephen Frail, while Burley watched on from the main stand, perhaps wishing, like the five members of the media in attendance, that he was in front of a television set to see if Colin Montgomerie could overhaul Tiger Woods at St Andrews and clinch his first major title.

Temperatures inside the tiny, enclosed press box topped 100 degrees as kick-off approached; fresh air was a necessity, but it became apparent that the windows were jammed shut and had probably not been opened since Berwick Bandits met Teesside Teessiders in a speedway league match at Shielfield on the warm spring evening of 22 April 1972. I have commentated in various degrees of heat over the years, both at home and abroad, but that day was unbearable.

The afternoon got progressively worse as the two teams produced an absolutely dreadful spectacle in the searing heat to go in 0–0 at the break. There is no get-out for commentators during a football match, but there was for George Burley . . .

Monty was giving Tiger a fright at the home of golf, witnessed by the gaffer in the boardroom during the half-time interval. Burley had a dilemma: another 45 minutes of dross in sweltering heat with chances at a premium and quality football long forgotten about or a seat in front of the television with a nice cold beer watching the golf. Not so much a dilemma as a no-brainer: 'Gaun yersel, Monty!'

At least Burley had a choice! Numerous substitutions in the second half added to the poor show, and I have never been as happy to hear a referee's full-time whistle in my life. There was just time for a quick post-match interview with Burley;

unbeknownst to us, however, he knew as much about what had happened in the second half as the supporters who'd decided to lie back and enjoy the sunshine at half-time and had forgotten (or simply hadn't bothered) to open their eyes again!

Hearts fans got their first chance of the 2005–06 pre-season to see their team in action at Tynecastle when English Premiership side Middlesbrough provided the opposition. A full house watched the action after chief executive Phil Anderton, with the agreement of the board, sanctioned free entry for all. This was the first opportunity for supporters to get a glimpse of three players who would subsequently join the club – Michal Pospíšil, Roman Bednář and Julien Brellier – and one, Rudi Skácel, who'd put pen to paper the previous day on a one-year loan deal from Marseille. It was also the first opportunity for the manager to assess the suitability of some of his potential recruits.

'George had particular people and agents he relied upon to help him bring players to the club,' said John McGlynn. 'His chief scout, Simon Hunt, was a very big part of that, helping him pick which players would be good additions to the squad. They had a list of signing targets they were looking at, including two more Czechs – Roman Bednář and Michal Pospíšil – after securing Skácel's signature. All came highly recommended, and all three started against Boro, making immediate impressions.

'The gaffer had never seen Bednář play in person – the striker was a recommendation – but at half-time in that game at Tynecastle I remember him saying to Roman in the dressing-room, "After that 45 minutes, son, you'll do for me." That's all it took to convince George he wanted to sign the lad. Anyone who was at the game would understand why!

'Julien Brellier also featured at Tynecastle that day, having played against East Fife [sub], Stirling and Berwick, and he was one of the signings of the season in my opinion. Edgaras Jankauskas and Takis Fyssas also came on board prior to the transfer window closing, and it quickly became apparent that we had brought in quality; we had a real chance of challenging for honours. Anyone in attendance at our games in Dublin would scarcely have believed it!'

George Burley's first month in charge was hectic, to say the least, with eight matches and five new signings. In came Bednář, Jankauskas, Pospíšil, Brellier and Skácel. Add a contractual wrangle that meant club captain Steven Pressley had to be listed as a trialist for the games at East Fife, Stirling Albion and Middlesbrough, plus Rangers' interest in Andy Webster, and it was all go at Tynecastle. There was much upheaval, which made Hearts' start to the season even more remarkable.

Travelling down to Kilmarnock for the opening league match of the new campaign, there was no way any Hearts supporter could have envisaged what lay ahead in the next ten months. The club had a new major investor, Vladimir Romanov, a new manager, George Burley, and new players in the team that would take some getting used to – not just the style of their play but also the pronunciation of their names!

Skácel, Bednář and Jankauskas all made their debuts for Hearts at Rugby Park that day – the first two even managed to get on the scoresheet in a 4–2 win. The performance, as much as the result, sent the visiting fans home happy that evening. They witnessed a display of pace and fluency that hadn't been seen from a Hearts team for some time.

'After the opening-day victory at Kilmarnock, we were on a roll,' said John McGlynn. 'The Scottish lads – the likes of Steven Pressley, Paul Hartley, Robbie Neilson, Craig Gordon and Andy Webster – very quickly accepted the foreign guys into the dressing-room, and it was amazing how quickly everything just clicked together. Momentum and confidence were there in abundance as we kept winning, and the backroom staff were all delighted with the way things were going. We could not have asked for a better start . . .'

AUGUST 2005

George Burley's reign was off to a good start after the victory over Kilmarnock, but that quickly became a flying start . . .

Hibs were the visitors for the Jambos' first competitive home game of the new league campaign. The first Edinburgh derby of the season also signified a huge positive for the supporters who had been involved in the Save Our Hearts campaign, aimed at keeping the club at Tynecastle. The group had been helped hugely by George Foulkes, and both the Hearts chairman and Gary Mackay shed a tear as the game started. Ninety minutes later, it was tears of joy all round as the men in maroon hammered the boys from the east of the city 4–0 – a scoreline to be remembered for later in the season . . .

Those first couple of results found the Hearts supporters in great voice, and fans received a further boost four days after the win against Hibs when one of the club's Scotland internationals put pen to paper on a new contract. Paul Hartley was a transfer target for Celtic, but the Tynecastle board quickly rejected a derisory £300,000 offer from Parkhead for the midfielder. (Wouldn't it be nice to give them a taste of their own medicine one day and slap in a bid of £125,000 for Jan Vennegoor of Hesselink and see how they like it!)

Hartley eventually put the speculation about his future to rest by signing a new long-term contract, committing himself to Hearts until the summer of 2009. Playing under George Burley, suggested Paul, had a lot to do with his decision: 'It was easy to see the players Mr Burley was bringing in were quality – Champions League and European Championship winners –

and he stressed to me how ambitious his plans were for the future. I was really enjoying my football with Hearts, and that was another main factor why I decided to extend my spell at Tynecastle.'

Paul confirmed he had thought about leaving Hearts for pastures new at the end of the 2004–05 season, but that all changed when the new boss came in: 'I was considering various options before I spoke to the manager – perhaps a spell in England – but as soon as he came in and I saw his plans and the way he wanted to play football, it changed my mind. I was sure I could be part of a winning team by remaining at Tynecastle.'

Over the coming weeks, the team continued to perform with a style and panache rarely before witnessed by those wearing maroon scarves. Five goals were scored in the next two games to secure comfortable victories against Dundee United at Tannadice (3–0) and Aberdeen at Tynecastle (2–0), while Edgaras Jankauskas grabbed his first two goals for Hearts in a CIS Cup tie against Queens Park at Hampden (2–0).

The routine for the players following a match was always the same under Burley. The entire first-team squad and all the backroom staff went to the seminar room at Riccarton on a Monday morning for a video-analysis session of the weekend's game. Positives and negatives were discussed and analysed, as was the shape of the team and its performance throughout the match. Despite the good results, the manager regularly stressed that he wanted his defence to hold a higher line. Burley also asked for thoughts on both individual and collective performances – good points were highlighted, as were areas that required improvement, with players encouraged to be self-analytical.

The concept of video analysis is not new to Scottish football; in fact, Hearts were one of the first teams north of the border to implement the system, as former boss Craig Levein explained: 'I was approached by a Scottish company called Elite Sports Analysis to find out if I would be interested in receiving a demonstration of their video-analysis system. It didn't take them long to persuade me, and we first used the system at the start of season 2002–03. It was a great help when trying to analyse matches with the players and also made sure that none of them could trick me by claiming, for example, that they had tracked back when it was clear that they hadn't!'

The incredible start to the season ensured a huge sense of optimism among supporters, with those who had placed their annual £2.50 bet on Hearts at 500–1 to win the SPL title suddenly looking out holiday brochures and checking where the Maldives were located on the map. There was also a sense of optimism among the coaching staff at Tynecastle, although privately they did have one worry, as John McGlynn explained: 'We were very concerned that the new signings were not at the same level of fitness as the other lads in the squad because they missed out on a full pre-season programme. The concern was mainly centred on their long-term fitness as the season progressed. George Burley did not want the new recruits to go through a pre-season and cram everything into a short space of time, as there would have been an increased risk of injury; therefore, our training was very short and very sharp. A ten-minute warm-up was usually sufficient due to the high temperatures at that time of year. We would then go into simple, high-tempo passing drills – which George liked a lot – and possession play, as well as different types of game situations. The players loved it.

'The gaffer demanded quality. He was not happy if a pass went astray or if a first touch was poor in training. He had very high standards, and the players were well aware of that from early on. I think our short, sharp training techniques helped the players get out of the blocks very quickly in matches, and we scored a number of early goals in the initial part of the season. This resulted in several games being virtually wrapped up by half-time. The likelihood that we were not going to concede many in the second half because of our strong defence also helped immensely.

'We were quickly becoming a formidable team under George Burley; however, it was always in the back of our minds that this type of fast football would eventually catch up with us. We were concerned that the wheels would eventually fall off the barrow because a number of players did not have a full pre-season under their belts.'

August ended with the visit of Motherwell to Tynecastle – not one of the best games of the season but still memorable for Craig Gordon's world-class save to deny David Clarkson an equaliser right at the end of the match. 'It was a good save,' said the ever-so-modest goalkeeper, 'and it was pleasing to keep the 100 per cent record going because we were top of the league and flying at that stage. A lot of people were waiting for our bubble to burst and that could have been the moment we dropped our first points of the season. Hopefully, I can look back at the end of the season and its significance will have grown . . .'

Five league games during the second month of the season had brought five more wins. It was a good time to be a Hearts supporter, with the fans witnessing fast, free-flowing, attractive football. Phil Anderton even hinted at a contract extension for the head coach: 'George signed a two-year deal, and we were delighted to bring him on board. He has already said he hopes and expects to be here longer than that. I would be happy to sit down with him to discuss that – we are expecting and hoping to keep George Burley here for longer than those two years.'

Talks never got under way with Burley to discuss an extension.

SEPTEMBER 2005

The Hearts bandwagon continued to gather momentum in September: four more league matches, four more wins. More than 6,000 fans made the short trip to Livingston to witness a comprehensive 4–1 victory, one of the biggest away supports ever carried to a league match by Hearts. The feel-good factor was very much alive at Tynecastle with record season-ticket sales and every home game a sell-out up to that point.

Two days after the win at Almondvale that maintained Hearts' 100 per cent start to the season, the squad gathered in the seminar room at Riccarton. Usually, analysis of the weekend's game would be one of the first things to take place on a Monday morning, but this time things were different, as John McGlynn revealed: 'George Burley sat everyone down and asked the squad, "How far do you think we can go this season?" wanting "The full 38 games" as an answer. However, Takis Fyssas simply said, "To the next game", and explained that the following match is always the most important one in his opinion and that he refused to look any further ahead than that. Takis is a very shrewd guy – it was probably the perfect answer to the question.

'George actually asked the same question just prior to the start of the season, and Steven Pressley suggested we should be aiming to win the league. Half the squad thought he was off his head! After those first six unbeaten games, though, a smug Mr Pressley was giving the "I told you so" chat to anyone who would listen!'

Later that day, the squad headed off to Musselburgh Racecourse for a bonding exercise aimed at letting the new players get to know their teammates in a different environment. The day out nearly backfired, though, when a number of foreigners sought retribution against several so-called 'racing experts' for costing them a fair bit of money courtesy of several dodgy tips!

The subsequent 1–0 victory over Rangers at Tynecastle the following Saturday was not only the first win at home against the men from Ibrox since August 1998, it also marked the first time Hearts had won their opening eight league matches since the 1914–15 season. The victory may have provided another reason to celebrate for everyone with a maroon association, but there were still some people who weren't entirely satisfied. 'The match could have been better,' said Vladimir Romanov, 'but the important thing was the result. It was a great victory for us, and I have no doubt we can now stay at the top of the league.'

Hearts moved 11 points clear of reigning champions Rangers at the top of the SPL, but there were still mixed responses coming out of Tynecastle when various people were asked if Hearts could really win the league. 'If we finish third, it will be a tremendous season,' said George Burley, keeping his feet firmly on the ground. Unlike Julien Brellier: 'The players are beginning to believe more and more that we can win the SPL and that Hearts can go far.'

Just when it seemed things could not get any better for the maroon hordes, with their team sitting unbeaten at the top of the league, rumours swept through the capital that everything might not be as rosy behind the scenes. It was alleged that all was not well between George Burley and Vladimir Romanov – cracks were apparently appearing in their relationship. Fuel was added to the fire when Burley admitted that four of Hearts' nine summer signings – Ibrahim Tall, Samuel Camazzola, Takis Fyssas and Edgaras Jankauskas – were not his choice.

'It is not ideal for me, but if Mr Romanov hadn't been involved with this club, then we wouldn't have the side we have at the moment,' said Burley. 'There have been a number of players I wanted to bring in, and he has looked for alternative ones. I have spoken to Mr Romanov, but I have never fallen out with him. It is just that he has different thoughts from me in terms of running a club.'

The speculation about the alleged fall-out intensified, so Burley took the opportunity at a pre-match press conference to publicly re-emphasise his overall satisfaction with the way things had gone since joining Hearts at the beginning of July. A closer inspection of his comments, though, revealed that the rumours were, in fact, not far from uncovering the truth: 'My everyday running of the club is absolutely fine, and I feel we have come a long way over the last couple of months. As a manager, I would like to be able to bring in a player and do it right away, but that is not the scenario here. We talk about signing targets, but, at the end of the day, Mr Romanov is the one paying for them, and I am happy with the players we have. The transfer deadline came up quickly, and we got two new signings; there were other targets we did not manage to get. It was a big gamble for me to come back to Scotland; however, I am enjoying Edinburgh and nobody could have imagined we could make this sort of start. But, of course, there are areas that Mr Romanov and I have to work at.'

Were the last 15 words a throwaway comment or something more revealing? The answer soon became apparent.

OCTOBER 2005

The month did not get off to the best of starts as Hearts dropped their first points of the season after being held to a 2–2 draw at Falkirk. The relationship between Vladimir Romanov and George Burley, meanwhile, got progressively worse behind the scenes. While the rest of the football world marvelled at Hearts' ten-game unbeaten league run, Romanov finally admitted that his relationship with his head coach was not ideal, mainly due to Burley's working relationship with some agents: 'I strive to cooperate with everyone at the club, but the reality is that there must always be conflict of opinions in any successful venture. Anyone who says they know best is a fool – you must consult others. The purchase of players must not be in the hands of agents. I have my own intelligence network reviewing the ability of players from as far afield as Chile and Japan.'

However, that was only the prelude to one of Romanov's most telling remarks: 'If you are building a house and you want it to stand for 1,000 years, it is sometimes better to build it yourself. As Tsar Peter the Great once said, half of the builders in Russia should be in jail. If it is your house, you need to maintain control over what goes on.'

If it wasn't before, that statement ensured it was now common knowledge that the major shareholder and the head coach did not see eye to eye. John McGlynn was also aware that things weren't right between the two. 'It had been speculated in the media on many occasions that things were not always rosy in the garden between George Burley and Mr Romanov,' he said. 'It was also reported by the press that George would speak to other managers after games about his situation and tell them he wasn't entirely happy with the way things were going. It was reasonably common knowledge that they weren't getting on too well, but the results were good, so it was assumed things would continue the way they were. I'm not exactly sure what the straw that broke the camel's back was.'

On the pitch, though, it remained business as usual as Hearts produced an excellent performance to secure a thoroughly deserved 1–1 draw against Celtic at Parkhead – preserving their unbeaten start to the season. However, Burley did not realise that it was to be his last match in charge.

At the time of his arrival in the week leading up to the Dunfermline game, the return of Valdas Ivanauskas to Riccarton failed to raise any eyebrows. The Lithuanian had taken a backseat role under Burley at the start of the season and had departed once the transfer window closed at the end of August. A few days after returning to Edinburgh, however, Ivanauskas would find himself in the dugout for the match against the Pars, assistant to John McGlynn.

'Valdas arrived back in Edinburgh a short time prior to George Burley's departure,' said McGlynn. 'However, I think it was more than just a coincidence that George left the football club two or three days later. In my opinion, there was more to it than that. I think Mr Romanov knew what he wanted to do, and he was obviously putting plans in place if George Burley moved on.

'It was actually business as usual on the morning prior to the Dunfermline game. We worked on [the team's] shape at training. It was unlikely that George would name the starting XI on a Friday, but the formation we worked on usually gave the players a good idea who was playing. I took a note of the set-piece routines, as I had to write them on the board on a Saturday. There was nothing to suggest that something was amiss . . .'

That Friday was also a significant day for Hearts behind the scenes. Vladimir Romanov announced his intention to increase his stake in the club to 55.5 per cent after agreeing to purchase the SMG and HBOS shareholdings and become the club's majority shareholder, much to the delight of George Foulkes: 'This is one of the most significant developments in the history of the football club. It is the biggest thing in ownership terms since Wallace Mercer sold out to Chris Robinson and Leslie Deans. This is one of the greatest days for Hearts. We are seeing great success on the field. We have taken a number of important decisions, such as staying at Tynecastle and the appointment of George Burley. Today, with Vladimir Romanov as principal shareholder indicating he would like to become the owner is the best news. It is our aim to end the duopoly enjoyed by the Old Firm.'

An early morning press conference was held in the Gorgie Suite to announce full details to the media, with former chief executive Sergejus Fedotovas making a welcome return to Edinburgh after being out of the public spotlight for a couple of months because of illness. Fedotovas had no more than a watching brief from the floor as Romanov and George Foulkes shared centre stage, and no one in attendance that morning had any idea that the director of the club was not only in the country to applaud his boss for taking a huge step towards obtaining complete control of Heart of Midlothian but also to attend a meeting later that day that would ultimately bring an end to George Burley's reign as head coach.

SATURDAY, 22 OCTOBER 2005

Hearts fans woke up that morning to what they thought was just another match day. Dunfermline were in town that afternoon, and the Jambos were odds-on favourites to extend their unbeaten league record to 11 matches. Shortly after 10 a.m., however, it became clear to John McGlynn that this was not 'just another day': 'I had gone up to the Academy at Riccarton early to prepare for an Under-19 match when I received a call from Phil Anderton. He told me something had happened and Mr Romanov wanted to meet me at Dalmahoy immediately. Phil more or less informed me that George Burley was no longer in charge of the football club.

'I went straight along to the hotel. Mr Romanov was there, Roman Romanov was there and Valdas was also in attendance. Shortly afterwards, Steven Pressley arrived, and it was then confirmed to us that George Burley had parted company with the football club. Mr Romanov had made his decision. It was then up to Steven and me to discuss the way forward from there, starting with the Dunfermline match that afternoon.

'We all knew it wasn't a bed of roses between the pair, but the timing of it on the day of a game was the biggest shock to me. I still do not understand why it was done when it was – Mr Romanov, though, took that decision, and he took the gamble. I don't think anyone with a British mentality would have done that because of the effect it could have had on the team. The players losing focus and dropping vital points was certainly a possibility.'

The players began arriving at the hotel for their pre-match meal at about 11.45 a.m. to be met by Vladimir and Roman Romanov; an impromptu meeting was held and the squad was informed what had happened. The visibly shocked players were not given a reason why George Burley had left – they were just told he was no longer involved with the football club.

The news soon spread to outside sources, and by lunchtime it was in the public domain, although many supporters still refused to believe what had happened, incredulous at the whole situation – no team gets rid of their manager when they are sitting proudly at the top of the table. 'I was in the dressing-room at Wyndham's Theatre in London preparing for *Heroes*,' said actor and Hearts fan Ken Stott. 'I really should have been preparing for that afternoon's matinee performance, but instead I found myself glued to the radio. George Burley had been sacked – I couldn't believe it.'

Supporter Ronnie Hare was preparing to head to Tynecastle from his home in Mortonhall when he heard confirmation of the news on Radio Forth: 'At first I thought it was a joke, but it soon became evident it was not. All sorts of things went through my mind, but the main thing was how the players would react.' It didn't take long for word to spread further afield as well – ex-pat Hearts supporter and one-time Livingston player Barry Wood also thought someone was winding him up when he heard the news at his home in Perth, Australia: 'I frantically tried to fathom out who was playing tricks on me. I must have checked the date a hundred times, but it wasn't April Fool's Day – it was true. It was a sad day for Scottish football, never mind just for Hearts. Burley's transformation of this completely new side into a well-oiled, attacking machine was amazing, and the team was fantastic to watch.'

In one of the most surreal atmospheres I can ever recall at Tynecastle, almost funereal at times, the Hearts players somehow put the dramatic events of the morning behind them to record a 2–0 home victory over Dunfermline. Supporters had been informed via the club's website at lunchtime that a further announcement would be forthcoming at 6 p.m. that evening to shed light on the day's events. The wait, however, was not exactly worthwhile as a three-paragraph statement, read to the assembled press following the match against the Pars by George Foulkes and broadcast live on radio, failed to answer any questions:

> Heart of Midlothian Football Club announced today that after discussions between the board of Heart of Midlothian and George Burley, it has been mutually agreed that because of irreconcilable differences George Burley will not continue at the club with immediate effect.
>
> The board is currently looking for a new top-class manager who is worthy to be the manager of Heart of Midlothian FC and who will be able to achieve the Champions League place in the SPL. In the interim, John McGlynn will be caretaker manager.
>
> The club, Mr Burley or any associated parties will make no further comment.

Foulkes then took part in a voluntary question-and-answer session with assembled journalists. 'Today, unlike yesterday, is not a great day. I would agree to that,' he said. 'We are now looking to the future. We have to put today behind us. Heart of Midlothian Football Club is greater than any one person. It's greater than me as chairman, and it's greater than managers of the past. It's important for the fans that we look to the future, and we are determined to get a top-class manager.

'I'm a fan and I'm still a shareholder, although I have agreed to sell my shares, and I am trying to give the supporters an explanation. What I can't tell them, however, is the circumstances of the parting of company with George Burley other than it was by mutual agreement and because of irreconcilable differences.

'I understand their [the fans'] bewilderment, and what I am saying to them is these things happen in football, as I have discovered in the last two years. We don't go into the details that have been agreed. We have given that promise to George Burley and he's given that to us, and I can't break that. What I can say is that we give a pledge to the supporters and everyone connected to the club that the club is going to go from strength to strength – we are determined to do that.'

They say a week is a long time in politics, as George Foulkes would well know, but surely not even politicians change their views as spectacularly quickly as this? In the space of 24 hours, it had gone from being, in the opinion of the club chairman, the best day in the history of Hearts to one of the worst.

Supporters demanded answers. What on earth was going on? One of the best starts to a season in living memory had now been completely overshadowed by the dramatic events off the field. George Burley had left Hearts having never lost a league match – but why?

Vladimir Romanov had some explaining to do – cue another official statement from the club:

> Heart of Midlothian Football Club majority shareholder Vladimir Romanov has reiterated that his vision for the future of the club remains intact. Mr Romanov is disappointed that a way could not be found to continue with George Burley at Tynecastle: 'I would like to place on record my thanks to George Burley for his input over the past four months. However, we will not be derailed from our ambition to deliver to the fans and the city of Edinburgh a club that is regularly competing at the highest levels of football in Scotland and Europe. I want us to be winning the Scottish Premier League title on a regular basis as well as playing top-quality football in the Champions League.
>
> I have kept all my promises to Hearts fans and want them to know that they and the club can look forward to further investment on and off the field. However, we will not be rushed into a decision on a new manager. I have always said we will pay for quality and professionalism, and that does not mean taking the first individual available.
>
> Can I also state quite categorically that, despite rumours to the contrary, Valdas Ivanauskas will not be a candidate to replace George Burley. He has been working at the club on a regular basis, assisting with the coaching duties, and this may continue in the future if the new manager feels it appropriate.

The departure of George Burley made both national and international headlines; even one of Scottish football's biggest names gave his view on what had happened. Kenny Dalglish passed comment on the situation, writing in the *Sunday Herald*:

> Vladimir Romanov in the dressing-room before kick-off, giving what amounts to a team talk?
>
> Everybody appreciates the Hearts owner is entitled to voice his opinion, but even a caretaker manager has to be allowed to manage come match-night . . . there is a line you just cannot cross.
>
> It seems apparent Romanov simply cannot resist being hands-on. He has spoken in one interview of addressing the team just before the midweek match against Kilmarnock, despite club officials warning against it.
>
> How often do unbeaten sides at the top of their leagues part with their managers? Far less in Scotland where that team is neither half of the Old Firm. Personally, I do not know who would be interested in taking up the position.

On the same day Dalglish's article appeared in the *Sunday Herald*, George Burley's wife Jill revealed to the *Sunday Mail* that a disastrous dinner with Vladimir Romanov at the Balmoral Hotel in Edinburgh (following the 1–1 draw with Celtic at Parkhead at the start of the month) could have sown the seeds for her husband's downfall:

> George had dinner with Romanov most Saturdays. The week before he was sacked he brought me along, too. I found Romanov a very rude man. Never mind anything else, when we arrived he had already eaten. I found that unbelievable, but maybe it's a Russian thing. We just didn't get along. He doesn't speak English and needs to speak through an interpreter, but it would be fair to say

we didn't bond. He didn't like me at all . . . It was so bad
I knew right there and then that George's days at Hearts
were numbered.

Even by the capricious standards of football management,
getting rid of Burley was an extraordinary decision. However,
despite all the turmoil, it was business as usual in the chief
executive's office at Tynecastle as Phil Anderton continued the
process of finding a top-quality replacement to fill the
managerial hot seat. 'I am close to finalising the list of potential
candidates, and every one of them is a manager with top-class
European pedigree,' said the chief executive. 'Much has been
made of the events at the weekend, but my sole concern at this
time is to ensure that the board is presented with a selection of
managers that can deliver the domestic and European success
that this great club desires. I strongly believe that we can look
forward to the future with immense confidence.

'We have top-class players and a first-class footballing
structure; it will only be a matter of time before we have a top-
class manager leading the team. The team and fans have been
exceptional this season, and I am sure that they will be further
rewarded with the appointment of a highly experienced top-
class manager who shares the ambition we all have for the club.'

That was to be the last public comment from Phil Anderton
in his position as chief executive of Hearts: he was sacked
following a board meeting on Monday, 31 October. Club
chairman George Foulkes resigned in protest. In the space of
ten days, Hearts had lost a manager, a chief executive and a
chairman. It was not exactly the stability required at a football
club that wanted to challenge for honours.

THREE

WHY BYE BURLEY?

IN THE END, GEORGE BURLEY LASTED 114 DAYS – BUT IT could have been just 12 from start to finish. Those 114 days – making him the shortest-serving Hearts head coach/manager in the club's 131-year history – contained plenty of success, drama in abundance and left an indelible impression at Tynecastle, but Burley's tenure might have been over before it had even begun.

Burley was sitting relaxing with Simon Hunt and Malcolm Webster in the Hilton Dublin Airport Hotel on the evening of Monday, 11 July 2005. The triumvirate were discussing the goalless draw with St Pat's the previous day and looking ahead to the following night's match against Bray Wanderers. They were also trying to come to terms with a decision by Vladimir Romanov to completely rebuff their list of transfer targets submitted for consideration.

A compromise was eventually reached and some of the players on the list were approved, but the initial snub led to early disenchantment among the trio. It was not the best start to their working relationship with Romanov, leading Webster to declare that having never been to Edinburgh before, he 'still might not get there!'

'THERE ARE MORE QUESTIONS THAN ANSWERS' (JOHNNY NASH)

Life is full of unanswered questions:

- What would have happened had referee Bill Crombie awarded a penalty for Hearts at Dens Park in May 1986? Dundee defender Colin Hendry apppeared to foul Hearts striker Sandy Clark in the box in the first half, but Crombie waved play on.
- Would Hearts have won the 1996 Coca-Cola Cup final at Parkhead if the linesman had flagged for a foul on John Robertson? Joachim Björklund clearly impeded Robbo in the build-up to Paul Gascoigne's goal to make it 3–2 to Rangers, but assistant referee Alan Freeland chose to ignore the offence.
- Why did George Burley leave Hearts? After an unbeaten start to their league campaign, Burley parted company with the club on the morning of another vital SPL fixture and after only 114 days in the job.

When Hearts chairman George Foulkes read out his pre-prepared statement in the most dramatic of circumstances following the match against Dunfermline at Tynecastle on Saturday, 22 October 2005, supporters expected to hear the real reasons behind Burley's dramatic exit. Already stunned, they were also disappointed by a distinct lack of any information. It quickly became apparent that both parties had verbally agreed a confidentiality clause and the real reasons behind his departure would not be revealed.

Until now . . .

*   *   *

Like the 23 permanent managers before him (from the point at which the board of directors ceased to run team affairs in 1901), George Burley is now part of the proud history of Heart of Midlothian Football Club. The former Scotland international moved to Tynecastle and signed on the dotted line on 30 June 2005, having been out of football for only 23 days after leaving Derby County. His record with Hearts was virtually impeccable, with the exception of a CIS Cup loss at Livingston, and the team played with a certain swagger and flowing style under his leadership that saw thousands of supporters return to Tynecastle for the first time in years. Even after back-to-back draws, at Falkirk (when the ten Hearts players showed tremendous spirit to come back from two goals down after Craig Gordon had been sent off) and at Celtic, everything in the Gorgie garden remained rosy as far as the fans were concerned.

However, things were not so propitious behind the scenes, as former chairman George Foulkes explained: 'George Burley was getting all the credit for the fantastic start that Hearts had made, and rightly so. The media were giving him credit, and the supporters were giving him credit. Of course they were – he was doing a good job. However, Vladimir Romanov has a problem with anyone who is in the limelight at the expense of him. He does not like it at all.'

The working relationship between Vladimir Romanov and George Burley slowly deteriorated throughout August and September, before reaching the point of no return in October. Burley was perplexed that players were signed without his knowledge or say-so (Samuel Camazzola and Ibrahim Tall being just two examples). The head coach was also annoyed when he put forward transfer targets to Romanov but was consistently knocked back.

There was also mounting disillusion from Romanov about

Burley for various reasons. He did not like the style of play under the head coach – he felt it was far too physical, despite the positive results – and he didn't think George was managing the team in the right way. Romanov also became increasingly annoyed about Burley's team selection. On several occasions, he thought the wrong players were chosen to play. In one instance, Burley was told by one of the Lithuanian directors, acting on orders from Romanov, that Saulius Mikoliūnas should feature more regularly (instead of Rudi Skácel), while Burley was harangued for not including Deividas Česnauskis in the first team more often. Romanov wanted his Lithuanian players to be in the shop window and on show for potential buyers, and it annoyed him when they were either on the bench or left out completely. Romanov was also paranoid about Burley's relationship with certain agents. He believed the manager was only picking players from a select group of representatives.

These reservations were confirmed by George Foulkes: 'Vladimir Romanov and George Burley disagreed on various matters during Burley's short spell in charge, including the relationship the manager had with certain agents and also which players George was selecting to play in the first team – for example, Julien Brellier.

'Romanov used to draw up a matrix on a continuing basis relating to the performance of the Hearts players, giving each a mark out of ten. He would regularly give Brellier three or four out of ten, saying he was useless on many occasions.

'There is no doubt in my mind that Romanov was looking for some excuse to get rid of the manager, other than his regular disputes with Burley and differences of opinion about which players were being chosen for the team.'

For his part, George Burley also maintained that his choice of agents was based entirely on the quality of the players they suggested and their efficiency and integrity.

The speedy deterioration of the relationship between Vladimir Romanov and both George Burley and Phil Anderton could certainly not have been predicted in the summer of 2005. Anderton was given the responsibility by Romanov of finding a new manager, while Burley got on fine with the owner when they met in Lithuania prior to his appointment.

'Things seemed to be going well with Vladimir, George Burley, Phil Anderton and myself for the first few weeks,' said George Foulkes, 'but during the course of the initial two months, things deteriorated. I think the overriding problem was that there were too many egos at the club. I did not have a problem if Phil Anderton and George Burley received a lot of credit, because as far as I was concerned the more credit they received, the more reflected glory I would get. This didn't matter to me . . . but it did matter to Vladimir Romanov. He came to the conclusion that Phil was in it to see what he could get out of it. Phil Anderton is an able publicist and understandably wanted to use his post at Hearts to build up his reputation – there is no doubt about that – although there is nothing wrong with that.'

In the end, it reached the stage where something simply had to be done as far as Romanov was concerned. He thought Burley was not right for Hearts and wanted rid of him. He got his wish, and the excuse he had been waiting for, following the monthly board meeting on Friday, 14 October 2005. Although Vladimir was not present, Roman Romanov relayed to his father the content of the meeting and informed him what was said in the boardroom. 'At every board meeting, Phil would provide his fellow directors with a report on what was happening at the club – that was his duty as CEO,' explained Foulkes. 'He would always tell us a whole range of things, including news of marketing and sales as well as commercial activities. I would chair the meetings, Phil Anderton would make his monthly reports and Chris Robinson would make a comment from time to time, while the Lithuanian who spoke the most was Liutauras Varanavičius – he is very clever, and his English is excellent. Roman Romanov never usually spoke. He hardly ever said a word – at some meetings, he would say nothing at all, just sit there.

'At this board meeting [14 October], Phil mentioned in passing – almost as an aside – that he had been made aware of a couple of comments relating to George and drink, and it would be worth keeping an eye on the situation. As soon as Phil had finished saying this, Roman picked up on it and said, "We must do something about this. We can't have that." I thought his response was very strange. He hardly ever spoke at these meetings, and then, suddenly, because of a throwaway comment, he was very active.'

As chief executive, Phil Anderton was contractually obliged to mention at board meetings any stories or gossip he had been made aware of that could potentially damage the club. He'd been alerted to three things relating to George Burley ahead of the October board meeting:

1. An employee of Hearts had mentioned to him that there was an occasion when he or she could smell alcohol on Burley's breath.
2. The media had informed the club that they had evidence of Burley's drinking.
3. Anderton was also told that the *News of the World* was preparing a story concerning Burley's private life – although nothing was ever printed.

This hearsay had to be brought up by Anderton at the board meeting to cover his back, based on the terms and conditions of his contract as CEO.

Phil Anderton, though, informed George Burley about the

media stories two days before the board meeting and told him to be careful. Anderton also checked with Steven Pressley that the players had no problems or issues with George. The reply came back negative – the squad loved Burley being in charge.

'I understand both Roman and Vladimir Romanov were talking to Phil Anderton at length about the drinking issue, asking him more questions about it and quizzing him,' said Foulkes. 'The way Phil mentioned it at the board meeting on 14 October, it was simply a case of "OK, let's just keep an eye on this", but the Romanovs were very keen to do something about it.'

In the UK at least, most football coaches enjoy a drink, and it is seen as being part of the culture. In Burley's case, there was certainly nothing to suggest that he had a problem that was affecting his ability to do his job. The Romanov's seemed to be overreacting, but, of course, they come from a different culture.

Vladimir Romanov flew into Edinburgh on Thursday, 20 October 2005 with a dual purpose. He would attend a press conference the following morning, at which it would be announced that he had agreed to purchase the shareholding of SMG and HBOS to become Hearts' majority shareholder, increasing his stake in the club to 55.5 per cent. Romanov would then meet the rest of the board following the press conference to inform them of his plans for George Burley.

A morning meeting subsequently took place at Tynecastle on Friday, 21 October, involving Vladimir Romanov, Roman Romanov, Sergejus Fedotovas, Phil Anderton and George Foulkes. It was suggested by the Eastern Europeans that George Burley should go to Lithuania with Vladimir Romanov for a week and undergo a health check. Phil Anderton suggested that this might be a good thing as it would also provide the opportunity for George Burley to discuss bringing players in during the January transfer window. It was then put forward that Burley and Romanov could go in November when there was a free weekend in the SPL due to the World Cup play-offs.

'We also explained to them that if it did turn out that George Burley had a problem with drink then they should try and give him support and help him deal with the issue in a sensitive and effective manner,' said Foulkes. 'This was accepted. I then spoke to Phil near the end of the meeting and asked him, as CEO, to explain to George what we had discussed. That was a mistake! Vladimir Romanov interjected and said, in English, "Leave it to me – I will talk to him . . ." I asked Phil if he was content for Romanov to do this, and he reluctantly agreed.

'Around this time, Phil Anderton was becoming increasingly unhappy about his role as chief executive being undermined by both Vladimir Romanov and Julija Gončaruk, among others. This task should have been carried out by Phil in his role as CEO; however, he agreed to let Romanov speak to George Burley that afternoon, fearing recriminations against him if permission was not granted.'

George Burley attended the pre-match press conference at Riccarton at 12.30 p.m. that Friday, as per normal. As well as previewing the match against Dunfermline the following day, he also welcomed a period of 'financial security' for the club after Vladimir Romanov's ŪBIG investment group announced plans that morning for a full takeover of the Tynecastle club: 'One of the reasons I came to Hearts was Mr Romanov after I went to speak to him in Lithuania. It is great for the club to have the financial security to try and push forward. We are all looking forward. It has been a great start from this team. It is unbelievable how we have progressed as far as we have on and off the field. Hopefully we can keep things progressing, keep developing and get stronger and stronger.

'It is all about trying to improve your club; it is not always about spending money. It is about getting the right players in that will suit your team, and, of course, if there is finance available to bring in more quality, then that can only help. I think the key is building things gradually, and I know Mr Romanov is not just going to throw money away for players who he thinks will not improve the squad.

'The players we have brought in have been tremendous. They have been great assets and have improved the squad. We have not paid silly money for them. These players have all done well for us. That is the key – progression.'

That press conference turned out to be George Burley's last as head coach of Hearts. It certainly wasn't obvious to the journalists in the seminar room at Heriot-Watt University that lunchtime, myself included, that something was amiss behind the scenes. Following my weekly Radio Forth interview with an enthusiastic Burley in the reception area at Riccarton at the end of the press conference, he asked if I could get him tickets for the upcoming Robbie Williams concert. For his wife, of course, as he was quick to point out, laughing. I told him I would see what I could do but explained that dates for the gigs had not even been announced yet, never mind tickets being available! There was certainly no sign at that point that within hours his tenure at Hearts would be over . . .

FROM ROBBIE TO ROMANOV

George Burley was called to Tynecastle that Friday afternoon to a private meeting with Vladimir Romanov (along with a translator). Burley quickly found out that Roman Romanov and Sergejus Fedotovas were also going to be in attendance – three Eastern Europeans and the head coach but no Phil Anderton, who was not invited to take part. George Foulkes, meanwhile, had left the club for the day and had driven back to his home in Ayr.

The meeting – in Anderton's office – lasted just over two hours. The topics that caused the disagreements between the head coach and the owner were discussed at this meeting, as they had been at previous ones. It's thought Burley was questioned about various things, including speculation that Simon Hunt had told Craig Gordon not to sign a new deal, as well as conjecture in the press linking the head coach with other clubs. It's also believed that Romanov asked the head coach to commit his long-term future to Hearts due to the speculation, but Burley felt there was no need to do so, having signed a two-year deal less than three months previously. This, though, was ultimately more ammunition for the Russian-born former submariner.

Instead of Burley being asked by Vladimir Romanov at the meeting what he thought about the idea of him going to Lithuania for a week, he was told that Romanov wanted him to go to Lithuania the following day. This would mean the manager missing the games against Dunfermline, Kilmarnock and Hibs. Burley, who has persistently denied allegations that he has a drink problem, dismissed the suggestion on the grounds that it was unnecessary and would also prove disruptive to the team.

Fedotovas eventually emerged from the meeting and told Anderton that Vladimir Romanov wanted to sack Burley. It was explained to Anderton that all four Lithuanian directors were in agreement with Romanov about the course of action to be taken; in other words, it didn't matter what Anderton and the two other Scottish directors (Stewart Fraser and George Foulkes) thought or how they voted, it was a done deal – the four (Fedotovas and Roman Romanov plus Liutauras Varanavičius and Julija Gončaruk by phone) had intimated they would vote in favour of Burley's dismissal.

Fedotovas asked Anderton to get in touch with Brodies, the

club's lawyers, to find out what the legal position was vis-à-vis George Burley. Anderton, on the advice of Fedotovas, then left Tynecastle for a short while to escape the mayhem and phoned Brodies from a nearby coffee shop. The chief executive explained what had happened with Burley that afternoon and sought advice from the law firm but was told that the club would have to go through the proper procedures to sanction such a move.

On his way back to his office, Phil Anderton phoned George Foulkes to update him on the situation. 'I went back to my house in Ayr after the meeting in the morning,' explained Foulkes, 'but on the way home I received a phone call from Phil telling me exactly what had happened. I said, "WHAT? He [Romanov] can't do that. He's not even on the board!"'

'Incidentally, at around the same time, we were getting complaints from other large shareholders – led by Calum Lancastle – that we were giving Vladimir Romanov too much say and that he should not have so much influence because he was only a 29 per cent shareholder. We were planning to meet with them to try and allay their fears – that meeting never took place, of course, as it was overtaken by events.'

By this stage, Burley had left Tynecastle, having told Vladimir Romanov he had to go to the airport to pick up his wife, allowing him time to speak to his agent to discuss his next step. In fact, his wife didn't fly north that day after Burley phoned her to explain what had happened.

Phil Anderton entered his office in a bid to try and sort things out with Vladimir Romanov, Roman Romanov and Sergejus Fedotovas and buy some more time for George Burley. A general discussion ensued, during which Phil went through the legal options provided to him by Brodies.

George Burley reappeared a short time later and re-entered the room, telling Romanov he wanted to remain at Hearts and take charge of the team the following day against Dunfermline. He told Romanov and the Lithuanians he would speak to his wife over the weekend and then let them know his decision at the start of the following week. Burley then stood up and left the room, much to Vladimir Romanov's annoyance.

Phil Anderton followed Burley out of the room and into his car for a chat. Burley explained to Anderton that it was clear the end was nigh and it was obvious Romanov no longer wanted him at Tynecastle; he suggested a compromise agreement would be in the best interests of both parties because his position as head coach was now untenable. This would ensure that the Romanovs or any other Hearts director would not be able to make public allegations that might besmirch his character, while he would not be able to talk to newspapers about the interference from above and the breakdown of his relationship with Vladimir Romanov. A compromise agreement also ensured there would be no sacking, which could have led to a messy court case with dirty linen being aired in public on both sides.

Following his discussion with George Burley, Phil Anderton went back to his office and explained the details of the conversation to Vladimir Romanov, Roman Romanov and Sergejus Fedotovas and outlined Burley's suggestion for an agreement. Anderton then suggested that Burley continue to take charge for the match against Dunfermline less than 24 hours later to allow everyone time to reach a compromise. At this point, Vladimir threw his toys out of the pram! Romanov disagreed with Anderton's recommendation, claiming that Burley was 'poisoning the team' and was 'wrong for the club'. He told Anderton, 'Burley MUST go – he must go NOW!'

From that point onwards, Anderton's days at Hearts were numbered, although he didn't know it at the time – Vladimir Romanov now regarded him as an enemy as much as an employee. Romanov demanded loyalty from his staff – he expected his chief executive to be devoted to him, not to the head coach, and felt Anderton had screwed up by suggesting other alternatives and coming up with his own recommendations following his discussion with George Burley.

Those present at Tynecastle eventually agreed that, from a purely legal requirement, Phil Anderton should contact Burley's agent Athole Still to ratify the agreed course of action. It was suggested during the subsequent phone conversation between the pair that something be put in writing to clarify the agreement. This was drawn up by the CEO, checked by Sergejus Fedotovas and Brodies, and emailed to Burley's agent. A compensation package would be agreed the following week due to the time constraints.

Anderton also checked with Brodies that the agreement reached that day was legitimate without having been voted on at a board meeting. He was told it was binding as long as the board convened at the earliest possible opportunity to formally ratify the decision. An emergency board meeting was organised and scheduled to take place at Tynecastle at noon the following day, prior to the match against Dunfermline. George Burley, though, would not be taking charge of the team against the Pars and was, in effect, no longer the head coach of Hearts . . .

Friday, 21 October 2005 was a dramatic day in the history of Heart of Midlothian Football Club. It was important because of the financial announcement in the morning and sensational due to the events concerning George Burley, but it was also the day when the pendulum effectively swung Vladimir Romanov's way for good in the boardroom with the departure of SMG representative David Archer from the board. Romanov now had the power to get his fellow countrymen and countrywomen to vote in his favour, knowing fine well he would get a majority, no matter what.

George Foulkes travelled back to Edinburgh on the Saturday morning for the emergency board meeting. His influence, however, was minimal, as Romanov had already made his mind up about Burley. 'Phil Anderton had informed me that Sergejus Fedotovas and Roman Romanov had already consulted with Julija Gončaruk and Liutauras Varanavičius on the telephone, and all the Lithuanians were in agreement that George Burley should go,' said Foulkes. 'It was four of them and three of us – Phil Anderton, Stewart Fraser and myself – and we had not even had a chance to vote on the issue or express our thoughts! That's when I spoke of my concern – and requested it to be in the minutes – that we had been faced with a fait accompli and there was nothing we could do. I was very unhappy about what was going on.'

The board formally rubber-stamped Friday's agreement that George Burley would not be in charge of team affairs for the Dunfermline game. They also sanctioned a compromise agreement to be drawn up the following week and to include a confidentiality clause and adequate compensation for the termination of Burley's contract – it would be negotiated between Phil Anderton and Athole Still. But Anderton's dismissal the following week meant that nothing was ever signed, even though the Romanovs did meet with Burley's representatives in London at the end of October 2005 in a bid to try and reach a sensible solution. Burley's claim for compensation was eventually dropped in October 2006, despite his own lawyers indicating he had a very good case.

'We agreed we should make a joint announcement – the famous 6 p.m. statement that the world and his uncle seemed to be waiting for – but I was unhappy I had to inform the media that the decision had been mutually agreed,' said Foulkes. 'A number of people who saw me make that statement knew that I wasn't happy doing so. I simply explained to them that I, perhaps, was not a very good actor . . .'

With Burley now gone, the search was on for his replacement. Coach John McGlynn took the reins on a temporary basis, assisted by Valdas Ivanauskas. 'Valdas was very helpful during the period,' said McGlynn. 'I discussed team selections with him, but I had the final call with regards to picking the team. During that short period of time, I selected what I thought was the correct side, I made the substitutions and I was not influenced by anyone, although I was more than happy to liaise with Valdas and use his knowledge if it benefited the team and the situation.'

Although he steadied the ship and helped prepare the players immediately before the match against Dunfermline on the day Burley left the club, John McGlynn's first proper game in charge was the 1–0 victory over Kilmarnock at Tynecastle four days after the dramatic developments. That was followed by a trip to Easter Road the following Saturday, the day Hearts' unbeaten start to their SPL campaign finally came to an end as a result of a 2–0 defeat at the hands of arch-rivals Hibs. The loss was a bitter pill to swallow for all connected with the club; it was also the catalyst for another incredible decision by Vladimir Romanov . . .

FOUR

BOARDROOM UPHEAVAL

MONDAY, 24 OCTOBER 2005

VLADIMIR ROMANOV ALWAYS USED A MONIKER TO REFER TO Phil Anderton in absentia: he was the 'Wunderkind'. Two days after the dramatic departure of George Burley, the Wunderkind was called into a meeting that Sergejus Fedotovas had organised with Brodies. Anderton was asked to recount details of the comments he had made about George Burley at a board meeting earlier that month. The chief executive was also asked if there were any other issues or stories concerning Burley that he could think of. Phil replied that he'd had a brief discussion with a director of a leading Edinburgh company after a completely unfounded allegation against George Burley had been made public, but the director confirmed that no such incident had ever taken place. Despite the confirmation that it was untrue, the allegation still found its way onto the list of reasons to get rid of Burley (several of which were incorrect) being prepared for Vladimir Romanov, which the Lithuanian hoped would ultimately ensure that he would not have to pay his former manager for the remainder of his contract.

It quickly became clear to Anderton that Fedotovas, on behalf of Romanov, was trying to find any possible means to justify the termination of Burley's contract on the grounds of gross misconduct in a bid to avoid paying the requisite compensation. Using Burley's alleged problems as the only reason for his sacking would not be acceptable from a legal point of view – Anderton had checked this out. The chief executive had also confirmed at a previous board meeting that there had never been any allegation of misconduct mentioned in connection with Burley. The head coach had done nothing wrong and the club had not invoked any disciplinary procedures against him – trying to proceed with a case for non-payment of compensation to Burley was nigh on impossible with the lack of evidence they had.

A chronology of events was subsequently drawn up for Romanov by Brodies, although it transpired a lot of the content that was supplied to the law firm was factually incorrect, including details of a meeting Anderton was supposed to have had with a director of Derby County in relation to Burley – Phil had never even met the man before!

THURSDAY, 27 OCTOBER 2005

Three days later, interviews took place with Sir Bobby Robson and Claudio Ranieri. This was the first occasion when Phil Anderton was introduced to Rolandas, a Russian lawyer representing Vladimir Romanov, who was also used as a translator for Romanov in these two interviews.

Talks finally broke down with Claudio Ranieri, following his exorbitant wage demands (reported to be in the region of £1.7 million per annum), but discussions were ongoing with Sir Bobby Robson. Phil Anderton was in attendance at the

Radisson SAS in Edinburgh, along with Romanov and Rolandas, when Robson was interviewed again. Romanov was asking Robson questions (through the interpreter) when suddenly Rolandas, on behalf of Romanov, asked Anderton to leave the room as Vladimir wanted a few minutes on his own with the former Newcastle boss.

Sir Bobby emerged a short time later and told Anderton that he had been offered the job but for a miserly amount of money. Robson announced his concern that his salary would not be paid from Hearts' bank account, while the former England boss also expressed his disappointment that Anderton was not allowed to sit in throughout the whole interview. Despite all this, Robson told Anderton that he remained very interested in the post if one or two things could be sorted out. The chief executive promised to get back in touch within twenty-four hours and the two men went their separate ways.

FRIDAY, 28 OCTOBER 2006

Phil Anderton attended a pre-arranged meeting at Brodies' offices in Atholl Crescent in Edinburgh with Rolandas and Iain Young, a senior partner at the firm. Rolandas asked Young, on behalf of Brodies, to sign the chronology-of-events paper to make it look more legitimate – but he steadfastly refused to put pen to paper. Phil was also asked to sign the document and refused to do so. When Anderton enquired why they wanted him to sign the paper, Rolandas – in front of Young – said that Vladimir Romanov would be negotiating with Athole Still the following week, and if he had a document with Anderton's (or Brodies') signature on it, then it would carry a lot more clout in their discussions.

During his time in Brodies' offices, Anderton, as promised, got back in touch with Sir Bobby Robson in a bid to strike a deal. Robson was still angry at the level of cash promised – it was reported at the time that he had been on £2 million per annum at Newcastle – and while he stressed that money was not his number-one goal, he claimed he had been insulted by the initial offer. Anderton explained that negotiations with Vladimir Romanov were sometimes like that until the two parties could come to an agreement. The chief executive asked if Robson still wanted the job, at which point Sir Bobby said yes, subject to an acceptable salary offer.

SATURDAY, 29 OCTOBER 2005 – EASTER ROAD
2.10 p.m.
After mingling with Hibernian directors on arrival at Easter Road, Phil Anderton made his way over to the other end of the boardroom for a chat with Vladimir Romanov to inform him that, following further talks, Robson had agreed to take the job as long as the club was willing to offer an increase in salary. Romanov, though, demanded that talks with all prospective candidates were put on hold until the Burley situation was sorted out.

At this time, George Foulkes, having witnessed Romanov's animated retort to Anderton, suggested it might be better if that specific discussion took place after the game . . .

5.00 p.m.
Hearts had lost their first league match of the season: a 2–0 defeat to Edinburgh rivals Hibernian. In the boardroom after the game, Vladimir Romanov, pointing his finger at Phil Anderton, told his chief executive that the team had lost because of George Burley, despite the former head coach having been away from the club for a week. Anderton countered this claim by suggesting the match was lost because Burley was no longer in the dugout . . .

The discussion from earlier in the day restarted, with

Romanov reiterating to Anderton that he would not appoint a new head coach until the situation concerning the old one had been sorted out. He told Anderton that he had to sort out the problem and sign the chronology-of-events paper. Again, fingers were pointed in the direction of the CEO, but Anderton informed the majority shareholder that he'd been told by a third party that Romanov was going to take charge of the Burley situation. At this point, things were starting to get heated – although no voices were raised – leading George Foulkes to intervene and suggest that it was not an appropriate place for a discussion of that nature. Vladimir Romanov shrugged, laughed and then walked away.

Phil Anderton knew the writing was on the wall for him. He'd been told to sack George Burley against his wishes and had been blackballed by Romanov for refusing to sign the chronology-of-events paper. Anderton was guilty of insubordination in Romanov's eyes. He was well aware he was not Vladimir's favourite employee . . .

The chief executive decided to inform George Foulkes and Roman Romanov that, although he wanted to stay at Hearts, it was his intention to resign when his contract expired at the end of that season unless things changed dramatically and the interference from Vladimir Romanov ceased.

Anderton left Easter Road for home, where he drew up a letter explaining his intentions. The letter was emailed to George Foulkes on the Sunday morning.

As he was leaving Easter Road, George Foulkes's mobile phone rang – Vladimir Romanov wanted to see him later that evening in his hotel suite at the Radisson SAS. This was a surprise, as the chairman had already suggested in the boardroom that they would reconvene the following day.

Four people were present in Romanov's suite that night:

George Foulkes, David Southern (Hearts' communications director), Rolandas and Vladimir. There had clearly been a breakdown in relations with Phil Anderton, so, needless to say, the chief executive's position was the only topic for discussion. 'I said to Romanov in the hotel room that it would perhaps be better to leave things alone until the following day when we could meet again to discuss the situation further,' said Foulkes. 'Following talks, Vladimir agreed to a meeting with Phil Anderton and myself on the Sunday, at which point I said my goodbyes and headed back to Ayr after another long day.'

It normally took George Foulkes about an hour and a half to get home from Edinburgh, less that night because the traffic was a lot lighter. As the chairman was heading along the M8, his mobile rang again. 'Roman phoned me as I was making my way back to Ayr to say that Vladimir was now unable to meet Phil and me the following day – he was going to Tannadice instead to watch Dundee United and Celtic.' It was agreed the discussion would continue on the Monday.

SUNDAY, 30 OCTOBER 2005
5.00 p.m.

The match at Tannadice had been finished for about an hour when George received another phone call from Roman Romanov. 'I was at home,' said Foulkes, 'but Roman asked if I could come to Edinburgh right away to meet Vladimir. The pair of them were on their way back from Dundee. I said, "Look, I am in Ayr – it's at least an hour and a half away. Anyway, I'm doing things tonight that I have not been able to do over the weekend because of my commitments to Hearts. I have other important work that needs done – I am doing it now, and I simply do not have the time to come up to Edinburgh."

'Roman said that it was vital that I met with Vladimir that

100

evening, but I explained that I could come up the following day after attending a funeral. "No, no. We must see you tonight," said Junior. "We will come to you."'

And so the Romanov magical mystery tour began . . .

'It was pouring with rain that day, and they managed to get themselves lost on the way down to Ayr,' explained Foulkes. 'They eventually arrived and presented my wife with a bunch of flowers and some chocolates that had been purchased at the BP filling station just up the road from my house!

'Liz had prepared some coffee, tea and smoked-salmon sandwiches – that sort of thing – but they got straight down to business. They were at my home to persuade me that Phil Anderton should be sacked. I told them they had no reason to do so, but they said he had to go for refusing to sign the document justifying George Burley's sacking.

'I explained to them that of course Phil had refused to sign the document – some of the allegations were wrong and others were impossible to verify. They had strengthened it, and they obviously wanted to use this as part of the justification for getting rid of Burley. There was no way I was going to agree to Anderton's sacking anyway, but for them to try and use this as evidence beggared belief, and I told them that I would not be agreeable to the sacking of the chief executive.'

Vladimir and Roman left soon after they ate the sandwiches. It is not known what route they took to get back to Edinburgh or, for that matter, how long it took them to arrive back in Auld Reekie . . .

'I was planning to go to a funeral in Cumnock the following day but was suspicious so pulled out and headed for Edinburgh instead,' said Foulkes. 'On the way, I received a phone call from Irene McPhee [club secretary] informing me that an emergency board meeting had been called by Roman Romanov for 12 p.m. – high noon, if you like. I said, "But the Lithuanians won't be able to get over at such short notice," to which she replied, "Oh, they are on their way or are already here!"

'The whole thing had been planned. That is why Vladimir had to see me on the Sunday night – he knew exactly what he was doing. It had all been set up to try to persuade me to back the sacking of Phil.'

When Foulkes eventually arrived at Tynecastle, he saw a member of staff crying and immediately knew something was up. 'I told Vladimir and Roman they could get rid of George Burley, even though I thought they were wrong doing that, because he could look after himself – but now they wanted to get rid of the chief executive and had also got a lady who had worked for the club for many years into a state,' Foulkes said. 'I told the pair of them I was not going to have that, and I poked a finger at Vladimir, to the utter amazement of Roman, who immediately shrieked loudly and looked as though he had seen a ghost because of what I had done to his father. Well, I soon realised I had gone too far – it's not like me – and it quickly became apparent that no one had ever stood up to his father before!'

The emergency board meeting was subsequently convened, and those directors who were involved made their way into the boardroom. Before they even got a chance to get comfortable in their seats, Roman Romanov immediately moved that Phil Anderton be sacked. 'Roman said it was time to vote on the issue,' explained Foulkes. 'I said, "No – we need to discuss this." Three times I asked for a reason, and three times they refused to give me one. Stewart Fraser, to his credit, made a very positive statement and backed Phil, even though I found out afterwards he and Phil did not always agree. I also mentioned that Phil had been doing really well and was, quite rightly in my opinion, getting a lot of credit for the increase in sales and in season-ticket holders. They still, however, refused to give a reason why they wanted Phil sacked, and a vote was taken. Inevitably, it was 4–3 in favour of Romanov and the Lithuanians, and that was that.'

At his home in Ayr the previous evening, Foulkes had told Vladimir and Roman that if they went ahead with the sacking of Anderton, he would intimate his resignation. They tried to persuade Foulkes to stay on as chairman, but he declined. 'The Romanovs also tried to persuade me to stay as a board member,' said Foulkes, 'but, again, I declined. Their advisers – British Linen Bank and Brodies – then phoned me and tried to persuade me to stay because they were worried about the whole share option/offer that I was recommending. Once again, I said no – I had made my decision and was sticking by it.

'In conversation before the board meeting, our lawyers told Stewart Fraser and me not to resign but to intimate our resignations, which we both did. Stewart and I then sought independent legal advice and submitted our resignations in the proper form so we were legally covered. Stewart was actually in a different position and needed more advice than I did because he was, and still is, an employee of the club, retaining his position as finance director, even although he ultimately resigned from the board.

'Perhaps I was naive in thinking that by threatening to resign I would head them [the Romanovs] off in a bid to keep Phil. That was a mistake. Soon after – in retrospect – I made another terrible mistake! In a moment of spontaneity, I said, "Since I plan to resign as chairman, would you care to nominate someone to replace me?" I was sure they had someone lined up – whether it was Leslie Deans, a local businessman or someone else.

'Roman said, "I nominate myself." I laughed. Of course, that did not go down well either, but by that time I was past worrying! It didn't take a genius to work out why I was not the most popular person in the Romanov household at that time – pointing a finger at Vladimir and chortling at Roman!'

The departure of Phil Anderton and the subsequent resignation of George Foulkes sparked further upheaval at the football club and led to increased chaos behind the scenes at Tynecastle, just over a week after the exit of George Burley. Caretaker boss John McGlynn was one of the first to express his bewilderment: 'I'm shocked and stunned, and it's hard to comprehend. Phil seemed to be the one who was trying to get a new manager in – that's what we were led to believe he was doing. But where does that leave us now?'

Vladimir Romanov tried to shed some light on the situation when he revealed he did not think that Foulkes and Anderton had done a good enough job for the club. 'They've had over one year and not been able to do the things I've wanted to do for Hearts,' he said, even though Anderton was only in office for seven months! 'They've had the funds and all my energy, but I've not had the response I've wanted.'

That explanation, however, did not go down well with many fans. John Borthwick, secretary of the Federation of Hearts Supporters Clubs, wanted additional answers as a result of Phil Anderton's forced removal. 'We talked about Mr Romanov arriving like a knight in shining armour last season when we thought Tynecastle was going to be sold,' he said, 'but we now need him to explain what is going on. We'd had record ticket sales, were unbeaten in 12 games before Saturday and the club was being marketed like never before. So, when Mr Romanov says the chief executive had not delivered what was expected, what I would like to know is – what was expected?'

Although Roman Romanov decided to get rid of Phil Anderton on Hallowe'en, the new Hearts chairman stopped short of dressing up and going round the doors of supporters in a bid to seek forgiveness. He did, however, ask fans for patience after a turbulent ten days. 'Sometimes, in order to continually progress, it is necessary to take action that may seem unpalatable at the time; however, we only ever act with the long-term interests of Heart of Midlothian Football Club [in mind],' he said. 'We were forced to take the decisions made in connection with the manager and chief executive's departures. In the short term, many people will ask why. However, we ask our fans to judge us on the results that we are determined to bring to the club. Despite the events of the last ten days and suggestions otherwise, I would like to assure all Hearts fans that we are still entirely resolute in delivering the success that we have spoken about throughout our involvement with this great club.'

There are two sides to every story, however, and although Anderton's exit may have left most Hearts fans bewildered, former Tynecastle director Liutauras Varanavičius believed the departure of the chief executive was necessary for the club to continue functioning properly. 'The problem with Anderton was that he was too proud of himself,' he said. 'He was not working as a team member – he was acting primarily for himself. Romanov not only values loyalty, but he demands that his employees always have the interests of the club as the number-one priority. If you are part of the team, then you do your best for the team. If not, then you dig your own grave. Anderton wanted to show everyone how professional a chief executive he was, no matter what it took, but Romanov did not appreciate this kind of approach.'

A letter written to the board by Phil Anderton before the Burley affair outlined the chief executive's concern at the club's financial position. That certainly didn't curry favour with Vladimir, but it wasn't the only thing that annoyed the majority shareholder. His constant refusal to sign the chronology-of-events paper relating to Burley's sacking was not appreciated;

neither was his involvement in the compromise agreement that was drawn up at the time of Burley's departure. That was, and still is, a major bugbear for Romanov, according to Varanavičius: 'That was a big annoyance, but it was not only that. It was how Phil Anderton handled the discussions with Burley. It was not only the compromise agreement – there were also a lot of other issues that were done the wrong way. I think that Romanov wanted to make the exit of Burley less painful for the coach, but the way the chief executive handled that situation was done in a very poor manner.

'Romanov's general plan is to ensure Hearts are successful in the long term – he will only accept good results if they are replicated on a consistent basis. He expects all the employees of the club to work together to achieve this goal. Individual achievement is frowned upon if it does not benefit either the team or the club as a whole. Maybe some of the people who were at the club during my time there did not respect this idea and that was why the club parted company with them . . .'

Ten Days That Shook the World was John Reed's classic account of the Russian Revolution. The brave new world of Heart of Midlothian, on the other hand, was shaken to the core by its own ten days of bloodletting, although on this occasion the Romanov dynasty continued to rule the roost . . .

FIVE

SAY HELLO, WAVE GOODBYE, GRAHAM

ON 15 NOVEMBER 2005, THE *DAILY TELEGRAPH* REPORTED that Vladimir Romanov offered George Burley his old job back just ten days after his acrimonious departure – on the Tuesday after the 2–0 loss to Hibs at Easter Road on 29 October. However bizarre and implausible that may sound, former Hearts director Liutauras Varanavičius confirmed that Romanov did indeed get in touch with his former boss and his representatives. 'The offer to George Burley of his old job back was related to the sacking itself,' he said. 'Romanov's proposal was a sincere one [but] both parties have now moved on, and I think the chances of Vladimir Romanov wanting to work with George Burley again are very slim. Burley depended too much on agents, and that is the problem in football in both Scotland and England – most of the teams are run by agents, not coaches or managers.'

So why, exactly, did Romanov offer Burley his old job back?

A close confidant of Phil Anderton claims that the former chief executive believed there were three reasons:

1. Vladimir Romanov was not expecting such a vociferous reaction from fans when he sacked George Burley. Anderton stood beside Romanov at the infamous Dunfermline game and thought that the majority shareholder's ego was bruised when supporters angrily gesticulated in his direction.
2. Once Phil Anderton was gone, Romanov could get George Burley back and blame his initial departure on the former chief executive. Vladimir would then be seen as the saviour.
3. Romanov looked at their flimsy legal case concerning the dismissal of Burley and came to the conclusion that it would be cheaper to reinstate the head coach instead of paying compensation.

Whatever the reason, Burley point-blank refused to return to Tynecastle, and after nearly three weeks without a permanent Hearts head coach, Graham Rix – a candidate for the vacant managerial position at English non-league side Crawley Town – was chosen as his unlikely replacement.

'Romanov believed that, because of his past, Graham Rix would not be influenced by agents as much as other coaches,' said Varanavičius. 'Romanov looked for someone who would be loyal to him and loyal to the team – that is why he appointed Graham Rix to succeed George Burley.'

The appointment of Rix as the new head coach of Hearts on 8 November 2005 was a huge surprise, especially after club officials had held talks with, among others, Claudio Ranieri and Bobby Robson. The lack of a big name was a concern for some fans, and Rix's past was clearly an issue for others, but it was the nationwide television coverage showing a small minority of supporters shouting abuse at the former England international and kicking Cossack hats in disgust at the appointment that made former chairman Doug Smith cringe. 'A lot of viewers outside Scotland saw the reaction of those fans. It got a lot of publicity in England and surprised a lot of people,' said Smith. 'Graham Rix was starting off on the back foot – it was never going to be easy for him after that. In my opinion, choosing Rix seemed to be more of a stopgap appointment until the end of the season, when his position would be reviewed, depending on performance and results.

'Whether the appointment of Graham Rix was a mistake is open to conjecture, but his friend Gianluca Vialli certainly didn't think so. I remember the Italian was a guest pundit on Sky Sports covering the Premiership match between Manchester United and Chelsea at Old Trafford, just two days before Graham's appointment as head coach of Hearts. Vialli certainly gave Graham a tremendous endorsement in front of a nationwide audience.

'It is never easy trying to find a quality manager during a season. As we found out when trying to replace Jim Jefferies, it can sometimes be awkward arranging to meet candidates – getting a time that suits both parties – and then sorting out follow-up interviews if necessary. As often as not, the top names have their own agendas. Sometimes, especially if you are trying to make the appointment mid-season, they are not available straight away. At other times, certain financial demands make you wonder why you even made an effort to approach the person in the first place . . .'

Graham Rix arrived at Tynecastle without bringing any backroom staff with him but quickly settled into his role with the help of John McGlynn, Valdas Ivanauskas and the rest of the coaching staff who had remained at Riccarton following the departure of George Burley. McGlynn had taken charge of team affairs for the four matches prior to the arrival of Rix but was more than happy to step aside for the new man, even though it meant getting used to a new coaching style: 'Working with Graham Rix was different from working with George Burley. Graham arrived on his own, whereas George came with an entourage. Graham had to rely on me, Valdas, Stephen Frail and John Murray at first to help him settle in and provide him with background knowledge of the way the club worked and was run, and we gave him information on players and opponents. Valdas was like his chauffeur initially – he would pick Graham up from the hotel every morning and take him to the training ground, then back to the Dalmahoy Hotel, where he was staying. He was with him a lot until Graham got his own club car and moved into his own flat. Valdas spent a lot of time socialising with the new gaffer and going for meals with him. It was a good way for them to get to know each other, and it helped build up a trust.

'It was also good to have Valdas as part of the team. He knew what the owner wanted. He has been there, in some capacity, since Mr Romanov first invested in the football club. Initially, I think he would have been letting Mr Romanov know how training was going, but I don't think he was going back telling tales. It was always handy having Valdas around, as he was able to pass on instructions to the Lithuanian players – he was very loud, very sharp, very abrupt and to the point, but he got his message across loud and clear.'

Rix demanded quality and complete professionalism from his players both on the training ground and on the pitch, as you would expect from someone who played for Arsenal and had a coaching role at Chelsea. He was in charge of the youth team at Stamford Bridge and presided over the likes of John Terry coming through the ranks. This meant he was able to relate to the young players who were coming through at Hearts, none more so than Calum Elliot. 'Prior to Graham taking over, he watched the Dundee United game at Tynecastle, and Calum did exceptionally well that day,' said McGlynn. 'Graham was very pleased with his performance. Calum had already impressed his soon-to-be new boss, and he didn't even know it! Rix was also very much a players' manager – he would talk to them a lot after training and spent a fair bit of time giving Calum, among others, plenty of encouragement. He also relied a lot on Steven Pressley and Paul Hartley – he would talk to them all the time.'

It's been suggested that the use of different training methods was one of the reasons why Graham Rix was unable to replicate the success of George Burley. Without being critical of his former boss, Steven Pressley confirmed that the training became 'more technical than intense'. The players, having been used to Burley's high-tempo approach, suddenly had to change mid-season, and Rix won just one of his first five games in charge of Hearts as the squad struggled to adapt to the new regime.

'Graham's training methods were different from George's,' said John McGlynn. 'Burley had particularly high demands; Rix's demands were possibly not quite at that level. I would say the players were more relaxed in their approach under Graham. Once things were finished with George, they were done and dusted. Graham, on the other hand, would pull players aside and talk to them either on their way off the training ground, in the changing-room after sessions or even in his office.'

The usual scenario at Riccarton the day before a match involved Graham Rix meeting the press in the seminar room before going outside for a quick Café Crème cigar, during which time I would interview him for Radio Forth – inhaling smoke, though, was not ideal when I was trying to ask him questions! Before the one-to-one interview got under way, he would always enquire – at least in the early stages of his employment – how he had 'performed' in front of the press, as if self-belief and self-confidence were still an issue for him when facing journalists he had yet to get to know and trust. Despite this, a cheery 'Hi, guys' was uttered weekly as he sat down for the press conference, and he usually tried to crack a joke.

Not too many, if any, of the press seemed to have an issue with Graham Rix as a person, but many of them had an issue with his managerial ability and felt he couldn't cut the mustard – some, right from the start. 'Appointing Graham Rix did not help Hearts following the departure of George Burley, and his ideas were quickly shown to be wrong, compared with his predecessor's,' said *The Scotsman*'s chief sports writer Stuart Bathgate. 'The first time I interviewed Rix, three or four days after his appointment, he said to me that the Hearts team had to learn to play more patient, slow-tempo football. That was a big mistake. The team had started the season extremely well with a fast-paced, fluent style that got results and entertained at the same time. Rix thought he was more sophisticated as he was coming from English football, which obviously is superior in technical terms. However, sometimes if you impose a sophisticated model in a crude market, it does not work.'

Graham Rix, Valdas Ivanauskas and John McGlynn regularly discussed possible signing targets with a view to bringing them on board during the January transfer window. With Roman Bednář on the sidelines for a few months after sustaining ligament damage in the match against Rangers in September 2005, the need for a new striker was more pressing than any other position.

'Jimmy Floyd Hasselbaink's name cropped up in one of those conversations after his agent enquired if we would be interested in signing the Dutchman,' said John McGlynn. 'Graham mentioned he was unsure how our tightly knit squad would react to the arrival of that kind of high-profile player. We decided not to take things any further because we did not want to risk disrupting the harmony and morale in the dressing-room. As much as I think the fans would have been very impressed with us bringing a player of that calibre to the football club, we did not want to lose the other good things that we had.

'We were keen to sign a striker when both Edgaras and Roman were out injured. Graham made an unsuccessful attempt to get Carlton Cole on loan from Chelsea. He also made an enquiry to see if Mikael Forsell was available, but when we realised he was on £30,000 per week, we quickly dropped our interest!'

FOOTBALL – IT'S A FUNNY OLD GAME

Legendary striker John Robertson spent 16 years at Tynecastle (with the exception of a short spell at Newcastle) trying to obtain a winner's medal with Hearts, eventually doing so in his last match in a maroon jersey against Rangers at Parkhead on 16 May 1998. How ironic, then, that it was Robbo who set Hearts on the road to Hampden, and ultimate success, on 10 December 2005 when he, along with Ally Dawson, made the third-round draw for the Tennent's Scottish Cup at Tynecastle. Robertson and Dawson paired Hearts with top-flight rivals Kilmarnock in one of two all-SPL ties in the third round. The match would be played on Saturday, 7 January 2006.

Meanwhile, Vladimir Romanov promised to splash the cash to boost the squad when the January transfer window eventually opened. Hearts fans were expecting one or two new faces, but no one, least of all John McGlynn, could believe it when the month ended with a total of eleven new players being brought to the club. 'It was remarkable,' he said. 'They just seemed to keep bringing players in before the transfer deadline at the end of January. Far too many new signings came in. In my opinion, three or four quality players would have been ideal. I honestly do not know why they went that far. Training the players became an overnight problem. To have more than 30 players, not including long-term absentees, meant there was no easy way to train everyone properly and keep them all happy.

'We ended up with a very basic, harsh way of deciding who trained where. Graham decided which players he wanted to work with, and I was left with the others. A list was pinned to the wall each morning – not very personal, but it was the only way to do it. Names in yellow would be on pitch one, names in red on pitch two.

'The new signings all came from clubs where they were playing regular first-team football, so it must have been hard for them if they were not involved in the main squad. But there was no way we could risk having too many guys in the main group preparing for matches because other players would suffer. It was a harsh way of doing things, but the number of players in our squad meant we had no option.'

Prior to the arrival of the 11 new signings, Hearts entertained Celtic in a league match on New Year's Day. The tall dark strangers from Parkhead brought their lump of coal and slice of black bun to Tynecastle and then disappeared with all three points thanks to two late goals that earned them a 3–2 win! Whether that was the match that ultimately 'decided' the destination of the league title is open to conjecture, but one thing is for sure: it was one of the games of the season, and it was witnessed by Hearts legend, former France keeper Gilles Rousset. 'I was only able to attend one match in season 2005–06, but what a match it was,' he said. 'I came over to Edinburgh on Hogmanay and saw in the New Year in Princes Street Gardens before my hangover and I went to Tynecastle to watch Hearts against Celtic. I had a smashing couple of days back in Scotland – it's always good for me to come back because I feel Edinburgh is like my home. The reception I got from people in the city centre on Hogmanay, and also from the fans at half-time during the Celtic match, was incredible. Everybody spoke to me and said nice things – it was wonderful.

'I think that game at Tynecastle summed up the whole of Hearts' season in just 90 minutes, with highs and lows and plenty of drama. It was a crazy match, full of excitement, but that was forgotten about following the loss of those two late goals. If Hearts had managed to hold on to their lead in that game, I think the title race may have been a different story. Hearts deserved to win; unfortunately, they lost, and the psychological difference between a one-point gap at the top and a seven-point gap was massive. I don't think it was possible to recover after that. It was a big blow for Hearts to lose that game, especially in that way.'

A Hearts win against Celtic that day would have taken them to within one point of their opponents at the top of the table – the defeat meant they trailed the Parkhead side by seven points. According to Gary Mackay, that was when Hearts' chances of winning the league title ultimately evaporated. 'Going into the game against the league leaders, we all believed that a win could reignite our title challenge and prompt a concerted push to dislodge Celtic from the top of the table,' he said. 'At half-time, and leading 2–0, it looked like this could be the case. Unfortunately, three things in the second half caused a complete transformation: the introduction after an hour of Celtic sub Stephen Pearson; the ridiculous red card shown to Takis Fyssas; and also something much more deep-rooted than either of those two incidents. The third reason, in my opinion, was that the team as a whole did not have the requisite level of fitness required to maintain a title challenge throughout the season. None of the summer signings, of whom most were regular starters, took part in a full pre-season training schedule with Hearts, and I think that was the first game where this problem was evident. With the 3–2 reverse, the league title had slipped completely from our grasp.'

There was a touch of irony and a sense of déjà vu as Hearts began their 2006 Scottish Cup campaign against Kilmarnock at Tynecastle the week after the dramatic Celtic match. The man who helped bring the trophy back to Gorgie in 1998 for the first time in 42 years – Jim Jefferies – was given the chance to knock out his boyhood heroes at the first hurdle. He had failed 12 months previously when the Jambos progressed in the competition following a replay at Rugby Park.

This was the fourteenth time in the history of the Scottish Cup that the two sides had been drawn together, and Hearts recorded their tenth win. Steven Pressley nodded home a long throw from Robbie Neilson in the first half before substitute Jamie McAllister added a second after 75 minutes. Colin Nish pulled one back for Killie with five minutes to go, but, despite some scary moments, Hearts held on to secure a place in the fourth round.

Their path to the final opened up considerably the following day after one of the biggest shocks in the history of the competition. First Division Clyde, made up of a group of players who were selected following pre-season trials, knocked out cup-holders Celtic in a day of drama at Broadwood. Roy Keane made his debut for the Hoops after joining the club at the start of January, but he and his teammates succumbed to goals from Craig Bryson and Eddie Malone as David conquered Goliath.

Broadwood was not the only venue that produced a cup shock, with three more SPL sides losing to lower-league opposition. Dunfermline lost 4–3 to Airdrie United in their replay at East End Park, Motherwell were hammered 3–0 by First Division leaders St Mirren, while Second Division part-timers Alloa won 2–1 at Livingston after a replay, former Jambo Robert Sloan scoring a late winner for the Wasps at Almondvale. Elsewhere, Aberdeen came from two goals down at Tannadice to send Dundee United packing, and, incredibly, half the teams from the SPL had been eliminated in just one round.

There was still a sense of disbelief at Broadwood after Clyde's demolition of Celtic when Scotland's First Minister Jack McConnell and Alex Smith made the draw for the fourth round. Robbo and Ally Dawson had paired Hearts with SPL opposition in the previous round – would this draw be a little kinder to Graham Rix and his players? The answer was no! Hearts were to face Aberdeen at Tynecastle, but at least it gave the Gorgie Boys a chance to settle an old score. No Hearts team had ever beaten the Dons at home or away in the competition; the Jambos' only victory was in the 1995–96 semi-final at the neutral Hampden, courtesy of goals from John Robertson and Allan Johnston.

The month, despite starting with defeat in the cruellest of fashion, ended with a very pleasing 4–1 victory over Hibs at Tynecastle. Yet another full house was crammed into the Gorgie ground, including Barry Wood back on holiday in Edinburgh from Perth, Australia. 'I was fortunate enough to return to Scotland for a holiday and was delighted to get the chance to savour the atmosphere at Tynecastle in person,' he said. 'A full house for every home game sounded fantastic on *Hearts World* through my broadband connection on the other side of the world, but when I walked into the stadium two minutes before kick-off in the Edinburgh derby (and only two hours after my flight from Perth had arrived in Glasgow!), the noise was possibly the loudest I had heard it since the night we beat Bayern.

'The applause for Wallace Mercer was a great sign of respect for a true Hearts man; he did plenty of good for the club and will never be forgotten. The pace, enterprise and determination of the team that day was a true reflection of what this Hearts team was all about, and it was just amazing being part of the atmosphere, albeit having just arrived from the Australian summer to a somewhat chilly Gorgie Road. I spent the next three days thawing out!'

February began with the fourth-round Scottish Cup tie against Aberdeen at Tynecastle, but Hearts were dealt a blow four days before the match when the SFA retrospectively suspended midfielder Paul Hartley for lashing out at Celtic defender Ross Wallace near the end of the league game at Tynecastle on New Year's Day. Match referee Iain Brines missed the incident, but it was captured by television footage.

Another fast start – Hearts' trademark in 2005–06 – and first-half goals from Michal Pospíšil, Calum Elliot and Steven Pressley (penalty) wrapped up a comfortable 3–0 victory and a place in the last eight.

In yet another shock, Rangers exited the Scottish Cup at the hands of Hibs before Hearts had even kicked off against Aberdeen. Tony Mowbray and his players went to Ibrox and recorded their second 3–0 victory of the season in Govan. For the first time since 1987, neither of the Old Firm would be represented in the quarter-final draw, which was made at Broadwood. Only four SPL sides were left in the competition – including Hearts and Hibs. The pressure was on ex-Scotland boss Craig Brown and former Clyde goalkeeper Tommy McCulloch to give Hearts a third consecutive home tie. They obliged as the Jambos were drawn against Partick Thistle (who beat Inverness Caledonian Thistle after a replay) for the ninth time in the Scottish Cup and the second time in as many seasons.

Graham Rix said, 'I'm pleased to avoid an Edinburgh derby.

Hibs are a good side, and the result they got at Ibrox was fantastic – I'm pleased for them. I was sweating a bit because we were one of the last teams to come out of the hat, but we can't really worry about Hibs, we can only worry about Hearts.'

The major talking point of the Graham Rix era occurred in early February 2006 prior to a league match against Dundee United at Tannadice. Six changes were made to the team that had beaten Aberdeen in the Scottish Cup three days earlier: new signings Luděk Stracený and Martin Petráš were handed their debuts, stalwarts Robbie Neilson and Andy Webster were demoted to the bench, and Christophe Berra and Rudi Skácel returned to the side at the expense of José Gonçalves and Lee Johnson. But it soon transpired that Rix had not had an input into team selection for the match – Vladimir Romanov had selected the starting line-up.

'Let's face it,' said John McGlynn, 'Mr Romanov had a big influence on which players came to the club during the January transfer window. He has a theory that players who play many games in a short period of time cannot perform to the best of their ability. I think he wanted to freshen things up for the Dundee United game at Tannadice.

'Jim Duffy [who had been brought in as director of football] had discussions with Mr Romanov leading up to that match, which he then relayed to Graham. Due to the interference, the gaffer felt the need to hold a meeting to inform the players that he had not selected the team and that there might be times during the game when substitutions would be made, not necessarily because someone was playing badly but because the changes had already been prearranged. Informing the players at that meeting, ultimately, may have cost Graham Rix his job . . .'

It's no secret that Vladimir Romanov had a large input into

which players were bought and sold by Hearts, but the revelation that he had also picked the team for the match at Tannadice should have been the final straw for Graham Rix in his position as head coach, according to Gary Mackay. 'The moment Rix was forced to tell the players that Mr Romanov had picked the team was when he should have contemplated resigning,' he said. 'It disappointed me greatly that the club became a laughing stock due to people not being able to deal with the circumstances. I think if Rix wanted to retain total respect among his squad, then he should have quit that day.'

Despite the behind-the-scenes turmoil, bookmakers installed Hearts as favourites to win the Scottish Cup following the elimination of the Old Firm, and the Sky cameras were at Tynecastle at the end of February to see if they could capture yet another cup shock. The tie involving Hearts was selected for live transmission following the quarter-final draw at the start of the month, with television executives no doubt expecting to cover the all-SPL clash between the Jambos and Inverness Caledonian Thistle. Instead, they got the big boys at home to Second Division opposition. This was the fifth live match of the competition for Sky, but, worryingly for Hearts, unfancied teams had beaten their more illustrious opponents in three of the previous four . . .

A sixth-minute header from Edgaras Jankauskas from a Paul Hartley cross helped settle the early nerves, but Partick belied their lower-league status and more than matched Hearts for long periods of the game. The Jags were on top at the start of the second half, as they pressed forward for an equaliser, but were caught by a sucker punch after 63 minutes and found themselves 2–0 down. Deividas Česnauskis cut inside from the main-stand touchline and unleashed a tremendous left-foot shot that left goalkeeper Kenny Arthur without a prayer.

Roman Bednář was shown a second yellow card (for 'simulation') after 71 minutes before Mark Roberts deservedly pulled a goal back for Partick 15 minutes from time. The ten men in maroon survived a late period of intense pressure from the Jags but managed to hold on to secure their place in the last four of the Tennent's Scottish Cup before the other three quarter-final ties were even under way (due to the 12.15 p.m. kick-off time).

Hearts were through to the semi-finals of the national cup competition, but their league challenge was faltering. It was now a case of ensuring that Rangers did not catch them in second spot, instead of Hearts trying to catch runaway leaders Celtic. The team recorded just one win in February, which did not go unnoticed in the boardroom. Two days before the league match against Rangers at Tynecastle in March, Hearts chairman Roman Romanov confirmed that Graham Rix's position would be reviewed at the end of the season. This 'vote of confidence' lasted just four days: Hearts drew the match against the Ibrox side on the Sunday and by the Tuesday Graham Rix was sacked after just 18 games in charge. Jim Duffy also lost his job as director of football. Valdas Ivanauskas was immediately appointed head coach on an interim basis until the end of the season, to be assisted by John McGlynn.

'Vladimir Romanov decided that results had not been good enough,' said Doug Smith. 'His aim was to finish second and secure a place in the Champions League, but he clearly felt this was being jeopardised with Graham Rix in charge. Romanov was both proactive by identifying the problem and reactive in doing something about it, giving the job to Valdas on a temporary basis until the summer. Once again, his decision was vindicated.'

Five days later, following the departure of Rix and Duffy, Hearts supporters were given an insight into exactly what had happened that fateful Tuesday at Riccarton, courtesy of Duffy's regular column in *Scotland on Sunday*:

> I didn't have any sense of foreboding when Graham Rix and I settled into our working day at Riccarton on Wednesday morning. On the way in, I even exchanged pleasantries with Roman Romanov – and I didn't read too much into the fact that he rarely makes an appearance at the training complex.
>
> When Valdas Ivanauskas appeared with the list of players for the session, his serious expression seemed merely an excuse for a laugh. 'He looks a real happy chappie,' I joked. I now know his sombre, sheepish demeanour was the result of knowing Graham and I were about to lose our jobs . . .

Graham Rix went upstairs to speak to Roman and was gone for around 20 minutes, during which time Jim Duffy helped Stephen Frail prepare the equipment for training – until he was called back upstairs to be told by Roman Romanov that his friend Rix had been sacked:

> The reasons given for the sacking seemed weak but in such situations there is no point in stamping your feet and throwing a hissy fit. When directors decide you are out of a club, all you can do is pack up your belongings and leave. It seems that a home draw against Rangers – even one that kept Hearts a pretty encouraging six points ahead in the chase for the Champions League place – caused the goalposts to be shifted, the demands to be altered.
>
> I tried to reason with Roman Romanov and asked that the club consider giving Graham just another ten days; let him take the team into the Scottish Cup semi-final

against Hibs and then see what happened. To that I was told in no uncertain terms that the decision was made and that was that.

It is understood that player power persuaded Vladimir Romanov to appoint a director of football, following that famous February meeting when five players – including captain Steven Pressley – expressed their concern about meddling in team affairs from above. The appointment of Jim Duffy, a former Hibs manager, received a mixed response from Hearts fans – but none of them could have guessed that his tenure as director of football would last just five weeks:

> I asked about my own situation and was told that, as I was part of the same team as Graham, the director of football post was no longer available. That was fine, I expected that. But while Graham received a letter outlining the reasons for the termination of his contract, I was given nothing in writing officially detailing the duties I had failed to perform to the club's satisfaction. No wonder. In five weeks in the director of football post, I had done absolutely everything asked and expected of me.
>
> I am angry, absolutely furious, about what happened. It is devastating to lose your job when there is absolutely no reason. It is insulting to be lectured on our area of expertise by businessmen who have absolutely no knowledge of football mechanics.
>
> Second isn't good enough for Vladimir Romanov. Not winning every game isn't good enough for Vladimir Romanov. I don't see any top-class manager being interested in a head-coach position that makes such impossible demands of its occupier.

Incredibly, for the third time in one season, Hearts were on the lookout for a new boss. In the interim period, Valdas Ivanauskas and John McGlynn were given a simple directive from above: qualify for the Champions League by finishing second in the SPL and win the Scottish Cup. Nothing less would suffice.

SIX

WALLACE MERCER, 1946–2006

SCOTTISH FOOTBALL LOST ONE OF ITS GREAT CHARACTERS IN January 2006 with the passing of former Hearts chairman Wallace Mercer. Here, his son Iain pays an emotional and personal tribute to his dad.

The referee blew his whistle and suddenly the stadium erupted in a cacophony of noise. There were 14,100 Hearts fans standing and clapping, and the chant 'There's Only One Wallace Mercer' began filtering around Tynecastle until it too was deafening. I spotted a banner in what looked like row 24 of the Wheatfield Stand that simply said 'Wallace Mercer RIP' – it was then I realised the enormity of what was taking place and how surreal it was. As I stood there in the second row of the director's box alongside my sister Helen and my mother Anne, I realised that they were also moved by the noise pouring from the three stands.

Meanwhile, the 3,200 Hibernian supporters in the School End were less euphoric in their celebrations, and many of them carried out their pre-match threat of turning their backs to the pitch. It was a pathetic attempt by a minority who were intent on showing defiance towards a man who tried to shut them down some 16 years previously. Even following the death of a person, there are some people in the world who cannot get past their own bitterness. I remember thinking after the match that they probably wished they had stayed standing with their backs to the pitch after their side was thumped 4–1!

TUESDAY, 17 JANUARY 2006

Dad was diagnosed with terminal liver cancer just before Christmas 2005, but he showed astonishing bravery and courage throughout his illness. He faced and won many battles throughout his life, but sadly this was one he was never going to win. To watch him wither away in such a short period of time was desperate and heartbreaking. It brought home to me, as if an example was ever required, just what a wretched disease cancer is and how it touches so many people's lives.

Despite not having had an active role in Hearts for 12 years, he always maintained a very public presence, and I think that was reflected in the press coverage he received following his death on 17 January 2006. It was extremely important to the family that the media got the story correct, and we released a press statement that afternoon through Quintin Jardine, the author of the extremely successful Skinner novels and a close family friend. Within an hour, the news was everywhere – on radio, television, teletext and online.

My mobile phone went berserk – I received lots of texts of commiseration, including one from Hearts legend John Robertson. It read:

> Hi Iain – John Robertson here. Sorry to hear the sad
> news about your dad. Please pass on my condolences to

your mum and sister. There is nothing I can say that will make you feel better, but he was a fantastic man who will live long in my heart, not only as chairman but also as a friend.

John Robertson is a hero of mine, and *he* was sending *me* a text. Soon after, it all hit home, and I burst into tears.

The club released a statement within an hour of the news being made public. I was impressed with the way the Romanovs reacted, as I was not sure how they would cope with or, indeed, appreciate the significance of the loss of a former club chairman. Vladimir's statement read:

> Our deepest sympathies go out to Wallace's family. I had the pleasure of his company on a number of occasions and found him to be a true gentleman.
>
> He was a great Hearts man who will always be in the hearts and minds of all directors, players and fans. He worked tirelessly to make Hearts a great club and dedicated so much of his time and energy in doing so.
>
> We are all deeply saddened by this loss; however, he will always remain part of the Hearts family.

I thought his comments were first class, and the Romanovs immediately went up in my estimation after that.

Journalists had somehow found out that my father was battling cancer about four weeks prior to his death and began contacting my mum and me to try and establish whether or not the rumours circulating Edinburgh were true. She asked for the family to be left in peace and, to be honest, we were. I believe that shows the respect the press had for him, but what happened the following day was unbelievable.

WEDNESDAY, 18 JANUARY 2006 – PRESS COVERAGE AND TRIBUTES

I knew the reaction was going to be widespread, but no one could have predicted the coverage Dad's death received. A friend of the family, and a good friend of my father, said he could not remember the Queen Mother's death being as widely reported in the Scottish press, and I don't think he was joking either.

I vividly remember the morning of 18 January 2006, waking up and seeing all the press coverage. I bought every paper available. Dad's death had not been officially announced until 4 p.m. the previous day, but to see page after page of text and photographs was absolutely overwhelming. A press-monitoring company had been instructed to collate all the articles across every media, and we now have them as a record to look back on.

The family has taken enormous strength and comfort from the many articles and letters of condolence that were written, the flowers that were received and the way the fans have remembered him. The club gave us all the scarves, shirts and messages of support that were left outside Tynecastle in tribute. They are in a box that will probably never be opened, but I wanted to keep them as a memory rather than having them disposed of.

We were also touched by the fact that Rangers, Aberdeen and Hibs sent wreaths to the club and also donated cheques directly to the cancer centre at the Western General Hospital in Edinburgh. That just showed how highly regarded he was and that his overall contribution to Scottish football did not go unnoticed. Various people that Dad had encountered over the years also paid tribute, and the family is extremely grateful to everyone who offered such kind words. Here are just a few:

Triumph in 1998: Cameron, Adam and Salvatori celebrate at Tynecastle after winning the Scottish Cup against Rangers the day before.

Turmoil a few years later as Gary leads the protests against the former chief executive Chris Robinson.

The message to Chris Robinson is clear . . .

Scottish journalists are introduced to Vladimir Romanov in
Kaunas, Lithuania, in July 2005. (Courtesy of the author)

Vladimir having a 'ball'
after becoming Hearts'
majority shareholder on
21 October 2005.

In happier times: George Foulkes
congratulates Vladimir Romanov
for agreeing to purchase the
shareholding of SMG and HBOS.

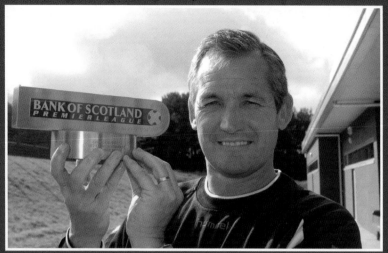

George Burley's second (and final) Manager of the Month award.

Romanov's defiant salute to the fans prior to the Dunfermline game on 22 October 2005. Just four hours later, the players were told that George Burley was no longer in charge of Hearts.

Chairman George Foulkes makes *that* statement: the first official confirmation that George Burley was no longer in charge of Heart of Midlothian Football Club.

Hearts chairman Roman Romanov welcomes new head coach Graham Rix to Tynecastle on 8 November 2005 – at least one of them looks happy at the appointment!

Stern faces in the directors' box after the 1–1 draw with Rangers – Rix's last match in charge.

Should have watched your near post, Zibbi: Hibs' Polish keeper Malkowski is beaten by Paul Hartley's free-kick as the midfielder gives Hearts a two-goal lead in the Scottish Cup semi-final at Hampden.

Three and easy against Hibs at Hampden: hat-trick hero Paul Hartley celebrates with Michal Pospisil after converting a late penalty in the Scottish Cup semi-final in April 2006. It finished Hearts 4 Hibs 0.

Coolness personified: Paul Hartley, watched by Aberdeen defender Kevin McNaughton and Hearts midfielder Bruno Aguiar, slots the vital penalty past Jamie Langfield at Tynecastle in May 2006 to secure Champions League qualification.

Sheer, unbridled joy at the end of the Aberdeen match.

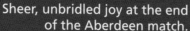

Robbie's cup-winning tackle: Neilson prevents Gretna substitute David Graham scoring the equaliser in the Scottish Cup final.

Gretna – over and out.

At long last: Hearts captain Steven Pressley lifts the Scottish Cup to end an eight-year trophy drought at Tynecastle.

Lucky mascot
Aaron Pressley.
(Courtesy of the
author)

Elvis and Mark Donaldson celebrating at the Saturday
night party at Murrayfield. (Courtesy of the author)

I did it my way: Hearts owner Vladimir Romanov
gets his hands on the Scottish Cup at the end of an
incredible season at Tynecastle.

Valdas Ivanauskas performs for the cameras after becoming Hearts' 25th manager on 30 June 2006 – exactly one year after George Burley arrived at Tynecastle.

Gary Mackay sitting on the (restored) old bridge in Mostar, Bosnia. (Courtesy of the author)

The night a dream died, yet we continued to believe . . . (Courtesy of Davy Allen at London Hearts)

I always enjoyed being in his company and found Wallace good fun. He was one of a breed of football chairmen who we don't see today. He led from the front and was always prepared to give his views. Whether you agreed or disagreed with him, he had a strong opinion, and people used to listen to him.

He cared passionately about what he did and was good for Scottish football as well as for Hearts. I think he should be remembered for that as well as for his acumen in the business world. Wallace had a very successful property portfolio, and it may have been his involvement with football that masked his business success. There may also be some negative recollections because he tried to take over Hibs. But he was a first-rate football chairman and a first-rate businessman.

Rangers chairman David Murray

Wallace was by far the most charismatic chairman Hearts ever had. He led the club with great panache for over a decade and helped them to enjoy tremendous success. Before he came along, the club was struggling and often relegated. He took them back into Europe and challenged for honours. It was a remarkable turnaround, and Wallace truly became a legend in his own lifetime.

He was a very good friend of mine, and I can reveal now that when I was chairman of the club he offered me advice on a number of occasions. Let me say it was always the wisest of counsel. He was a very kind and generous man. In fact, the private man was quite different from the public image. I liked him immensely and will miss a good friend.

George Foulkes

The club was in the gutter at that time and could not have gone any further down. Hearts needed a white knight to come to the rescue, and they were fortunate to find one in Wallace. For six or seven years as chairman, I thought he did absolutely everything right. He was passionate about the club, and I can't think how anyone could have done any better.

Donald Ford, who was instrumental in bringing
Wallace to Tynecastle in 1981

I never met anyone else quite like him. I first knew him as a client, but he quickly became a friend. Wallace was a unique guy.

Quintin Jardine, the successful author and former PR
consultant to Wallace Mercer

Strangely enough, Dad never thought he was that highly regarded in Scottish football. He would never have understood why they would recognise him in such a way, which is quite strange, given the amount of coverage he used to receive and considering his ego was the size of Scotland – I am sure he won't mind me saying that!

I am also sure that he would have loved the wonderful tribute penned by Mike Aitken in *The Scotsman* the day after his death:

MISJUDGED MERGER ONLY REGRET OF AN EXCEPTIONAL LIFE
As the most high-profile and newsworthy chairman in the club's history, Wallace Mercer, who has died aged 59 after a short illness, played a pivotal role in the promotion and development of Heart of Midlothian. In the Eighties, it was his vitality that helped revive Hearts when the club faced extinction.

A successful businessman, who rebuilt his career as a property developer after selling his shareholding in Hearts to Chris Robinson and Leslie Deans, Mercer had just enjoyed his most profitable year as an entrepreneur in 2005. Sadly, the significance of that achievement was clouded, a few days before Christmas, when it was learned he was suffering from cancer.

Although frail, over the past few weeks he survived long enough to see the birth of his granddaughter Jessica, enjoy a short visit to Spain and make one last pilgrimage to Tynecastle for the New Year's Day match against Celtic. He was warmly welcomed back that day by all connected with the Hearts family, where his stock among the club's supporters had risen immeasurably in recent years, partly because of his opposition to playing at Murrayfield.

Respected by Vladimir Romanov, the current owner, as a sage friend of the club, Mercer enjoyed his return to the boardroom and was optimistic about the future. Like the Lithuanian banker, Mercer was also seen as a saviour of Hearts 25 years ago, when, thanks to the intervention of Donald Ford, he was persuaded to challenge Kenny Waugh, an Edinburgh bookmaker who went on to become chairman of Hibs, for control of the Gorgie club.

Although Wallace and his wife Anne had bought a few shares a year or two earlier, they only chose to become directly involved when the club's bank warned that unless a significant amount of new capital was raised then Hearts might have to close. Mercer was at the Royal Garden Hotel entertaining clients in London before an England v. Scotland match when Ford telephoned the young businessman and asked him to top Waugh's bid of

£255,000. He eventually put down a personal cheque for £265,000 and with £85,000 in support from a consortium was able to buy all the shares after narrowly winning the support of the board.

The battle between Waugh and Mercer for the ownership of Hearts was played out through the media, and it was at a supporters' club meeting in Slateford that Mercer's talent for mixing grand gestures with business acumen first made an impression on the media. Later fondly nicknamed by scribes as either the 'Great Waldo' or 'Wireless' Mercer – he once hosted a TV chat show as well as a regular programme on Radio Forth in Edinburgh – Wallace Mercer's approach to running a football club turned out to have more in common with Phineas T. Barnum, the great American showman, than the 'blazerati' who populated the boardrooms of Scottish football at the dawn of the Eighties.

Born and raised in the west of Scotland – prior to taking control of Hearts his only connection with football was that he'd been a milk boy who delivered a pint to the former Rangers manager Scot Symon – Mercer was just 33 when he took the reins at Tynecastle.

Over the next 13 years, Mercer would call more press conferences than any of his peers and make headlines, some on the front pages of Scotland's newspapers, and many more on the back. If, in the beginning, he didn't know all that much about football, he understood enough about business to immediately ensure Hearts received compensation when Bobby Moncur left the club to become manager of Plymouth. It was the start of a more business-like era.

Otherwise, the early days of Mercer's reign at Hearts were blighted by low crowds, hooliganism, poor facilities and indifferent football. The late journalist John Fairgrieve, in a seminal column, once suggested Tynecastle might as well be turned into a car park. Only when Tony Ford was dismissed and Alex MacDonald, then the Hearts captain, was appointed as player–manager, did the situation improve.

Mercer and MacDonald were the same age and, thanks to the steadying influence in the boardroom of Pilmar Smith, who would become a lifelong friend, Hearts began the long ascent back to the summit of the game. A natural salesman – he always referred to supporters as 'customers' – Mercer was brimming over with ideas. Hearts were the first club in the country to admit the unemployed free of charge and the first to raffle a house as a prize in a half-time draw. Within five years, Mercer's Hearts were transformed from a yo-yo club, always bouncing between the divisions, into genuine title challengers.

But for a cruel twist of fate on the last day of the season in 1986 at Dens Park, the outstanding Hearts side that featured John Robertson, John Colquhoun, Gary Mackay, Craig Levein, Sandy Jardine and many other fine players might have nudged their way into immortality by winning the championship. As it was, Hearts never won a major trophy under Mercer's command, and his reign is still best remembered for the divisive attempt to buy Hibs and merge the two clubs. Weary of seeing the Edinburgh clubs play the role of 'nearly men' to the Old Firm as well as to Aberdeen and Dundee United, Mercer believed the emergence of just one professional club in Edinburgh, playing in a new, purpose-built stadium at Hermiston Gait, was the way forward.

While there was some merit in this idea, it was not so much a merger as a takeover. Understandably, the reaction of Hibs' followers to Mercer's £7.5 million bid was one of outrage. While most of the demonstrations were heated but peaceful, one extremist did smash the windows at his city-centre offices.

Years later, he told me, 'I suppose the scale of the backlash against that idea should serve as a warning to anyone in football that social engineering is not a wise move. Looking back, maybe that idea wasn't thought through properly, and I could have done things differently. It's something I regret. That whole episode took a lot out of me, and by the time I was 46, 13 years after I first walked into Tynecastle, I was emotionally and physically spent.'

If he didn't succeed in bringing silverware to the boardroom, Mercer raised the profile of Hearts as no chairman had done before him. There were tussles in Europe with giants such as Bayern Munich as well as close shaves in cup finals. He also greatly improved the value of the business and was proud of the fact that shares in Hearts bought for £100 in 1981 were worth £750 in 1993.

The sale of his holding to Chris Robinson for £2 million and the subsequent legal squabbles between the men was also something he regretted and, during the years when he split his time between homes in North Berwick and Mougins in the south of France, Mercer was a trenchant critic of his successor's business management of Hearts.

Perhaps I should declare an interest here. For a quarter of a century, Wallace was a generous and loyal friend of mine. We wrote a book together, *Heart to*

Heart, which was published by Mainstream in 1988, and were good companions on the golf course, in restaurants and over a glass or two of Sancerre. I last played golf with him in late November at Archerfield where we started planning a golfing holiday to Lisbon in April.

That day, we met John Colquhoun, now a successful agent, and Lawrence Donegan, *The Guardian*'s golf correspondent, in the clubhouse and enjoyed a typically robust conversation before lunch about recent turbulent events at Tynecastle.

A man of keen intelligence, sometimes wilful single-mindedness and a wonderfully kind heart, Wallace lived a full and rich life. He was full of paradoxes. On the one hand, he could be quite formal and always preferred writing letters to email. Yet, while he liked to be in control, he had a great sense of fun and was engaging company.

Blessed with a strong marriage to Anne, his loyal partner in business and life, Wallace couldn't have been more proud of his children Helen and Iain and his grandchildren Oliver, 3, and Jessica. His health had deteriorated over the last year or two, but the illness that ended his life was only diagnosed in December. It was typical of this larger than life character, when forced to count the hours rather than weeks, that he should defy the advice of the medical profession last week and jet abroad to enjoy a couple of lunches in Spain. It's fitting to think of him still, raising a glass in fond remembrance.

SATURDAY, 21 JANUARY 2006 – THE FUNERAL, MORTONHALL CREMATORIUM

We knew there would be a lot of people in attendance at the funeral to pay tribute, but we did not think anywhere near as many would turn up as did. Mortonhall Crematorium seats 250, and we basically doubled that number to get a rough estimate of the attendance, but I have since been told that it was probably more than 500. It was standing room only inside, and there were many more people standing on the grass outside. When we arrived in the funeral cortège, the first thing I saw as we turned left into Mortonhall was a police motorbike with two police officers stopping the traffic and directing us in. Then I saw a battery of cameras and film crews up on the hill, but, to be fair, they kept their distance, which was very much appreciated by the family.

Following the service, Mum wanted to stand at the entrance to the chapel to meet everyone and thank them for coming. It was something she was determined to do. Despite being the grieving widow, she showed enormous strength and courage to greet and thank every single person there. My sister Helen and I stood with her as people filed past, and we saw faces we had never even seen before, many of whom were supporters coming to pay tribute. There were a lot of people I had not seen since I was a child: friends from school who I had lost touch with. A number of people also came up to us with Hearts scarves on and simply said, 'I am just a fan, but I had huge respect for your dad,' and 'Hearts wouldn't be here without your father.' That really touched us all.

The wake was held in the George Hotel in Edinburgh, and it was great to see so many ex-Hearts players and staff there. From John Robertson to Charles Burnett, the former commercial manager, many of the staff from his time at Tynecastle came along. Unfortunately, former flying winger John Colquhoun had been slowed down to a mere hobble as he limped around on crutches after rupturing his Achilles tendon whilst playing five-a-side football. I told him he should have stayed retired, concentrating instead on his transfer dealings as an agent!

Representatives from many of the SPL clubs attended the funeral, but as it was a Saturday and they had matches to attend it was understandable that they could not come to the wake. Sir Tom Farmer, the owner of Hibs, did come to the George Hotel and took time to take me aside and offer words of advice and speak of his admiration at what Dad had achieved in his life in both business and sport. I had only ever met him once before, but I really appreciated his comments.

SATURDAY, 28 JANUARY 2006 – THE ONE-MINUTE APPLAUSE, HEARTS V. HIBERNIAN

The club invited the family as their guests to the match against Hibs, the first home fixture following Dad's death, and I could not think of more fitting opponents. During his spell as chairman, he presided over the unbeaten 22 games in a row and set out every season to ensure that the team picked up maximum points against their nearest rivals – nothing less would suffice. The fact Hibs were well beaten 4–1 that afternoon was very pleasing.

A number of people in the boardroom came up to me after the game with comments ranging from 'Wallace would have enjoyed that' to 'I bet he was up there watching with a big smile on his face' – I agreed with all of them. There was something in the air at Tynecastle that day; the atmosphere was electric. It made the hairs on the back of my neck stand on end, and I said to my sister before the match, 'If the players are not up for this match, then they will never be up for it!' They came out of the traps full of passion and guile and, despite a nervy opening ten minutes, destroyed Hibs with the match all but wrapped up by half-time.

We preferred a minute's applause instead of silence at the match because we felt it was far more of a celebration of his life. There had been a one-minute silence at Rugby Park the week before when Hearts played Kilmarnock. We were all immensely moved and proud to be there, but, in some ways, it was almost like an out-of-body experience.

I remember watching the George Best funeral on television and the subsequent tributes across the country. I never knew the man, and I am not trying to compare the two – Best was an iconic figure around the globe – but to be standing in a football stadium with the majority of a capacity crowd standing and chanting my father's name was truly surreal.

On reflection, it was also quite ironic because I remember sitting behind him in the director's box 12 years before when the supporters chanted 'Mercer Must Go' just prior to the end of his reign. I felt mixed emotions: having sat there when the Hearts fans were trying to get rid of him, the same fans, albeit a younger generation, were now, more than a decade later, singing something completely different. That, for me, sums up the fickleness of some football supporters.

WALLACE AND THE ROMANOV REVOLUTION

Dad was a supporter of Vladimir Romanov and enjoyed going back to Tynecastle during the 2005–06 season to watch the influx of new signings, such as Rudi Skácel, who took the season by storm. But he was not as impressed with the way Romanov chose to deal with certain situations – the way Burley, Foulkes and Anderton were dealt with, for example, appalled him. It was certainly not how he would have treated people, but, having led the club from the front for 14 years, he knew how difficult those decisions were to make.

He was a close friend of George Foulkes, and I think a part of him thought that it was perhaps no bad thing that Foulkes left, although certainly not in the manner in which he did. Foulkes had removed the Robinson regime, he had stopped Tynecastle from being sold to CALA property developers and he had attracted the investment from Romanov. He did great things for Hearts and had probably taken the club as far as he could in a short space of time. When all is said and done, he is a politician, and there were times when Dad felt Foulkes should have known when to say nothing.

One of my father's lasting legacies at Tynecastle is the three stands he began redeveloping in the 1990s to ensure the stadium complied with the Taylor Report. He put the initial funding in place through the successful 500 Club and that allowed the construction of the Wheatfield Stand to commence in 1994. The capital resources required for the next two stands, the School End and Gorgie Road Stand, were also put in place before he sold his interest in the club to Chris Robinson and Leslie Deans. Sadly, they tried to take all of the credit themselves and never invited him back to see the completed stands, which was a bitter disappointment. Now, the new regime is planning to redevelop the stadium further and raise the capacity beyond the 20,000 mark. This is a project that Dad supported wholeheartedly, because he saw it as a way of eventually bringing more revenue into the club by tapping into Edinburgh's corporate scene, which is not as well catered for as it could be at Tynecastle.

From a financial perspective, Vladimir Romanov and Wallace Mercer are poles apart. I have heard suggestions that Romanov's fortune ranges from anything between £200 million to £1 billion, which puts my father's wealth so far in the shade it is dark. But Dad was a self-made millionaire with an entrepreneurial instinct, as is Romanov, who used to sell bootleg LPs from the back of a car. Dad certainly had energy and a ruthless streak in his business life that assisted him in achieving the results and success that he did. In that respect, parallels can be drawn with Romanov. Wallace certainly admired the way Romanov travels to and from Lithuania on a regular basis to watch matches.

Football is a personality-led business, and the man at the helm needs to have both character and bravado to carry it out. Let's face it, there are not too many people in Scottish football who are particularly colourful. Dad certainly was and Hearts were predominantly on the back pages for the right reasons during his tenure. This all helped to raise the profile of the club as he drew it back from the brink during the '80s and '90s. There is no doubt his ego grew steadily over the years, but I think Romanov's is twice the size and seems to go off the scale at times!

Dad said to me on a number of occasions that he thought Vladimir Romanov was living in a fairytale land if he thought Hearts could win the Champions League within ten years. At the same time, he also remarked that Vlad should be applauded for at least showing the vision and ambition to get that far, because if you don't have dreams in life, you can never fulfil them. Romanov must be credited for splitting the Old Firm in his first full season and reaching the Champions League qualifiers, although he sometimes gets pilloried because he is bucking the trend and challenging the parameters that people accept as normal. He refuses to bow down to Rangers and Celtic – quite right. He is breaking the mould, and it is the shake-up that Scottish football has been screaming out for.

When Dad was chairman in the late '80s, Hearts were starting to lose touch with the Old Firm – it has taken from then until now for the club to be in a position to challenge Rangers and Celtic once again. In the end, one of the main reasons he gave up his position at Hearts was because he could no longer compete financially with the Old Firm – it was as simple as that. He could not keep throwing more money at the club, and the figures were simply not stacking up. There was not enough cash coming in from gate receipts to make it worthwhile, compared to the tens of thousands of supporters going through the turnstiles at Ibrox and Parkhead every week.

Vladimir Romanov's ruthless and brutal way of dealing with people is not everyone's cup of tea, and we are not used to that type of culture, but there is no denying that he has achieved success in a short space of time by taking the second Champions League place and winning the Scottish Cup in 2006. Dad agreed with the way Romanov wanted to take the club forward, just not with the manner in which some of the steps were taken.

SEVEN

V FOR VALDAS AND VICTORY

THERE HAVE NOT BEEN TOO MANY CONSTANTS AT Tynecastle since the turn of the century when the nineties became the 'noughties'. Jim Jefferies, Craig Levein, John Robertson, George Burley and Graham Rix all warmed the managerial hot seat before heading for the exit door, but one member of the coaching staff remained in place throughout and was employed in a variety of roles. He's been in charge of the Under-16s, Under-18s and reserves; he has also taken charge of the first team on an interim basis on no less than three occasions.

John McGlynn is the unsung hero at Hearts. He has no official nickname but, to borrow a moniker often used to describe Gary Mackay, 'janitor' would surely be applicable. McGlynn is usually one of the first people to arrive for work in the morning and is often the last to leave: '. . . and turn the lights out when you're finished please, John'.

McGlynn is one of the most down-to-earth and likeable people you will ever meet, the safe pair of hands that every football club needs. He's one of a dying breed who is in football not just to make a living but because he loves the game so much.

When Robbo left, McGlynn and Steven Pressley teamed up to guide the team through the last few games of the 2004–05 season. When Burley made his way through the by-now revolving door, McGlynn was in sole charge for four matches – won three of them. When Rix was sacked, John joined forces with Valdas Ivanauskas to try and guide the team through until the end of the 2005–06 season, but this time he had to settle for the title of 'interim assistant boss'. Although he was overlooked for the role of 'number one' in favour of Ivanauskas, he did not complain. John McGlynn is quite content simply to play a part at Tynecastle – any part . . .

'Being involved with Hearts has been amazing,' he said. 'I started out at Tynecastle in the mid-'90s, working with the Under-16s on a part-time basis because I was also a plumber. When Jim Jefferies offered me a full-time job, I can remember saying to my boss at the time that the gig with Hearts could be for six weeks, six months or six years – you never know what is going to happen in football – and that I may ask for my old job back if things did not work out!

'It's been a lot of work for me to get to where I am now. I have climbed the ladder step by step but have loved every minute. I consider it an honour to have been able to do the things I have done with Hearts over the years – it has been an incredible experience. The job satisfaction is enormous – waking up each morning and being part of a successful club is a dream come true for me.

'There were a lot of developments behind the scenes during the [2005–06] season. I saw things prior to George Burley leaving; I saw things prior to the departure of Graham Rix. I felt it was better as the year went on just to keep my head down and get on with my work. I felt this approach would give me a chance to remain at the football club for a longer period of time. It seemed there was more chance of being shot down if you were on the front line, so maybe it wasn't so bad that I helped Valdas out once Graham left, instead of the other way round!

'Valdas Ivanauskas is Lithuanian, he speaks the same language as Mr Romanov, he understands the culture and he knows the way Mr Romanov works. I think that is a massive thing for this football club. The football culture in Britain is to play your best team in every game, but that is not necessarily how they do things abroad. Specific players are sometimes identified for specific games, and squad rotation is also a big thing in some countries. Mr Romanov is not a fan of his best players playing three games in one week if there is a midweek game – he wants his best players fresh and able to perform.'

The appointment of Valdas Ivanauskas and John McGlynn as the club's new interim management team was welcomed by the players, who, by this time, just wanted a period of stability. Vladimir Romanov put his faith in the pair to deliver second spot in the SPL and to win the Scottish Cup, something he felt the previous incumbent in the managerial hot seat was clearly incapable of doing. 'It was my mistake to wait too long for Rix to produce better results,' said Romanov. 'The results had not been satisfying the board for some time, and the loss of so many points in the league was disappointing. I even suggested we say goodbye to him as head coach earlier, but the guys in the team insisted on letting him stay, and I followed their wishes. However, I feel I've made a mistake by not acting sooner, as we lost 24 points in the league since he took charge, as well as precious time. If we had stuck by him, we would have put ourselves in danger of losing our second-place position and failing to qualify for the Champions League.'

26 MARCH 2006 – FALKIRK V. HEARTS

Ivanauskas and McGlynn teamed up in the dugout for the first time for a league match at Falkirk. The short trip along the M9 had provided Hearts with plenty of problems earlier in the season; indeed, it was where the Jambos dropped their first two points of the season after Craig Gordon was sent off in the first half. In the second trip west, a goal from Paul Hartley gave Hearts the lead midway through the first half, but Falkirk were awarded a penalty just before half-time. For a split second, there was delirium in the away end as Alan Gow's spot-kick was saved, but he managed to score from the rebound, and the game was back on level terms. It was still goalless at Ibrox at half-time in the match between Rangers and Dunfermline, so the six-point gap between second and third place remained intact at that stage.

Hearts suffered a blow at the start of the second half when captain Steven Pressley failed to reappear after suffering concussion in the opening 45 minutes. More bad news was set to follow shortly . . .

News filtered through from the south side of Glasgow that a Sotirios Kyrgiakos header had finally breached Dunfermline's 5–5–0 formation and Rangers had broken the deadlock after 70 minutes. Not to be outdone, though, Hearts got themselves back in front at Falkirk with eight minutes remaining when a shot from Edgaras Jankauskas was blocked by goalkeeper Mark Howard but ricocheted back off the Lithuanian and found its way into the back of the net. Three vital points had been secured to maintain the six-point lead over Rangers, and Hearts remained in pole position in the race to finish second in the Bank of Scotland SPL with just seven games remaining.

HEARTS	62 pts
RANGERS	56 pts

The press interest in Hearts had grown throughout the season because of the remarkable series of events that had unfolded at Tynecastle. While Vladimir Romanov continued to seek perfection on the pitch, a very different team was being assembled off it. A small group of ex-national-newspaper journalists based in Ayr, including Shaun Milne (former deputy editor of the Scottish *Daily Mirror*) and Mark Smith (former news editor at the same title), launched a new publication. It was called *Planet Hearts* – a 32-page, full-colour tabloid newspaper published on a weekly basis.

Some people questioned the wisdom of launching a newspaper at a time when advertising revenue for papers was down, while others were sceptical about whether *Planet Hearts* could sustain a high-quality weekly content. Those doubts were quickly dispelled when Graham Rix was sacked. Despite having less than 24 hours before copy was due at the printers, the team produced comprehensive coverage of events at Tynecastle and also provided reaction from fans and players. *Planet Hearts* had arrived, and with it came even greater scrutiny of the Jambos from a source over which the club had no control whatsoever.

2 APRIL 2006 – LOS ANGELES, 4.15 A.M.

Film star Dougray Scott, a lifelong Hibs fan, had to rely on a very early alarm call to ensure he was awake in time to watch the eagerly awaited Scottish Cup semi-final against Hearts at Hampden. The Glenrothes-born actor was filming in California and was unable to return to Scotland in time for the game. Had he known exactly what was in store for his team at the national stadium, he might have decided that the snooze button on his alarm clock was a far better option, allowing him to roll over and go back to sleep! It really was 'Mission Impossible' for the Hibees.

With a place in the Scottish Cup final against Second Division Gretna now in the bag, Hearts' attention turned back to their league campaign and trying to secure second spot in the SPL and the Champions League place that went with it.

While the players were busy preparing to travel west to face Celtic at Parkhead – a must-win match for the Jambos to delay the home side winning the title – a journalist and broadcaster was also busy in his London study. Although it was never publicly stated by Vladimir Romanov, it was widely accepted that Valdas Ivanauskas would have to win the cup and finish second to ensure his coaching career continued at Tynecastle. A tough ask for anyone, so BBC presenter Nicky Campbell – a Hearts fan since childhood – decided to chance his arm and apply for the role of head coach in case Valdas failed in his mission:

Dear Vladimir,

I am Edinburgh born and bred and have followed the Jambos for a long time. Please could you fix it for me to be their new manager? I don't have any experience of first-class football, as such, but I am sure my enthusiasm for the job would more than compensate. Don't waste your money on anyone else. I will do it for nothing. I currently work on a breakfast programme in London but could be at Tynecastle by midday and work with the squad for a few hours every afternoon except Tuesday, when I present *Watchdog*, and Friday, when I take lunch with my wife.

To be honest, I don't feel qualified enough to actually pick the team, choose the players or do any hiring and firing, and I would be grateful if someone else could fulfil this role. Is this a problem? Basically, I see my job as having a kick-about with the lads during the week on the training pitch, shouting and gesticulating from the dugout on match days, and, of course, giving media interviews – something which, may I modestly suggest, I will be rather good at.

The pressure of the forthcoming cup final against Gretna holds no fears for me, either, as very recently I sang 'Edelweiss' live on national television with Beverley Knight.

Oh, and I promise I won't look at the books. When would you like me to start?

Nicky Campbell

The letter was passed on to Vladimir Romanov's UK spokesman Charlie Mann, who felt sympathy for Nicky after spotting him singing 'Edelweiss' with Beverley Knight on the television programme *Just the Two of Us*. Mann sent the following response:

Dear Nicky,

Thank you for your letter dated 4 April and for your application to join the Hearts management team.

I have discussed your approach at length with Mr Romanov, and while it is clear you share his strength of feeling and vision for the club, we are unable, at this stage, to place your name on the list of those likely to be considered for the role of either director of football or first-team coach.

News of your singing had in fact reached him in Kaunas, and once I had convinced him that you were unlikely to be a significant challenger to the Lithuanian entry for the Eurovision Song Contest this year, he felt a little more relaxed in considering your application.

Your obvious communication strengths and ability to

quickly pick up on new skills from others with arguably superior talents (we were thinking particularly of Beverley Knight and Julia Bradbury!) were obvious plus points, but he did feel you were unlikely to be in a position to fulfil the commitment levels required to become a success at Tynecastle.

Vladimir is also a man with strong family values, and he felt it would be wrong of him to deprive your wife of the obvious enjoyment you take from sharing lunch with her on Fridays. That is the day on which he would want you to take notes on the shape and style he expects the team to play the next day.

It is very good of you to use your Radio Five Live and other media outlets to spread the word of Hearts' success both on and off the pitch this season, and Mr Romanov wanted to assure you that his ambition to deliver the Hearts fans a club which would be challenging for domestic honours regularly and competing at the highest-possible levels in European competition was as strong as ever.

He does not seek to be compared with what Roman Abramovich has achieved at Chelsea but does see it as a personal mission to bring Heart of Midlothian Football Club up to that level of success, and he will be investing further to achieve those goals.

In short, he was delighted to receive your approach, grateful to read that you felt you could help him with his ambition to achieve great things for the club but unable to take things any further with you at this moment in time. However, as you have witnessed with Hearts this season, things can change quickly, so never say never!

Please continue to advise audiences south of the border that Hearts will continue to push the previously accepted boundaries, and people like you were certainly in his thoughts when he stated after the 4–0 Tennent's Scottish Cup semi-final victory over Hibernian at Hampden that, 'The Hearts fans are the golden fans of this country and worth more to me than all the oil and gas reserves of Russia!'

Yours in sport,

Charlie Mann

Now big boys are not supposed to cry, but the reply to Mr Campbell's application left him very upset, as he revealed to readers of his weekly column in *The Guardian*:

HEARTLESS RESPONSE FROM ROMANOV LEAVES ME FEELING DESERTED

A couple of weeks ago I sent a letter to Vladimir Romanov, applying for the Hearts job. Since then, I don't mind telling you, I have been a nervous bunny. Every time the letterbox has clattered, my heart has fluttered. I now understand what it's like being Alan Curbishley. And then, at last, I got a response from the Lithuanian's official spokesman, Charlie Mann. It was like opening that little envelope with my exam results in it. He thanked me for my letter, but his words then hit me like a juggernaut: 'I have discussed your approach at length with Mr Romanov, and while it is clear you share his strength of feeling and vision for the club, we are unable, at this stage, to place your name on the list of those likely to be considered for the role of either director of football or first-team coach.'

The letter is long and gives various reasons for their decision, but my other commitments seem to have been significant . . . It is crushingly disappointing, although despite the rejection, Mr Romanov's mouthpiece concludes, '[A]s you have witnessed with Hearts this season, things can change quickly, so never say never!'

I'm not banking on it. I'm holding out for *Desert Island Discs.*

5 APRIL 2006 – CELTIC V. HEARTS

While Hearts were busy hammering Hibs at Hampden in the Scottish Cup semi-final, Rangers closed the gap on the Jambos to just three points with a 4–1 victory against Dundee United at Tannadice. On the following Wednesday, Valdas Ivanauskas took his squad west to face champions-elect Celtic at Parkhead, hoping to once again increase his side's lead over the team from Ibrox. Despite a decent performance from the visitors, John Hartson scored the only goal of the game to clinch the title for the Hoops in Gordon Strachan's first season in charge. The race was now on to finish second . . .

HEARTS	62 pts
RANGERS	59 pts

Nine hundred Hearts fans left Celtic Park, having watched their team produce one of their best performances at Parkhead for many years, despite failing to get a result. At least they got a ticket – Ken Stott tried desperately to get time off filming an episode of *Rebus* but eventually had to admit defeat and ended up watching the game on television in a spit-and-sawdust drinking den in Greenock with his maroon scarf hidden underneath his coat. 'I was determined to watch the match, even although it led to a fall-out with my driver,' said Stott. 'He told me *not* to go into that particular establishment, as my safety could not be guaranteed, but I told him, "It'll be fine!" He said to me, "You think you can do anything and go anywhere – I'm telling you, you'll be in trouble if you go in there." I replied, "Ah, to hell with it", before getting out of the car and heading inside.

'I pretended to be one of the regulars by shouting "C'mon Celtic" and "They're making you look rubbish", but that couldn't disguise the fact they knew I was a Jambo. The locals actually behaved like perfect gentlemen, and there was no bother whatsoever, probably because Celtic won. It took a while before my driver spoke to me again, though!'

8 APRIL 2006 – HEARTS V. DUNFERMLINE

The final round of fixtures before the top six split saw Hearts at home to Dunfermline and Rangers at home to Motherwell. The previous time the Pars visited Tynecastle was one of the most dramatic days in the history of the football club, following the departure of George Burley, but there was no such drama this time as goals from Pospíšil, Bednář, Mikoliūnas and Juho Mäkelä secured a comfortable 4–0 victory over Jim Leishman's side. Meanwhile, Kris Boyd scored the only goal of the game at Ibrox, as Rangers beat Motherwell 1–0. Hearts would take a three-point lead into the final five fixtures of the season, with both the Old Firm still to play.

HEARTS	65 pts
RANGERS	62 pts

15 APRIL 2006 – HEARTS V. KILMARNOCK

They say one week is a long time in politics, but one minute ultimately decided the destination of the second Champions League spot.

4.28 p.m. – Hearts were failing to break down a resolute Kilmarnock rearguard and it remained goalless at Tynecastle, while Rangers were leading Aberdeen 1–0 at Ibrox thanks to

Kris Boyd's 51st-minute goal. As it stood, Alex McLeish's side would move to within one point of the Jambos.

4.29 p.m. – Paul Hartley scored for Hearts with a superbly executed free-kick at Tynecastle, while Scott Severin equalised for the Dons at Ibrox at almost exactly the same time. His shot from distance took a wicked deflection off Julien Rodriguez and found its way past Ronald Wattereus.

Christophe Berra, with his first goal for Hearts, secured all three points three minutes from time when he prodded the ball home from close range. The gap between the two teams was now five points when it could quite easily have been just one, and there were only four league games remaining.

HEARTS	68 pts
RANGERS	63 pts

22 APRIL 2006 – HIBS V. HEARTS

It was derby weekend in the SPL: the Edinburgh version was first, with Celtic v. Rangers being played the following day. Victory at Easter Road would have taken the Jambos eight-points clear of the men from Ibrox with only three matches remaining; however, a defensive injury crisis meant that Steven Pressley and José Gonçalves missed out, so Ibrahim Tall came in for his first start for Hearts. Rudi Skácel and Julien Brellier could only find a place on the bench, while Edgaras Jankauskas was not involved despite being fully fit. A Lithuanian 'mystery woman', known only as Rima, was practising her new-age therapy at the club and persuaded the Champions League winner to put his thumb in a machine for tests before the match. It's alleged that she told Jankauskas she believed he would injure his hamstring if he played at Easter Road. When this news was relayed back to Vladimir Romanov, it's understood the owner insisted the player was removed from the squad.

The absence of Pressley, Gonçalves, Brellier, Skácel and Jankauskas from the starting line-up was too much for Hearts to handle, and they slumped to a 2–1 defeat at the hands of their bitter rivals. It could all have been so different, though: an unmarked Ibrahim Tall somehow managed to head wide from close range following a corner when the score was 1–1. His miss was punished 12 minutes from the end when Hibs sub Abdessalam Benjelloun scored the winner.

The result at Easter Road handed Rangers a huge incentive ahead of their trip across Glasgow to face Celtic 24 hours later, knowing victory over their fiercest rivals would close the gap on Hearts to just two points. After a goalless first half in the east end of Glasgow, Rangers had a period of sustained pressure just after the break: Chris Burke blasted over from close range while Celtic keeper Artur Boruc did well to turn a Dado Pršo header onto the post. It ended scoreless at Parkhead, and although Rangers closed the gap on Hearts to four points, it could have been a lot worse . . .

HEARTS	68 pts
RANGERS	64 pts

With Pressley and Gonçalves both injured, questions were asked after the match as to why Andy Webster was not involved at Easter Road. It soon became clear: Vladimir Romanov confirmed that the Scotland international had been placed on the transfer list after refusing to sign a new contract with Hearts and was surplus to requirements. 'The coach is not sure that the player can give his 100 per cent best to win more points for us,' said Romanov. 'There have been statements in the media that Webster is looking for another club – I heard Rangers were among those he is supposedly looking at. My opinion is that the club should not work any more with agents like this because they start winding up the players. It does not benefit the club or the players. For the club, it means that our only option is to put him on the transfer list.

'I'm sad all this has emerged so late in the season. If that was the agent's intention, why wasn't this made clear before the January transfer window, and we could then have had a fair and open discussion? No one would have stood in Webster's way if that had been his choice. Instead, it feels like an unfair game with the club, and this saddens me. What I want at Hearts – just like our great fans – are players who are giving everything to the club, not those who are looking over their shoulders at Rangers, at a time when we are battling for the Champions League.'

The decision to ostracise Webster after more than five years and one hundred and eighty-four appearances for the club gave others a chance to stake a claim for a regular first-team spot alongside Steven Pressley, but it didn't find favour with Hearts assistant boss John McGlynn. 'I have to say, I didn't particularly agree with what happened to him approaching the end of the season,' he said. 'Andy Webster was at Hearts for a long time. I was one of the people who went to watch him when he was playing for Arbroath just prior to us signing him. He matured into an excellent defender. He is a very good all-round player and was good for the team. Andy also had a good relationship with Steven Pressley and Craig Gordon at the back, which was so important.

'I believe Andy Webster was our best football-playing centre-back and should have played. On the other hand, Mr Romanov wanted the player to commit his long-term future to the football club, and his refusal to do so at that time was the reason why he did not play.'

30 APRIL 2006 – HEARTS V. CELTIC

Hearts went into the match against Celtic at Tynecastle with only a one-point lead over Rangers – the Ibrox side had closed the gap the previous day following their come-from-behind 3–1 victory at Kilmarnock. The introduction of Marvin Andrews (as a half-time substitute for Alan Hutton) got Alex McLeish out of a very large hole, the big defender scoring twice after a first-half goal from Colin Nish had given the Ayrshire side a half-time lead.

Any thoughts that Celtic boss (and well-known Hibee) Gordon Strachan would rest several key players against Hearts with the SPL title already in the bag were dashed when the team sheets were handed out at Tynecastle. The big guns were playing, and Petrov and Hartson were on the bench, ready to come on if Celtic found themselves in bother. Maybe it was just as well the wee ginger-haired manager chose to play a near-full-strength side against Hearts: exactly four years earlier, a makeshift Celtic team, featuring several youngsters, arrived at Tynecastle for a meaningless fixture at the end of the season and promptly hammered the Jambos 4–1!

The start of the match at Tynecastle virtually mirrored the game on New Year's Day: for Jankauskas and Pressley, read McManus (own goal) and Hartley – Hearts were 2–0 up in the opening ten minutes again! Déjà vu, anyone?

When Rudi Skácel hit the post shortly afterwards, more than a few doubts were raised that failure to kill off the opposition would once again come back to haunt Hearts. This time, however, there was no such capitulation in the second half. Roman Bednář's 63rd-minute goal secured all three points and entitled the Hearts fans, in yet another capacity crowd, to savour the last half-hour of the match and enjoy the Jambos' first victory over Celtic at Tynecastle since Austin McCann scored a screamer in injury time way back in April 2003.

The four-point lead over Rangers remained. The scenario was now simple for Hearts: beat Aberdeen three days later to secure second place and the coveted Champions League spot.

HEARTS	71 pts
RANGERS	67 pts

It would be fair to suggest that there has been no love lost between Hearts supporters and Celtic captain Neil Lennon over the years, especially at Tynecastle. It therefore came as something of a surprise to hear him praise the Jambos just 24 hours before their comprehensive 3–0 victory. 'I think the Hearts players have handled all the things that have gone on through there this season very well,' he said. 'If I was in their camp, I wouldn't be happy at all. It has been one circus act after another.'

Of course, Lennon couldn't help but add some fuel to the fire at the end of his comments to the press, which Vladimir Romanov quickly picked up on. After watching his side demolish the new champions, he felt a retort was necessary. 'The circus is on track,' he said with a smile . . .

3 MAY 2006 – HEARTS V. ABERDEEN

The mid-week match against Aberdeen was one of the most important in the history of Heart of Midlothian, but, incredibly, it was not shown live on television. Hearts v. Aberdeen was, however, broadcast to a nationwide audience on BBC Radio Five Live – the first time a Scottish game not involving either of the Old Firm had ever been selected for live network commentary instead of a Premiership match.

'The policy at Five Live is to cover every English Premiership game and every match involving the Old Firm, while cherry-picking the best games from the English Championship and the rest of the Scottish Premier League card,' said the station's Scottish sports correspondent Andy Gillies. 'However, Bolton were playing Middlesbrough on the same night as Hearts faced Aberdeen. The match at Tynecastle was selected for commentary ahead of the Bolton match – that shows the level of impact made by Hearts since the arrival of Vladimir Romanov, and our agenda has subsequently been changed as a result.'

A goalless first half did nothing to help settle the nerves of the 17,327 supporters crammed inside Tynecastle, but the pendulum swung in Hearts' favour after 52 minutes. Roman Bednář flicked Robbie Neilson's long throw towards the back post at the Gorgie Road end of the ground and Russell Anderson inexplicably handled the ball. Referee Stuart Dougal immediately pointed to the spot.

After waiting a couple of minutes while Zander Diamond received treatment for an injury, Paul Hartley calmly placed the ball on the spot. He had never missed a penalty for Hearts . . . now was not the time to do so! Calm as you like, the Scotland international midfielder stroked the ball home to maintain his 100 per cent record from the spot and notch his 14th-consecutive penalty in a maroon jersey.

Stuart Dougal later conceded that Anderson should have been shown a red card for 'deliberately preventing a goalscoring opportunity' but didn't think so at the time – he only cautioned the Aberdeen centre-half, saving him from an early Radox bath. However, Aberdeen did go down to ten men. With 12 minutes remaining, Scott Severin helped out his former club · by curiously lunging at Bruno Aguiar in a vain attempt to play the ball and found himself first in the soapsuds in the visiting dressing-room.

Eventually, the shriek of referee Stuart Dougal's whistle pierced the air for the final time, much to the delight of everyone in the ground, especially Paul Hartley! The insufferable tension was relieved, fingernails were removed from mouths and Tynecastle prepared for a party like never before. It was time to make some noise because the Gorgie Boys were going to Europe.

HEARTS	74 pts
RANGERS	70 pts

Hearts had secured a place in the Champions League for the first time in their history, and the celebrations began immediately as Tynecastle experienced an atmosphere that many consider to be the best ever at the famous old stadium. The players returned to the dressing-room to change into specially printed T-shirts with 'Champions League: Here We Come . . .' on the front and 'Believe!' on the back, before returning to the field of play to take the acclaim of the jubilant supporters.

It had been 14 seasons since Hearts had finished as runners-up in the league and all of 46 years since they had taken part in European football's premier club tournament. It was also 20 years to the day since the dramatic events in Dundee when the Jambos had been heart-wrenchingly pipped at the post by Celtic. The ghosts of that day will never be exorcised completely, but the achievement of the 2005–06 season certainly made up for a lot of the heartbreak experienced by those Dens Park veterans.

'It feels great,' said Roman Romanov. 'It was a very tense night. We knew Aberdeen would be a very difficult team to beat, and I would therefore like to thank all the fans. I think they carried us through the whole season, especially tonight. Everybody could sense the tension with Rangers not far away, and I think the fans were our extra player on the pitch. Vladimir said we would achieve this at the beginning of the season. He believed it. We did it.'

Captaining the first side to split the Old Firm for 11 years ensured it was also a very proud occasion for the Hearts skipper. 'I have been at the club for eight years and waited a long time to experience a night like tonight,' said Steven Pressley. 'I spoke to Mr Romanov 18 months ago, and he expressed his dreams for the club. I suppose a lot of supporters were sceptical, but the dream has come true.'

He may have had to watch the match against Celtic at the start of April on a television set in a pub in Greenock, but there was no way Ken Stott was going to miss being at Tynecastle to see if his team could create history against Aberdeen. 'I've experienced great nights at Tynecastle in the past – including the memorable 3–3 draw with Real Zaragoza in January 1966 – but that was something quite special,' said the actor. 'Every Jambo loves Tynecastle Park, and it was like a family affair that night when Hearts celebrated a fantastic achievement in front of their "ain folk". Nobody left the ground for ages after the celebrations – everybody just wanted to hang around! If Murrayfield had been the venue for Hearts against Aberdeen, which might have been the case if some people had had their way, it wouldn't have felt the same – it's doubtful if we even would have had the chance to compete for second spot if we had moved there.'

Clinching second spot against Aberdeen rendered the final league match of the season – a trip to Ibrox – meaningless, allowing 800 Hearts fans the chance to head west and gloat for 90 minutes. A banner was unfurled by the visiting supporters prior to kick-off, letting the Rangers fans know where the 'Champions League Section' was located, while beach balls and rubber rings were gleefully thrown around the corner section. However, the best was yet to come . . .

When referee Iain Brines blew his whistle to indicate the start of the match, the Hearts supporters proceeded to start reading newspapers to signify they had no interest in how the game panned out – their team was in the Champions League and the job had already been done. That certainly bemused the Rangers fans, but not as much as witnessing the celebrations in the *away* end when Kris Boyd scored twice for their team!

The Hearts supporters at Ibrox that day did not care if their team lost the match, and neither did Valdas Ivanauskas: nine changes were made to the team that started against Aberdeen in a bid to keep the players fresh for the Scottish Cup final the following week. The first part of Vladimir Romanov's wish had been achieved; now the small matter of beating Gretna at Hampden was all that was required to keep Vlad happy and secure silverware at the end of an incredible and dramatic season.

EIGHT

SCOTTISH CUP SUCCESS

A GLANCE AT THE HISTORY BOOKS REVEALS THAT HEARTS do rather well in the Scottish Cup when the year ends in a '6' – winners in 1896, 1906 and 1956, and runners-up in 1976, 1986 and 1996. The 2006 competition also marked the 50th anniversary of the club's magnificent 3–1 victory over Celtic at Hampden to lift the famous silver trophy.

They say you need a bit of luck as well as ability to win a cup. Well, the omens were certainly good for Hearts in 2006 after being drawn at home in the opening three rounds – a replica of their winning campaign eight years previously. Having seen off challenges from Kilmarnock, Aberdeen and Partick, the boys in maroon were through to their 30th Scottish Cup semi-final.

Elsewhere, in the most open competition for years, the Old Firm failed to reach even the quarter-final stage, while lower-league sides Gretna and Dundee joined Hearts and Hibs in the draw for the last four at the end of February.

27 FEBRUARY 2006 – THE SCOTTISH CUP SEMI-FINAL DRAW AT HAMPDEN

Numerous debates took place in pubs across Edinburgh prior to the semi-final draw. The question being asked was, 'Do we want Hibs now or in the final?' (It was, of course, assumed that both clubs from the capital would dispose of lower-league opposition, if required!) Victory against your nearest rivals in a cup final would secure the ultimate bragging rights, but what would happen if your team lost? You would never hear the end of it!

Opinion was pretty much divided among the maroon half of the city, but one thing was certain: Hearts would go into the game as favourites, no matter who the opposition were. However, this tournament has proved that favourites don't always win . . .

It was the turn of Walter Smith and Tommy Burns to make the draw for the last four, and Hearts and Hibs were the last two teams drawn. It was an Edinburgh derby in the Scottish Cup for the first time since 'Wayne, Wayne, Super Wayne' in February 1994.

'It's the biggy!' said Graham Rix, unaware at the time that he would be watching the match from the comfort of the Sky television studio in the North Stand at Hampden. 'There is absolutely no doubt that the fans will be excited from now right up until the game for a whole variety of reasons. We have two very good teams in Hearts and Hibs, and if both sides play to their potential, then it will be a tremendous advert for Scottish football and the city of Edinburgh. It'll be a great day out for the fans with a trip to Hampden, and we're 90 minutes away from a cup final.'

The 28th capital clash in the cup – and the most eagerly awaited – was still more than a month away; plenty of time, then, to start a campaign to get the match played at Murrayfield

Stadium and prevent 52,000 fans needlessly travelling through to the 'Home of Scottish Football' when the 'Home of Scottish Rugby' was an ideal venue. Hearts promptly released a media statement giving their backing to the game being played at Murrayfield; Hibs boss Tony Mowbray, on the other hand, wanted the match to be played at Hampden. He felt Murrayfield would give Hearts an unfair advantage because they had used the stadium for three UEFA Cup games in 2004, even though only seven players who featured in that campaign were still at Tynecastle in 2006!

The SFA confirmed that a change of venue would require the agreement of both teams, among other things, so the campaign was effectively over before it had been given a chance to gain momentum. The Scottish Cup semi-final between Heart of Midlothian and Hibernian would take place at Hampden Park in Glasgow on Sunday, 2 April 2006 with a 12.15 p.m. kick-off to accommodate live satellite-television coverage. Traffic chaos was predicted, as 52,000 fans would be forced to make their way along the M8 on a Sunday morning – meanwhile, the Hearts team bus would head through the night before but minus yet another head coach . . .

2 APRIL 2006 – SCOTTISH CUP SEMI-FINAL, HAMPDEN PARK

The cup semi-final saw the fourth Edinburgh derby of the season and, incredibly, the fourth different Hearts head coach to get the chance to pit his wits against opposite number Tony Mowbray in less than eight months. Temporary boss Valdas Ivanauskas would be the latest to come up against the Englishman.

The Hearts players were greeted on arrival at Hampden by a sea of maroon-and-white-clad supporters, many of whom had been in Glasgow for most of the morning after having left early to avoid the expected traffic chaos. The Hibs squad, on the other hand, could not have failed to notice the alarming number of empty spaces in their section – either that or thousands of their fans had come dressed as plastic seats . . . First blood to Hearts before the game had even kicked off.

Psychological pre-match advantage number two arrived following confirmation of the two starting line-ups. With Derek Riordan already suspended, the Hibs team sheet showed that they were also without Chris Killen, Scott Brown, Michael Stewart, Paul Dalglish, Guillaume Beuzelin and Dean Shiels through injury. Tony Mowbray was even forced to give a debut to untried Moroccan striker Abdessalam Benjelloun.

Meanwhile, a couple of miles from the national stadium, Ken Stott was filming an episode of *Rebus* in Glasgow city centre, frustrated at not being able to get time off work to be at Hampden. 'I know it's not very professional, but I just had to know the score,' explained Stott. 'The car radio was right there in front of me – even although I was filming, I was still determined to keep up to date with news of the biggest Edinburgh derby in my lifetime.

'I watched most of the first half in a pub in the Merchant City in Glasgow, even though I was in full costume in preparation for filming, and, luckily enough, I was able to witness Paul Hartley giving us the lead before it was time for me to begin work.

'Military precision was required to plan the whole morning. I had to be in costume early and ready for work, enabling me to jump in a car heading to the city centre to watch the opening 45 minutes – the vehicle remained outside the pub until I was called onto the set. The things you do for your football team!

'Although it was frustrating not being able to be at Hampden, the particular scene I was filming was mainly in a car. I took it upon myself to listen to parts of the second half during breaks in filming! It was manic – I was trying to pay attention to the director and other cast members, while at the same time turning the volume back up on the car radio if no one was speaking to me!'

Claire Price – who plays DS Siobhan Clarke in *Rebus* – was in the car with Stott that day but took it all very well and never once complained that her co-actor's mind was not entirely focused on the job in hand: 'She could quite easily have said, "Listen, will you please concentrate on your work, you crazy man", but she was very accommodating and took pity on me! I turned the volume down when we went for a take (very thoughtful, don't you think?), but the minute the camera stopped rolling I had the radio back on to listen to the game.

'I actually missed one of the goals – I only thought we'd scored three, and I got a real surprise when the commentator on the radio said that Hartley had a chance to score his hat-trick from the penalty spot and make it 4–0. Luckily enough, the editor back at SMG in Glasgow was making a DVD of the game for me, so I watched the match in full after filming – and have watched it numerous times since!'

Back at Hampden, Hearts and hat-trick hero Paul Hartley were celebrating a stunning win over their city rivals, the Jambos' first victory in a Scottish Cup semi-final for eight years and their first at the national stadium for ten. The perfect day, then, for Vladimir Romanov. 'Today I have seen what I have been dreaming about,' said the Hearts owner. 'My team were playing football as I have dreamt it. The supporters are the golden fans of the country, and I appreciate them more than all the oil and gas of Russia. Glasgow has been the football capital, but I will do my best to ensure that Edinburgh takes that crown.'

Paul Hartley's hat-trick was the first of his career, taking his tally for the season against Hibs to six goals. The Scotland international somehow manages to find an extra gear when facing one of his former sides and this time kept a self-appointed date with destiny. 'I don't want to sound stupid here,' he said after the match, 'but I looked in the mirror this morning and told myself it was going to be my day. It just doesn't get any better than this – to score a hat-trick and win 4–0 against Hibs. We just had a feeling in the camp all week that it was going to be our day, and it was.

'I think the derbies mean more to me because I used to play for Hibs – I get really hyped up for them. My time at Easter Road was terrible, but over the last couple of seasons I've proved that I didn't really do myself justice there. Since I've joined Hearts, everything has gone right for me. That was for the Hearts supporters today, because they have been fantastic with me from day one at the club. When we rolled into Hampden at about 10.30 a.m., there were already thousands of them there, and you could just sense from the atmosphere that it was going to be our day.

'Everything went for us today, especially for me. I take the penalties in any case, so there wasn't going to be any argument about who would take it. Big Edgaras Jankauskas actually told me to try and chip the keeper with it, but I didn't have the bottle for that. I just can't wait for the final. It will be the first one of my career, and I'm really looking forward to playing against Gretna at the national stadium on 13 May.'

It was a 'Super Sunday' for everyone connected with the football club, and celebrations lasted long into the night as fans in pubs and bars across Edinburgh painted the town maroon. 'The supporters have earned the right to celebrate,' said Robbie Neilson after the semi-final. 'They were absolutely fantastic out there. When we made our way to the stadium prior to the match, I couldn't believe how many were here so early. We arrived about an hour and a half before the game, and they were all here outside waiting to get in. I thought there would be a few people here, but that is the best I have ever seen it. It gave us a massive lift, and we spoke about it in the dressing-room prior to going out. Valdas told us not to send them home disappointed – they spent a lot of money on tickets and coming through – and we were determined to make sure our fans were happy going back along the M8 after the final whistle.'

Gary Mackay featured more times against Hibs than any other Hearts player in history, suffering just eight defeats in fifty-five matches. However, the 4–0 win at Hampden eclipsed any of those games, and it was finally payback time as far as he was concerned. 'As a Hearts supporter, I have had to take some unbelievable stick about the 7–0 reverse in January 1973,' he said, 'but this result – in such a massive game – blew that result into oblivion. I have to admit to shedding a tear or two of joy as I looked at the huge Hearts support thoroughly enjoying themselves away to my left, right underneath the large electronic scoreboard that proclaimed "Hearts 4, Hibs 0".'

Gretna's 3–0 victory over Dundee the previous day meant Hearts would face Second Division opposition in the final – surely not even the Jambos could blow this opportunity . . .

13 MAY 2006 – SCOTTISH CUP FINAL, HAMPDEN PARK

Only Gretna stood between Hearts and a seventh Scottish Cup win, and pre-match predictions of 3–0, 4–0 and 5–0 were rife in Gorgie as confident Hearts supporters set off for Hampden on the Saturday morning of the final. With Scotland's second-best team taking on little Gretna, it seemed as though there could only be one result; surely it was a case of how many goals the boys in maroon would score.

More than 32,000 Hearts fans took their seats at the national stadium for what they hoped would be an enjoyable and worry-free afternoon, including Iain Mercer: 'I remember Dad saying to me in the autumn of 2005 that he did not think Hearts would win the league, even after their unbeaten start, but he had a feeling that they would win the Scottish Cup if they could stay clear of injuries. It was typical of him to have a gut feeling as to where the season was going, and he turned out to be right. The team he followed in England was Chelsea, so he would have viewed it as a hugely successful season both north and south of the border!

'In recognition of Wallace's contribution to Hearts, the club invited the whole family as their guests to the cup final, but, for one reason or another, we did not take them up on their kind invitation. My mum was over in Spain visiting friends, which had been organised long before the team had reached the final, while Helen and I had already arranged to go with some friends. We cheered the team on from the North Stand, although both of us had nagging doubts that it might not be our day once the game reached extra time . . .'

The fact that Hearts even had the chance to take the game to extra time was down to one of the best tackles ever made by a player wearing a maroon jersey. Bobby Moore's challenge on Pelé at the 1970 World Cup quite rightly goes down in history as one of the best ever, but, from a Hearts perspective, Robbie Neilson's sensational tackle on Gretna substitute David Graham was equally noteworthy. 'I just wanted to get back and try and stop him shooting,' said Robbie. 'Craig [Gordon] did well, as he managed to make him [Graham] go wide, and then I was able to get back in time and make the tackle. It was a relief when I timed it right, as I didn't want to concede another penalty. It was disappointing to give away the first penalty, because they never really threatened from set-pieces and hadn't created too much inside the box. The linesman put his flag up immediately after the penalty was taken, and we thought there was something happening, but Craig had come off his line. I think if they hadn't equalised then, the referee would have allowed them to retake the spot-kick.'

5.30 p.m.

Things had not gone according to plan. By half past five, the Hearts players should have been back on the team bus drinking cans of the sponsor's product, toasting a seventh Scottish Cup win, and the contract cleaners should have been out on the pitch cleaning up all the maroon-and-white ticker-tape from the post-match celebrations. Instead, a penalty shoot-out would decide the winners of the 2006 Tennent's Scottish Cup after Gretna midfielder Ryan McGuffie fired home the rebound of his missed penalty from close range – Craig Gordon had saved his second-half spot-kick – to cancel out Rudi Skácel's first-half opener for Hearts.

It seemed quite ironic that the song 'Crazy' by Gnarls Barkley was number one in the charts at the time because it had been a crazy afternoon: the previous 120 minutes at Hampden had virtually mirrored Hearts' entire season! Stephane Adam – Hearts' goal hero in '98 and the *Hearts World* summariser at the national stadium – nearly made a crazy decision of his own before the shoot-out began, but he quickly came to his senses. 'I cannot believe the thought even crossed my mind!' explained Adam. 'Penalty kicks were about to decide if the Scottish Cup would be draped in maroon-and-white or black-and-white ribbons, but I told Mark and Gary that I had to go – they would have to commentate on the spot-kicks for *Hearts World* themselves. The chance for Heart of Midlothian Football Club to win the national cup competition for only the seventh time in its history was potentially only moments away, but I would not be around to see it.'

Understandably, Stephane had not considered that Hearts would need extra time and penalties to beat Gretna when he had accepted an offer from Setanta to commentate on the final French league match of the season: Rennes v. Lille. Both teams needed to win to qualify for Europe, and Stephane had to be at the television studios in Glasgow city centre for 6 p.m. 'It should have been simple,' said Adam. 'Commentate on the cup final for the official club website, enjoy watching the celebrations when Hearts won by a couple of goals, get a taxi to the Setanta studios for the French game then head out in Glasgow afterwards for a party.'

The best-laid plans . . .

'When the referee blew his whistle to signal the end of extra time at Hampden, I looked at my watch – it was 5.30 p.m. I had a decision to make. If I left the stadium, I would get a taxi outside the ground without a problem and be at the studios in good time for 6 p.m., but I would miss the drama. If I stayed to watch the penalties and Hearts lost, there would be no chance of a quick getaway, as thousands of supporters would also be leaving – it would be chaotic.

'I initially decided it was better to be safe than sorry and, against my better judgement, said my goodbyes. It just didn't feel right, though. There was no way I could sit in the back of a taxi and listen to the penalties on the radio, especially after having experienced every emotion imaginable in the previous two and a half hours. The look of disbelief on the faces of both Mark and Gary following my initial decision also persuaded me to stay!'

When Paul Hartley became only the fourth player in the 132-year history of the competition to be sent off in a final (retaliation towards Derek Townsley at the end of extra time sealing his fate), Hearts were without their regular penalty taker and a man who had scored every one of his 14 spot-kicks in a maroon jersey. 'I thought I had maybe cost Hearts the Scottish Cup after getting sent off,' he said. 'I tried to get out to watch the penalties from the dugout, but the officials said I wasn't allowed, so I had to go back to the dressing-room and watch it on the telly with our press officer Clare Cowan. I was pretty confident when Big Elvis stepped up, as he's taken plenty of spot-kicks before, but I wasn't so sure about Robbie – I knew he had a great throw, but I didn't realise he could kick the ball that far!'

The omens weren't good for Hearts either. The three other players sent off in the cup final – Jock Buchanan of Rangers in 1929, Celtic captain Roy Aitken in 1984 and Hearts skipper Walter Kidd in 1986 – all picked up loser's medals . . .

Three of Hearts' five penalty takers were to be defenders in the absence of Hartley. Steven Pressley would take the first spot-kick, Robbie Neilson the second and Takis Fyssas the fifth, if required.

Penalty shoot-out

Player	Team	Score
Steven Pressley	Hearts	1–0
James Grady	Gretna	1–1
Robbie Neilson	Hearts	2–1
Mark Birch	Gretna	2–2
Rudi Skácel	Hearts	3–2
Derek Townsley	Gretna	3–2 (penalty saved)
Michal Pospíšil	Hearts	4–2
Gavin Skelton	Gretna	4–2 (penalty missed)

Hearts had won the 2006 Scottish Cup final, sparking scenes of joyous relief among the 32,000 maroon-and-white-clad supporters inside the national stadium, and also out on the pitch, as the players celebrated a victorious conclusion to a remarkable season. A certain midfielder who'd been stuck in the dressing-room for the previous ten minutes rejoined his teammates on the park. 'No one was going to stop me getting onto the pitch to join the celebrations,' said Paul Hartley. 'It was a fantastic feeling. I've waited a long time for this – to win a major trophy – and celebrating with the rest of the lads is something I'll never forget.'

One of the first players Hartley encountered when he ran onto the pitch was Robbie Neilson, and the pair exchanged some banter about Robbie's penalty. The defender, though, insisted he was always confident of scoring from the spot. 'I put my name forward straight away to take a penalty,' said Neilson. 'Elvis was taking the first one, and I said I would take the second. I just wanted to make sure I made good contact and not worry about any of those stupid videos you see about how to take a penalty. It was just a relief to put it away.'

If anyone had suggested during George Burley's time in charge at Tynecastle that Ibrahim Tall would be one of the recipients of a Scottish Cup winner's medal, they would have been scoffed at. The player was completely out of favour at the start of the season but worked hard behind the scenes and was rewarded with a place in the starting XI to face Gretna – only his fifth appearance in a maroon jersey. 'It was a very good way to end the season, as I played very little during the previous eight months,' said the Senegalese international. 'When the gaffer gave me the chance to play against Gretna, I was determined to give it everything I had. It's been a very good season because we won the cup and came second in the league.'

Edgaras Jankauskas added a Scottish Cup winner's medal to his Champions League gong with Porto but revealed he was in agony by the end of the game. 'We had plenty of chances to score, but with it being a final maybe we were nervous,' he said. 'Gretna were making things difficult for us, and it wasn't an easy game – it cost us a lot of energy. Several players had cramps – I couldn't move by the end – but unfortunately we had no more substitutions to make, so I had to stay on the park. I couldn't leave my mates with one less! It was a great feeling to win, no matter how it was achieved.'

Fellow striker Michal Pospíšil also picked up a medal after coming off the bench with 20 minutes remaining in normal time to replace fellow countryman Roman Bednář. It was the fourth time the Czech player had tasted success in his career. 'I won a gold medal at Under-21 level in the European Championships with the Czech Republic, and I also won a league title and cup over there,' explained Pospíšil, 'but the Scottish Cup is also very special for me. It was one of the best days of my career. I was a little nervous before taking my penalty in the shoot-out because I knew it was very important, but it was 3–2 at that stage, and I knew that if I scored, it would really make it easier for us. I was quite confident because I had actually scored from the spot in the European Championship final against France Under-21s, and I knew that I wanted this cup too much to miss! I was relieved to see it hit the back of the net. All of the pressure was gone, and I was delighted just to score.'

Takis Fyssas, the joker in the Hearts squad, had it easy during the penalty shoot-out – he simply had to watch before going up the steps to pick up his winner's medal. 'I was very sorry at the penalties because I had the fifth spot-kick to take, and I would be the legend of Hearts – I'd be the hero!' said the Greek international, laughing. 'Joking aside, I'm very happy we won this cup – it is an unbelievable moment. For me, it is very important because I came to this club and I've lived through some incredible moments. Winning this cup, after eight years for Hearts, is incredible.'

The cup win was also a personal triumph for Valdas Ivanauskas, who had begun the season arranging bibs and sorting out the markers for George Burley's training sessions. It was a roller-coaster ride for him as much as anyone, but the man who always seemed to look so serious was finally able to crack a smile. 'We won the cup, and so, for me, it is the biggest day of the season,' said the caretaker boss. 'The players were very strong. We have had a very long and hard season. It has been a great season, and I think it has been the best season for Hearts Football Club. I know how difficult this final was, but it is all about winning. In the game, we had so many chances, but if you don't take the chances, you can lose the game. If we had scored the second goal, it would have been so much easier, but we didn't, and we had problems with Gretna. Thankfully, it all worked out well in the end.'

When Steven Pressley moved to Tynecastle in the summer of 1998, the club was still celebrating winning the Scottish Cup for the first time in 42 years, following the 2–1 victory over Rangers at Parkhead. He didn't expect to have to wait eight more years before realising his ambition to win a trophy with Hearts. It had been a long wait for Elvis – too long, as far as he was concerned – so there was no way he was letting the trophy out of his sight following the players' party at Murrayfield Stadium on the Saturday night. 'The cup came back with me,' explained the captain. 'I decided to take it home and had a nice little party in the house! It was a very memorable moment for me as captain of Hearts to lift the cup. There aren't many occasions like that in your professional career. It's been a long time in coming, and I don't intend to give it up without a fight.'

The whole weekend for the Pressley family was memorable. Pressley's four-year-old son Aaron was the Hearts mascot at Hampden when Daddy lifted the Scottish Cup for the first time. The following day, however, provided the only downside for the Jambos captain. Elvis was accompanied onto the pitch at Tynecastle for the celebrations not by Aaron, but by his niece

Morgan. His son decided he would rather go to a birthday party instead because there was a bouncy castle. Nothing, however, was going to deflate the Hearts captain that weekend . . .

Stephane Adam, meanwhile, managed to get to the television studios in time for the start of the French league game he was commentating on. 'It actually worked out really well for me,' explained the cup-final hero of 1998. 'I got to see the penalties, and the minute Gavin Skelton hit the bar, I quickly hugged my co-commentators and made a dash for the exit. As I was going down the stairs at Hampden, I got a phone call from Setanta to inform me that there was a car waiting for me outside!'

However, in his rush to leave the national stadium, Stephane had forgotten to fulfil a prior agreement with a Sunday broadsheet. 'Amidst all the emotion that day, I completely forgot that I had agreed to do a column for *Scotland on Sunday* with my thoughts on the final. I was to meet one of their journalists, Andrew Smith, in the media centre following the game, and he would ghost-write my copy. Due to the match finishing late, and my subsequent dash into the city centre, things did not quite go according to plan. He was unable to phone me before I went on-air, as he was doing the post-match interviews at Hampden. By the time he called, I was broadcasting. He eventually got hold of me . . . at 8.45 p.m.!

'As I was leaving the studios at Cowcaddens in Glasgow, I was met by a frantic-looking Mr Smith – he had been waiting outside the front door, having made his way there from Hampden. It was then that it dawned on me about the column . . . I had completely forgotten! Perched against a vehicle in the car park, I explained to him my thoughts on the game as he scribbled away frantically in his notebook. Unbeknownst to me, he had a 10 p.m. copy deadline for his main edition, having missed the first. Pleasantries were quickly exchanged before I watched him literally sprint back to his office on West Regent

Street. Having read my article in the newspaper the following morning, I can only assume he was able to type as quickly as he could run!'

Victory in the Scottish Cup final was a wonderful way to end a remarkable season, and even though the celebrations at the end of the game were not quite as intense as they had been in 1998, it still meant as much for a club who had only experienced winning the Scottish Cup on six previous occasions. A lot of the newspapers that weekend understandably focused on Gretna's hard-luck story, but that in no way detracted from the ongoing celebrations in Gorgie. Sore heads were prevalent throughout the capital and surrounding areas the following morning as Jambos woke up after an evening of partying, while through in Glasgow city centre a certain Frenchman awoke on Sunday morning and immediately headed straight for his kitchen to partake of a couple of obligatory Alka-Seltzers!

Stephane Adam, the Hearts player, partied long into the night in May 1998 after scoring the winning goal against Rangers at Parkhead, and the celebrations were equally jubilant eight years later as Stephane Adam, the Hearts fan, painted Scotland's second city maroon – despite some wind-up merchants in the west trying to belittle the achievements of the Jambos for failing to hammer the Second Division champions. 'I can understand why they said that to me, but there are no easy games in cup football – especially in finals,' said Stephane. 'Just because you are favourites does not mean you have a right to win. I think that was a problem in 2006. Immediately after the 4–0 victory over Hibs in the semi-final, the Hearts players knew they would be facing a Second Division side in the cup final. During the six weeks between the two games, the media coverage was all about little Gretna enjoying their day out and simply hoping to keep the score respectable.

'There is no way that Hearts intentionally underestimated Gretna; however, players read newspapers, they listen to the radio and they watch television. It was impossible to avoid. There is no doubt in my mind that those six weeks' worth of coverage had something of a subconscious effect on the Hearts players. They all said at pre-match press conferences that they would give Gretna the utmost respect, that they expected a tough game. Of course they did – everyone in that situation would. However, it is one thing saying it but another thing entirely actually believing it.

'To me, the mental attitude and spirit of a player makes up 50 per cent of his performance – the rest is down to fitness, technique and ability. A lot of Hearts players turned up at Hampden expecting to go home with a winner's medal – what they did not count on was the performance of their opponents. Granted, Gretna had been playing Second Division football all season, but this was the biggest match of their lives – never to be repeated. No point being called "plucky" and "gallant" if you go home with a loser's medal. Gretna were right up for it.'

Stephane Adam experienced what the Gretna players went through prior to the match in 1998, going into the Scottish Cup final as underdogs. Where the two differ, however, is that the underdogs triumphed in '98, while they were beaten eight years later. 'All credit to the Hearts players for turning round what, at one point, was looking like a dire situation,' he said. 'The mental strength shown by certain individuals was fantastic. Collectively, as a team, it is impossible to simply flick a switch during a game and produce that extra yard when you find yourselves up against it.

'Let's get one thing straight. Hearts had enough chances against Gretna to win out of sight. They struck the woodwork and players missed opportunities they would normally score. They had so much pressure but could not find a way past the opposition keeper and their three central defenders. At times like that, you sometimes get the feeling it is simply not going to be your day.

'The Hearts players kept going, though, and deserve immense credit for winning the cup after producing a performance that fell well short of what had been produced earlier in the season. Perhaps it was a game too far for the squad at the end of a dramatic season, but they did what they set out to do – they won the Scottish Cup. Sorry, Gretna, but you do not get your name engraved on a trophy for a hard-luck story . . .'

So, the curtain was brought down on the 2005–06 season with a successful, if nervy, afternoon for Hearts at Hampden Park. Perhaps the luck they say you need to win a cup was in evidence for the Jambos at the national stadium that day – maybe even a little assistance from above helped ensure the silverware returned to Gorgie. 'I thought of Dad as I made my way to Hampden, and I was thinking about him throughout the game,' said Iain Mercer. 'It was bizarre: the sunshine came out during the second half of extra time and stayed that way until we won. His spirit was certainly at Hampden that afternoon, and I would like to think he had something to do with the result. Perhaps he urged them to victory, but that's all *Roy of the Rovers* stuff . . . isn't it?'

NINE

FROM RUSSIA . . . WITH CASH

THE DEBATE RAGED ON FOR MANY MONTHS. A LEADING member of the board of Heart of Midlothian Football Club felt the only way forward for the organisation was to sell Tynecastle and move to a much larger stadium. A dissenting voice from Eastern Europe, however, claimed there was no need to up sticks and decamp elsewhere; he felt the club could continue to survive and prosper playing at its spiritual home, and that all avenues for expanding Tynecastle had not yet been explored. The year was 1939!

Hearts chairman Alex Irvine wanted to move from Tynecastle to a brand-new stadium with double-tiered stands on both sides of the pitch to be located in the Sighthill area of Edinburgh. Plans were drawn up to build on a site which we would now call Saughton Mains, while the corporation agreed to extend the bus routes to the stadium; the railway company also gave the go-ahead to open Saughton Sidings on a match day.

Scotland's capital city had failed in a bid to host the 1938

Empire Games (now the Commonwealth Games), but plans remained on the table to build a 100,000-capacity arena that would be the focal point of any future bid. It was to have been shared by Hearts as well as being an alternative to Hampden Park for hosting international football. (The plans were later shelved once war broke out.)

The dissenting voice was that of Elias Henry Furst, a 66 year old who was twice chairman of Hearts between 1912 and 1935. Born in 1873 in Russia to an immigrant rabbi, Furst became a Hearts supporter from a young age after his family moved to Edinburgh via London, Hull and Middlesbrough.

Furst's early promise and financial acumen ensured his appointment as club auditor at Tynecastle in 1902 at the age of just 29. His foresight and administrative ability then secured him a place on the board five years later, followed by promotion to the position of chairman in 1912. He stepped down in 1922 and was reappointed in 1933. Despite again stepping down from the role in 1935, and resigning from the board, Furst remained a shareholder in the club and continued to make his voice heard. He felt the proposed move away from Tynecastle was a non-starter because of the enormous cost involved – he feared it would cripple the club. The Russian was also concerned that supporters might not travel to the new stadium and was convinced that Tynecastle could be successfully expanded.

At the Hearts AGM of 1939, the club announced that all debts had finally been cleared after many years in the red. Furst, according to Hearts historian David Speed, was adamant that moving to a new stadium at Sighthill would not only put the club back into financial difficulties but perhaps even bring about the threat of bankruptcy. 'Furst urged the board to make sure they explored every possible avenue with regards to the plan to move,' said Speed. 'He told them that the cost of moving – £100,000 to £130,000 – was too great for the club, even after the announcement at the AGM that they were finally debt free, and that leaving Tynecastle could signal the death knell for Heart of Midlothian.

'Some of the board felt that, with no financial millstone around the club's neck, it was a gamble worth taking, but Furst much preferred the more fiscally prudent idea of redeveloping the existing stadium at Tynecastle.'

Furst was ultimately proved correct, although his influence in ensuring that Hearts remained at Tynecastle was minimal. Fast forward more than 60 years and that is not something that can be said about the second Russian-born businessman to get involved with Heart of Midlothian Football Club . . .

Vladimir Romanov was born to parents Zinaida and Nikolai in the province of Tver, northwest of Moscow, in June 1947. His mother and father survived the brutality of the Stalinist regime, and in 1956, when young Romanov was nine, his father Nikolai was posted to a new army base in Lithuania, a country which had been annexed by the Soviet Union. The family lived together in Kaunas, Lithuania's second city, for seven years until Nikolai died of a massive heart attack in 1963 when Vladimir was only 16. The teenage Romanov then had to take over as head of the family, which gave him a thorough grounding in survival techniques, although he had to get special permission from the Communist authorities to start working before the minimum age of 18 in order to provide for his mother Zinaida and sister Olga.

He was officially a taxi driver, but Romanov used his entrepreneurial skills to set up another business to ensure he had enough funds to properly look after his family – bootleg copies of LPs by the Rolling Stones, Elvis Presley and The Beatles were sold from the boot of his Volga GAZ-21 car. After two years spent trying to dodge the authorities, it was time for the 18-year-old Romanov to undertake national service. He was drafted into the Russian navy and travelled to Murmansk, the main homeport of the Russian nuclear submarine fleet. During his six years there, first as a submariner and then in the merchant navy, he met and married Svetlana.

In 1971, aged 24, Vladimir Romanov and his new wife decided to return to Kaunas, and within a few months he had started his first company as the Soviet Union began to relax restrictions on private enterprise. Over the next few years, Romanov was behind several successful businesses, buying in raw materials from Russia and turning them into goods back in his adopted homeland of Lithuania.

Just how much money he made during the Communist era is unclear, but it was enough for him to take advantage of the break-up of the Soviet Union. Lithuanian entrepreneurs, like others in the rest of the old Soviet Union, ruthlessly exploited the lack of laws and business regulations in the early years of independence. The Baltic state became a market for all manner of goods and materials, from metals to textiles.

Vladimir Romanov's wealth multiplied as he benefited from state enterprises being sold off to the highest bidder, not only in Lithuania but also in other burgeoning nations, such as Ukraine and Bosnia and Herzegovina. He then teamed up with other rich Lithuanian entrepreneurs to create a bank named Ūkios Bankas and its investment offshoot. Eventually, amassing a paper fortune of almost £260 million in banking, textiles and metals allowed him to spend money on one of his main hobbies – football.

History is littered with many examples of erroneous decisions, albeit made without the benefit of hindsight, as well as plenty of cases of 'what might have been'. No one wishes to have their mark on the world framed by an honest miscalculation, but certain errors of judgement are always likely to be remembered.

Although not exactly fondly remembered north of the border, the 1966 World Cup final at Wembley Stadium was one such occasion associated with a major faux pas. The BBC World Service broadcast radio commentary of England v. West Germany but omitted to make provision in their schedule for the possibility of extra time. At the end of the nail-biting match, with the score poised at 2–2, they returned to the studio and carried on with the advertised programme, a recording of a Beethoven symphony. For listeners around the world, it was all over a bit earlier than it was for Kenneth Wolstenholme.

In Scotland, supporters of Ayr United still have cause to gnash their teeth when casting an eye in the direction of Ibrox and the sight of Rangers' progress under David Murray. The steel magnate's initial plan was to gain control and invest substantial amounts at Ayr's Somerset Park, but his advances were met with fierce resistance in the struggling club's boardroom.

Another example of 'what might have been' came in January 2004: Dundee United chairman Eddie Thompson and two other directors from Tannadice met a Lithuanian businessman by the name of Vladimir Romanov in Edinburgh to discuss possible investment in their football club. Thompson, according to Dundee *Evening Telegraph* football writer Tom Duthie, knew that Romanov had plenty of cash to invest but was not willing to turn over complete control of the club to the Lithuanian businessman. 'Eddie had only been in charge at Tannadice for just over a year, and while he was willing to accept Romanov's investment, there was no way he was going to step down after such a short spell at the helm,' said Duthie. 'He wasn't prepared to give up on his dream of rebuilding

United so soon after the titanic effort to gain control had finally come to fruition in 2002.

'There's no doubt it was a missed opportunity for Dundee United – it's up there with Derek Rowe from Decca Records deciding he didn't like the sound of The Beatles in 1962, claiming guitar music was on the way out!'

Vladimir Romanov could also have become involved with Dundee, just across the road from Tannadice at Dens Park, having been willing to invest a substantial amount of money, but his plans did not get off the ground because the club was in administration. 'Both the bank and the administrator were willing to accept Vladimir Romanov's cash,' explained Duthie, 'but they insisted that any money he was planning to spend or invest had to be lodged in a Bank of Scotland account in his name so that they knew he was genuine. Giovanni di Stefano had pledged money to Dundee shortly before administration – the cash never materialised and that made them sceptical of foreign investors. Romanov disagreed with this course of action. He had his own bank and felt this was not necessary.'

Romanov's desire to get involved with both Dundee and Dundee United convinced sports writers in the city that the Lithuanian was interested in more than simply investing in the two football clubs. 'Whether or not it was his intention, there was a considerable body of opinion within the city, and also within Dens Park and Tannadice, that Vladimir Romanov eventually wanted to merge the clubs,' said Duthie. 'United chairman Eddie Thompson was always against a merger – when he decided against giving up control, the issue was immediately put to bed.'

Vladimir Romanov's initial interest in Scottish football was not, in fact, with either club from Dundee, but with Dunfermline. Pars chairman John Yorkston, along with Jim Leishman, met the rich banker and his close confidant Liutauras

Varanavičius in Lithuania in 2003 and entered into discussions regarding a possible tie-up with the Lithuanian Football Association.

The pair from Dunfermline spent five days in Eastern Europe, but their intended involvement with the Lithuanians was limited to bringing players over from the former Soviet republic and giving them a more visible platform – there was never any mention of a takeover, according to Yorkston. 'The negotiations eventually faltered because Romanov and Varanavičius started talking to both the Dundee clubs about investing there, and we drifted away from them,' said the Dunfermline chairman. 'As far as I am aware, they also spoke to numerous teams in England and Germany.'

Exactly how Vladimir Romanov became involved with Hearts remains open to conjecture. Chris Robinson, Leslie Deans and Dundee director Jim Connor all claim to be the first to have brought him to the table in Scotland, but Romanov's initial involvement with a Scot was with Edinburgh's Deputy Lord Provost, Councillor Steve Cardownie, a lifelong supporter of the Tynecastle club, though not a shareholder. Cardownie, through business contacts in Eastern Europe, was introduced to Romanov at a European Championship qualifier between Lithuania and Scotland in Kaunas in 2003.

Later that year, in the return match between the two countries at Hampden Park on 11 October, a conversation between Lithuanian Football Association president Liutauras Varanavičius and John McBeth, his counterpart from the SFA, set the wheels in motion for Eastern European involvement in Scottish football. 'I spoke with Mr McBeth and explained to him what we were trying to do,' said Varanavičius. 'Initially, we wanted our clubs to become feeder teams for organisations in the West, providing us with a platform to showcase our players;

however, nobody showed much interest in that plan. We had spoken with people from Celtic when they played FBK Kaunas in July 2003, but they had no interest in getting involved.

'Mr McBeth told me it may be a better idea to try and buy a club in Scotland that was struggling financially. On my return to Lithuania, I mentioned to Romanov what McBeth had said. Immediately, he was very interested in the possibility of doing something – he wanted me to investigate which clubs he could possibly invest in.

'This started to become a serious project for Romanov, and he was very keen on the idea because it would not only give him a chance to open the market for Lithuanian players, but it also seemed a very viable business opportunity as far as he was concerned. Romanov wants to be the first to do everything, and when he takes an interest in a new venture, then you know he is serious and means business.'

Discussions with Dunfermline, Dundee and Dundee United all failed to produce a positive outcome for Romanov at the end of 2003 and start of 2004, but the seeds of involvement with Hearts were planted at a meeting in April 2004 – brokered by Steve Cardownie – between former Hearts chairman Leslie Deans and the Russian-born multimillionaire from Lithuania. Edinburgh's Deputy Lord Provost was convinced that the businessman was genuine and a man of financial substance, and, despite the breakdown in talks with the two teams from Dundee, Romanov was encouraged to get back round the table with representatives from another Scottish club. The rest, as they say, is history.

Vladimir Romanov lives an extremely busy life and has business interests in many European countries, yet he still has time to entertain influential statesmen, such as Ukrainian president Viktor Yushchenko, at his summer retreat in the Lithuanian resort of Nida. Romanov is not, therefore, the kind of person you would immediately think would take an interest in Heart of Midlothian – so why did this Eastern European millionaire want to get involved with a Scottish football club who hadn't won their national championship since 1960? 'There appears to be a complex variety of motives,' said George Foulkes. 'Romanov is genuinely interested in football, and is enthusiastic and passionate about it. I remember once being in his hotel suite in Edinburgh, and the televisions in the room were all showing football. He has tasted success in business and now wants the same in football, along with the glory and recognition that comes with it. He wants to win the Champions League, and he believes that is possible with Hearts. It's a huge ask, but anything can be done with the right resources – just look at Chelsea, for example.'

Edinburgh's reputation as a major financial city in the United Kingdom may also have persuaded Romanov to invest in Hearts, giving him a platform to showcase his Lithuanian bank and expand it Europe-wide, according to Doug Smith. 'There is an increasing number of Eastern European businessmen who are willing to invest in football clubs and generally get involved in the sport,' he said. 'Take Roman Abramovich at Chelsea – he felt safer and more secure being in London, as well as being more high profile. In the case of Mr Romanov, he wants to have banking interests here.'

However, Liutauras Varanavičius disagrees: 'In my opinion, obtaining banking facilities in the United Kingdom was the least important reason for Romanov investing in Hearts and in Scottish football. Primarily, the idea was that all the Lithuanian players went directly to the Western market instead of having to go via the likes of Russia or Poland.'

It might seem strange that someone from Lithuania should be passionate about Hearts, but it was evident from some of his actions in the directors' box during the 2005–06 season that Vladimir Romanov quickly built up strong feelings for his adopted club. 'A successful football team can provide successful business people with experiences they will never be able to replicate, even when brokering deals worth many millions,' said Doug Smith. 'Vladimir Romanov has achieved many things in his life and become extremely wealthy as a result of what he has done, but I doubt he will ever have experienced the joy and the sensation caused by his team winning the Scottish Cup and finishing second in the SPL. I do not think Vladimir realised how big Hearts were when he first expressed an interest in investing in the club or even how big Hearts could be.

'In fairness, does it really matter what his reasons are for getting involved? Looking at the situation from the point of view of where Hearts were prior to his arrival, I think supporters should be grateful to him for his investment and also thankful for his ability to provide substantial financial resources to ensure success.'

Vladimir Romanov was reasonably well-known in Lithuania before his involvement with Hearts but mainly as a businessman associated with the country's first private bank, which he helped set up in 1989. He is less well-known for being a sponsor of FBK Kaunas, despite the bank's emblem being emblazoned across the front of the team's yellow-and-green strips. Coverage of Romanov in the sports media in his homeland increased dramatically, however, following Hearts' start to the season and the subsequent departure of George Burley; but it was the burgeoning international exposure afforded to the Hearts owner that amazed many people in Lithuania, according to journalist Gintautas Dulskas from monthly Lithuanian sports magazine *SPO:*). 'The attention he received in Scotland, the UK, Europe and worldwide has been staggering – all because of his involvement with Hearts,' explained Dulskas. 'That would simply not have been possible if FBK Kaunas was his only interest.

'There was no way he was going to be able to invest in an English Premiership club of similar size to Hearts – it would have taken a lot more money to do this. Also, there are only two very big clubs in Scotland – Celtic and Rangers – and he knows if he provides funds for Hearts to challenge the Old Firm, that could also open many doors for him.

'Mr Romanov has two main passions in life – football and money. With Hearts, he can own a major part of an excellent football club and also earn money from the venture at the same time. He wants to bring in quality players for Hearts, put them in the shop window and then sell them for far more money than he paid for them. The players have the incentive to get a move to a bigger club if they do well every week, the supporters get to see their team full of quality on a regular basis and the club receives money if the player is sold on that can then be reinvested in another target.'

UEFA has tried on several occasions to clarify Vladimir Romanov's involvement with FBK Kaunas in Lithuania and MTZ-RIPO in Belarus as part of their multi-ownership investigation; the governing body for European football strictly forbids one individual from having a direct influence on more than one club simultaneously. However, Romanov, under the current legislation, has not broken any rules and actually has no 'official' connection with either club. FBK Kaunas and MTZ-RIPO are municipally owned clubs that are backed financially by a number of corporate sub-sponsors, the main one being ŪBIG, in which Vladimir Romanov is heavily involved as a major shareholder. Officially, as far as UEFA is concerned, Romanov has no direct involvement with either club and is simply a sponsor – unofficially, he has the potential to pull the strings at both organisations, and there is nothing European

191

football's governing body can do about it. This enables him to invest directly at Hearts without breaking any rules. It is a similar situation to Chelsea owner Roman Abramovich and his Sibneft Oil company's role as main sponsors of CSKA Moscow until the multimillionaire sold the company at the end of 2005.

Romanov's funding of FBK Kaunas ensures the team regularly win the Lithuanian league title, but even that fails to generate much publicity in the national press. Kaunas have played in the Champions League qualifiers on a number of occasions – including a match against the reigning champions Liverpool in July 2005 – yet the coverage in Lithuania remains lukewarm. 'That is another reason I think he decided to invest in Hearts: he knew if he was able to help bring success to the Edinburgh club, then that would open many doors for him,' said Dulskas. 'It would also make his name known to a lot more people than would have been possible in Lithuania. I think he has made a very clever decision, becoming the owner of Hearts.

'He is a very clever man and is nearly always able to deliver promises. When he said he believed Hearts could split the Old Firm, a lot of people were sceptical, but he has done it already. He also said he believes Hearts can win the Champions League within three years – I would not want to bet against Mr Romanov doing this!'

Others may have their own thoughts about why Vladimir Romanov invested in Hearts, but his reasons for getting involved were simple and there were no complex motives, according to the man himself. 'My Lithuanian club Kaunas was drawn against both Celtic and Rangers in European competition,' said Romanov, 'and the cult status of football in Scotland made a big impression on me. I had long thought about expanding my interests in the football business. Without fans, there is no real scope for progress – that's the situation in Lithuania. In Scotland, the ground is there, it simply needs decent investment to "fertilise" it – that was the main motive behind my decision. The fact that Lithuania has joined the European Union made my task a lot easier.

'Why would I invest money [in Hearts] if I didn't think I could make the club number one in Scotland? Hearts is situated in the capital of the country, and its quality is something different from the clubs in Glasgow. We believe very strongly that Hearts could get an even better support – this is another of my motives for investing. My next mission is to get a bigger fan base than either Celtic or Rangers.'

Vladimir Romanov is like Roman Abramovich in a variety of ways: they are both very successful self-made Russian-born businessmen; one is using his cash to help stir things up in a Premiership turned stagnant by the Arsenal–Manchester United duopoly; the other is doing likewise in the SPL with the Rangers–Celtic dominance. And although the Chelsea owner is infinitely richer than the Hearts owner (with an estimated personal fortune of £7.5 billion), both men have reached the top the hard way after starting at the foot of the ladder.

They have another thing in common – their PR advisers share the same surname: both Abramovich and Romanov have a Mann by their side . . .

In the blue corner – looking after Roman Abramovich – is John A. Mann II. No ordinary public-relations executive, John Mann is a veteran spin doctor from the political cauldron of Washington DC, and former vice-president of US PR giant Burson-Marsteller, the company that represents Ford and Coca-Cola, and has, in the past, acted for Union Carbide following the 1984 Bhopal disaster in India and the ExxonMobil oil company after the *Exxon Valdez* oil spill.

In the red (maroon) corner is Huntly's very own Charlie Mann, the head of public-relations agency Weber Shandwick's

Glasgow office and a man with a reputation for playing it straighter than most in his business. In the past, he has led the PR campaigns for the launch of the Tennent's Scottish Cup and the Bell's League Championship.

It's questionable if John A. Mann II has been called 'a muppet', 'beleaguered' and 'dishonourable' in his time working for Roman Abramovich, but Charlie Mann has during his employment as Romanov's UK representative. 'That's what I mean by polarised views,' joked Chazza, as he's affectionately called by Graham Spiers in *The Herald*.

In a survey carried out by Weber Shandwick, it was revealed that Vladimir Romanov received 4,623 mentions in the Scottish press between May 2005 and May 2006. When you consider that this was second only to Scotland's First Minister Jack McConnell, with 4,870 in the same timescale, it becomes apparent that these statistics show just how much of an impression the Russian-born Lithuanian has made on our society in such a short space of time since arriving on these shores from Eastern Europe.

Ironically, Romanov received very little publicity in the press when the Hearts board first approved his takeover at the end of January 2005 and his subsequent purchase of a 29.9 per cent stake in the club – but that was due to Barry Ferguson returning to Rangers and Craig Bellamy signing for Celtic at the same time. How times have changed!

Before Romanov came to town, discussion about Hearts in pubs and clubs outwith Edinburgh and the Lothians was usually limited to the few days before and after the Jambos were in opposition against the local team. That soon changed when the former Soviet nuclear submariner got his feet under the table at Tynecastle and started making his mark with a series of incredible decisions that, whether right or wrong, certainly had everyone talking. The fact that Vladimir Romanov was able to make such controversial decisions, despite not even being on the board, was due to the events of July 2005. Despite selling his shareholding to Romanov at the start of February that year, Chris Robinson remained on the board until the summer before eventually being replaced by Vladimir's niece. The boardroom finally saw the back of the chief executive but not before one last twist. 'It was obviously important for Vladimir Romanov to get a Lithuanian majority on the board to make it easier to make decisions,' said George Foulkes. 'The way he got that majority was by appointing Julija Gončaruk, his niece, as a non-executive director. I was given her CV and told she was a suitable person. She was Lithuanian but working in Rome and had experience in fashion and marketing which would be useful to the board. At no point, however, was I told that she was Vladimir's niece – no one ever mentioned this.

'Robinson intimated to me that he was not going to resign until we appointed Julija Gončaruk onto the board, and he made it a condition of his resignation that she become a non-executive director. Why he did that – [whether it was on] his own initiative or in consort – I do not know, but that is what succeeded in getting the Lithuanian majority onto the board.'

In the week before the start of the 2005–06 season, I was part of a small group of Scottish journalists invited to travel to Lithuania to interview Vladimir Romanov in a PR exercise arranged by Charlie Mann and Weber Shandwick. We were going to try and unmask the 'character' who was making headlines back in Scotland. Our group retraced the steps taken by George Burley exactly one month previously as we visited Romanov in his grand office in the Ūkio Bankas headquarters in Kaunas. A question-and-answer session took place during which the journalists were given carte blanche to ask anything they wanted, while Vladimir tried to be as open as possible with his responses. Unfortunately, the session backfired slightly when Chris Robinson, not Vladimir Romanov, made back-page headlines in Scotland the following day. 'Overall the trip was very successful,' said Rob Robertson from *The Herald*, 'however, the matter that came to the fore during the question-and-answer session was that Robinson – who had resigned from the board the previous week – was still being employed by Romanov as a consultant to help provide local knowledge when dealing with the council regarding stadium redevelopment.

'This probably came as a bit of a surprise to the public-relations company that helped organise the Scottish journalists' visit to Lithuania. They would have expected the headlines the following day to be about Vladimir Romanov and his vision for the future!

'Prior to the trip, I was not the only journalist with doubts about Romanov's financial clout and the wealth he purported to have, but those doubts were quashed the minute I walked through the front door of his bank and climbed the marble staircase to his sumptuous office. The negative feelings were put to bed completely, so, overall, the PR exercise served its purpose and blew away any doubts about Vladimir Romanov's validity.'

Romanov was very complimentary about George Burley throughout his discussion with us, but it's unlikely the former Hearts manager would have been given the opportunity to head down to the bank's basement for a tour of the vault after his chat. It was a case of 'after you' as all ten of us nervously made our way down a spiral staircase, while at the same time being told by our English-speaking guide that no member of the public had ever been afforded the privilege of visiting the basement vault before. When I think back, maybe I misheard and she actually said no member of the public had ever emerged from the basement vault after having been given the chance to look around. Perhaps if Vladimir Romanov had prior knowledge of the way his relationship with George Burley was going to deteriorate throughout the following three months, then an invite might have been extended to the manager to peruse the facilities in the basement . . .

While Hearts fans enjoyed their best season in years, spare a thought for supporters of FBK Kaunas. A host of big-name players signed for their club during the 2005–06 season – Edgaras Jankauskas, Roman Bednář, José Gonçalves and Bruno Aguiar among others – but immediately moved to Scotland on loan on the instruction of Vladimir Romanov. Despite their S. Dariaus ir S. Gireno Stadium having a capacity of just 7,432, FBK Kaunas only average about 400 fans at home matches – less than Meadowbank Thistle used to get – as football plays second fiddle to basketball in Lithuania. Because of this, Romanov's involvement with Lithuanian football was only ever intended to provide him with a step onto the European football ladder. 'There was never any question that Romanov would not concentrate fully on Hearts, despite his involvement in Kaunas,' said Gintautas Dulskas. 'It is natural that all the best players go directly to Edinburgh because he has invested most money in that project; however, the Kaunas fans do not mind at all. Their club is getting global exposure for the first time due to Mr Romanov's investment with Hearts, and the supporters are happy with this – they still get to see their hero Jankauskas and others on a weekly basis, even although it is on television after Romanov bought the rights to show Hearts games on Tango TV.

'I doubt that any more than 5 per cent of the viewing public actually watch the matches in Lithuania – football is simply not that popular in our country. For example, if our national basketball league finals were on television at the same time as a

Hearts match, the basketball game would have at least ten times more viewers than the football. In saying that, Romanov should be applauded for trying to make soccer as big as basketball in Lithuania. It is unlikely it will happen in the short term, but at least he is giving it a go.

'If all the owners of clubs got together and tried to increase the popularity of Lithuanian football, then maybe they would succeed, but I'm afraid Mr Romanov on his own has no chance of making football more popular in Lithuania than basketball over the next few years. Who knows what will happen in ten years' time? For now, though, nothing is likely to change.'

For a long time there has been talk of fan representation on the Heart of Midlothian board. That representative would most likely come from the Supporters Trust, which now owns around 2 per cent of the shares in the club after purchasing them from Leslie Deans. George Foulkes is a member of the trust – number 82, to be exact – but it's unlikely he'll be putting his name forward for consideration for a return to the boardroom. 'However tempting it is, I don't think it would be right for me to go back,' said the former chairman. 'I think Vladimir Romanov really does need to get new board members – he needs to get Scots on the board – but I think he also needs to look forward, rather than back. There is no point thinking of Les Deans, myself or Chris Robinson – certainly not Robinson – but people who could be seen as Hearts through and through – Scottish and fresh. They would be able to go in with their eyes open and know Romanov is not a person who you can have a big influence on.

'I think anyone who accepts a place on the Hearts board in the current arrangement has to do so with the clear knowledge that they are not taking part in the decision making – that all decisions are made by Vladimir Romanov and backed up by his

Lithuanian majority. Whatever they do, they are the public face of decisions made by Romanov, and they have to be absolutely sure they are happy about everything that is being done in the club, then go out and explain it to supporters, players and the public. When I did it before, I agreed with most of the things Romanov was doing – his criticism of some agents, some referees and the fact the SFA can be niggling, difficult and awkward at times – but I wasn't sure about the complaint the club submitted regarding the assistant referee Andy Davis when they questioned his integrity after he awarded Rangers a penalty on the night of the infamous "Mikoliūnas incident". It was not a clever statement to make – using the word "integrity" was, in my opinion, a mistake. In my opinion, [it was] Chris Robinson [who] influenced Sergejus Fedotovas to put in the complaint.

'There were two further examples [of things] we simply could not agree on. The sacking of George Burley was the first one – that was a week before I resigned – and then, of course, the second was my resignation in protest at the sacking of Phil Anderton. In retrospect, I should have resigned over the Burley issue, but hindsight is easy.'

Getting rid of George Burley was the most contentious decision made by Vladimir Romanov: sacking a manager while the team was undefeated in league competition and flying high at the top of the table. Incredulity greeted the news that Burley's time at Hearts had come to an end, but Romanov felt the exit of Burley from Tynecastle was the best option available to him. 'I've got an agreement with George Burley whereby I'm not going to comment on him personally,' he said. 'But I would say this: if the agents who were involved were still on the scene, then Roman Bednář, Craig Gordon and Paul Hartley wouldn't be here. They would have been sold; there would have been agitation behind the scenes to get them sold off. Perhaps we would have had one victory more over the season, but what we wouldn't have is Hearts as we have now.'

It wasn't just Romanov's decision to sack Burley when the team was top of the league that surprised everyone but also the speed at which the Hearts owner went about his business, according to Doug Smith. 'As soon as he realises he has to make a decision, he is decisive and does not waste any time doing so, especially if he feels that is what the club requires to ensure success,' said Smith. 'If you are putting in the money that Vladimir Romanov is, you are entitled to do what you want – within reason.

'I think one of the things that surprises everyone about Romanov's decision making is the speed at which changes are made. Top of the league, George Burley doing well, Phil Anderton and George Foulkes getting results off the park – everything looked rosy from the outside. Suddenly, it is all change within the space of ten days. When you look back at the season, however, it seems to me that Vladimir Romanov's decision-making, no matter how it has been perceived and what reasons have been given, has been vindicated. You can take the view, "Yeah, he probably made a few mistakes during the season" – don't we all in our own lives – but you have to look at the end product, and it has been one of the most successful seasons for Hearts in a long time.'

The BBC broadcast two documentaries about Vladimir Romanov in just seven months: a *Frontline Scotland* investigation into Romanov's business dealings in Eastern Europe, aired in December 2005; and *King of Hearts*, a behind-the-scenes look at the Russian-born Lithuanian shown in June 2006. A claim by Vladimir that the match against Celtic in October 2005 was fixed (made public by George Foulkes but subsequently proven to be unfounded) helped publicise the latter, but it was the former that ruffled more feathers in the Romanov camp – it included allegations of tax evasion in Bosnia – and ultimately led to Charlie Mann quitting his other role as a football reporter with BBC Radio Scotland after he was seen on camera attempting to stop an interview with Mr Romanov. Mann insists that he was not pressurised or forced into making a decision that cost him in the region of £8,000 per annum but claims he was left with no choice. 'I felt I had no alternative but to terminate my employment with the BBC, where I worked on a freelance basis at the football most Saturdays,' he said. 'I would always side with my client, and when the choice came between the two, there was always only going to be one winner.

'I have offered, on more than one occasion, to debate the issue publicly with the BBC about why I stopped the interview. I have absolutely no problem with what I did and the way I acted – it was the third time I had mentioned to them that it was time for us to leave. I had arranged for Vladimir to attend the Scottish Parliamentary Awards, where he would get the chance to meet the First Minister Jack McConnell for the first time.

'Romanov was not changed, and he had to go to the Radisson SAS to get ready before heading down to the Museum of Scotland for the awards dinner, which started at 7.30 p.m. It was 6.20 p.m. by this time. The BBC thought we were trying to mess them about – they did not understand that you cannot get an appointment in Romanov's diary at the drop of a hat, as he has businesses all around the world.

'He told me he could do the interview at the allotted time – on the same day as the awards – as he was in Scotland and had space for a half-hour appointment before heading off to meet Mr McConnell. I phoned the BBC and explained the situation, telling them when Romanov would be available, but the lady I was dealing with, Dorothy Parker, told me that the people doing the documentary were in Bosnia filming at Vladimir's Birac aluminium plant.

'I told her once again of Romanov's availability and explained that there were no guarantees when he would be free for another interview if they missed the initial time-slot allocated to them because he was leaving Scotland following the awards dinner. I explained to her that the interview would have to be done through a translator anyway, so why not just get a camera crew there, get a reporter to ask the questions that had been prepared and then use the cuts as normal? That is all they would have done anyway, so it did not matter if it was Ross McWilliam or another reporter posing the questions. She did not agree with this, so I told her that was the date, that was the time and Mr Romanov would be there waiting for them. They thought I was being awkward, but I was actually being helpful.'

The *Frontline Scotland* crew had to fly back from Bosnia earlier than planned and went straight to Tynecastle from the airport. Romanov was in a meeting and was ten minutes late for the 5 p.m. appointment – this, of course, did not go down well with the BBC! 'I explained to them prior to Romanov's arrival that they should get on with things straight away when he sat down and only ask the questions they wanted answers for,' explained Mann. 'They were warned not to spend ages going into the background of the situation, as Romanov would go off on all sorts of tangents. They had only been allocated a 30-minute slot and Vladimir was heading to the dinner afterwards.'

The interview eventually started at 5.15 p.m. At 6 p.m., Mann tried to bring the interview to a close: 'I politely asked the producer to wind things up, but the guy basically ignored me. Five minutes later, I told him that the interview should be stopped as soon as possible – we were due at the awards at 7 p.m. for a 7.30 p.m. start, and Mr Romanov still needed to go back to his hotel and get changed. The producer said the reporter would only ask two more questions. I kept my voice down at this stage, as the interview was going on at the other end of the boardroom table.

'[At 6.20 p.m.] there was still no sign of the interview ending, so I took the producer to the far corner of the boardroom and told him that if it was not ended at that precise moment then I would end it for him. He asked for a final question, which was grudgingly approved, but it soon became obvious that the reporter had no intention of stopping the interview, so it was stopped for him.

'The fact that they chose to show me on camera stopping the interview made my relationship with the BBC very awkward indeed. They chose to ignore several of the positive things Romanov was saying about the factory in Bosnia, instead choosing to try and dig up dirt on him.'

Incidents such as this one demonstrate that Charlie Mann's job as Romanov's UK spokesman is never dull. As one of the men charged with receiving copy from Lithuania and then making the Russian-born businessman's opinions suitable for public consumption via the media, Mann is also exposed to some of Romanov's more bizarre claims and ideas. Sometimes, however, the diktat from Eastern Europe makes it perfectly clear that the wording must not be changed. This was the case when Romanov's programme notes arrived in Scotland ahead of the match against Falkirk on Boxing Day, 2005 – an alternative to the Queen's speech, if you like, from Lithuania . . . with love:

> Dear Supporters,
>
> Even the most sacred places on this earth, the places that house the remains of Christ, are blighted by profiteers and moneygrabbers. Likewise, in the football world, which is sacred for those who love football, there are also

those – be they agents, journalists, jealous hangers-on or other 'wunderkinds' – who seek to ruin all that is good about the game. But it is the Devil that is driving them forward, and they are not going to stop. All that will remain for me is to step aside and bid them farewell on their road to Hell.

His Christmas message certainly raised a chuckle in the press box prior to the 5–0 victory – even Gary Mackay managed a laugh, despite being listed in two of Vlad's bad categories as both an agent and a journalist. 'I suppose the only thing I can't be accused of is being a jealous hanger-on!' said Gary.

Hearts' 3–2 defeat at the hands of Celtic on New Year's Day may have been the match that ultimately decided the destination of the title, but it could have been so different. Takis Fyssas was wrongly shown a red card by referee Iain Brines, with just over ten minutes remaining at Tynecastle, for allegedly fouling Shaun Maloney when Hearts were leading 2–1. The dismissal was subsequently overturned, but not before another rant from the owner: 'We should invite Celtic to play in the Lithuanian league. To win something there they should bring the three referees we had from our games with Hibs, Rangers and the New Year's Day game.'

Until recently, Vladimir Romanov more or less had free rein to say what he liked about anything to do with Scottish football in the knowledge that he was untouchable: he officially held no position of power at Tynecastle, despite being the club's majority shareholder. This quickly became an issue with the SFA, although they found themselves unable to do anything until their AGM at the start of June 2006 when the relevant rules and regulations were altered. 'I knew he was angry at the Scottish Football Association ruling attempting to gag "shadow directors", but I advised him not to say anything to avoid falling into a trap,' said Charlie Mann. 'It was blatantly obvious to all concerned that the governing body had *not* mentioned Vladimir Romanov's name when they announced their new ruling following the Annual General Meeting. Everybody knows he was a target for this SFA ruling, but so was Brooks Mileson, Dermot Desmond and others involved in the game but not actually employed as directors of their respective clubs.

'I immediately knew what was coming and spoke to and emailed people in Lithuania to make it very clear that neither the association nor chief executive David Taylor had mentioned Romanov and that it would not be appropriate for him to say anything in reply. It was better to leave it alone and deal with it at a later stage. The next morning, I got emails and calls from Lithuania saying there was a problem after a copy of the back page of *The Sun* had been faxed out to them, showing Romanov with two Elastoplasts over his mouth. He had seen this image, which was what provoked his reaction.'

Charlie got in touch with Will Stewart, a freelance reporter based in Russia, and told him it would not be appropriate to seek comments from Romanov on behalf of Scottish journalists because it would simply get Vladimir into big trouble with the SFA. However, Romanov was extremely angry at the back page of *The Sun*, as Mann explained: 'I reiterated my stance to the Lithuanians: do not let Romanov go public with his thoughts on the SFA. My advice, however, fell on deaf ears. An angry Vladimir Romanov spoke to Will and instructed him that he wanted the following comments released into the public domain back in Scotland on his behalf in response to the new gagging order – there was nothing I could do about it: "Do the new regulations mean I'll need to keep silent until the end of my life? Or will this rule only apply while you [Taylor] are in your post? I hope you won't leave your position for another

80 years because without you there's no one to think up such ingenious regulations. In case I do get fined for what I say, I'd like to know how you are going to spend the money? If it goes to pay bonuses to the referees, then which ones – those who just happen to be Celtic fans or those who monitor the direction of Skácel's spitting? Or should we establish some foundation to conduct spitting contests? You have already accumulated quite an experience in this field so I suggest you become the general director of this new Spitting Federation. I guarantee there will be not a word of criticism from me. I am even prepared to forget that you never apologised after an 'independent from you' referee wrongly sent off Fyssas. Instead of apologising, you disqualified key Hearts player Hartley for three games before decisive matches in the SPL. Maybe you just forget that he's the real pride of the Scottish national team, unlike you or me. Well, I understand that one's own interests are above everything else.'"

Mann was pragmatic about Romanov's outburst. 'All I can do is deliver advice to my clients,' he said. 'It is up to them to decide whether or not to take it on board. Lawyers do the same, accountants do the same, architects likewise – you can only point clients in a certain direction. There is no point throwing the toys out the pram if your client does not listen.'

Clinching second spot in the SPL ahead of Rangers was one of the main highlights of the season, not just for Hearts, but for Vladimir Romanov as well. Being at Hampden to witness the Scottish Cup returning to Tynecastle for the first time in eight years was a joyous occasion for the multimillionaire, especially as he was able to invite some Russian former submariners who served during the Cold War to the national stadium. 'These men helped save the world from the most awful catastrophe that any of us could ever imagine – an explosion on a nuclear submarine,' said Romanov. 'On its maiden voyage in 1961, there was a disaster on the K-19 submarine when the sealing on the starboard nuclear reactor's cooling system sprang a leak off the coast of southern Greenland. These men were among the submariners who made the vessel safe, risking their lives in the process. Some of their comrades died in this act of sacrifice, but, like any submariner, they did their duty, not thinking of themselves. To say they saved humanity from an awful nuclear disaster is no exaggeration.

'If I feel an affinity to these retired sailors it is because some years after this horror I served on this same K-19 submarine as a young conscript in the Soviet navy – by then, the submarine had been repaired. I was proud and honoured to serve there, even though it was called the sailing Hiroshima. When I joined the crew, I was told of the bravery of these remarkable men, but it was only recently, in Moscow, that I met them for the first time. Their feat puts football into perspective. Thankfully, the world has changed so much since then. People in the East and West now count themselves as friends, as I know from my own experience in Scotland.'

In the summer of 2006, Romanov purchased the Soviet submarine just weeks before it was due to be scrapped. He plans to move it to a berth in Moscow and turn it into a museum and meeting place which will help to build links between submarine veterans from Russia, Scotland and other countries. 'The vessel is very dear to my heart,' he said. 'I wanted to rescue it for world history as a symbol of those heroes who prevented a third world war.'

In Vladimir Romanov's first full season at Tynecastle, he certainly captured the public's imagination and was even named the eighth most-powerful man in the country in *Scotland on Sunday*'s annual 'Power 100' supplement:

Even Messrs George Burley, Phil Anderton and Graham Rix are likely to agree. No single individual has changed the face of Scottish football more than Lithuanian banker Romanov in the short time since he took the reins at Tynecastle. For the first time in 11 years, Celtic and Rangers have been split at the top of the Scottish Premier League and neither Old Firm team appeared in the Scottish Cup final. Further evidence that his influence has spread to the west coast is that Hearts, not Rangers, qualified for the Champions League in a seismic shift in the Scottish football firmament.

Sage observers scoffed when Romanov outlined his determination to pour his millions into creating a European super club. Few are scoffing now. Romanov also represents a growing phenomenon: the influx of Eastern Europeans into Scotland. From the Poles flooding into the construction and hospitality industries to the billionaire Russian oligarchs buying country estates, their influence is rapidly increasing.

Not only that, but Romanov finished ahead of J.K. Rowling (9), HBOS chief executive James Crosbie (20), Cardinal Keith O'Brien (24), Stagecoach chief executive Brian Souter (40), David Murray (63) and a certain Sir Tom Farmer (87)!

Romanov's actual day-to-day involvement at Tynecastle is minimal because he is rarely in Scotland apart from on match days. He leaves the running of the club to the chairman, his son Roman, although a hotline is frequently utilised. 'It cannot be easy being the son of Vladimir Romanov and also being thrown in at the deep end,' said Doug Smith. 'However, I think he has handled himself very well, especially with the Graham Rix appointment that evoked a lot of emotive feelings in

Edinburgh. Although Roman is chairman of Hearts, I do not think there is any doubt that his father pulls the strings; and now the club is once again a private company, Vladimir Romanov has the right to make whatever decisions he wants.

'[Vladimir] Romanov has now set the benchmark – it is up to him to take things forward because the expectation levels of supporters are now increased as a result of the team's achievements in the 2005–06 season. Hearts fans will probably be disappointed now if they do not at least match that success in years to come.

'There is a tremendously deep support for Hearts – we have seen that it is possible to fill the stadium week in, week out if there is a successful team on the park – but if Romanov can successfully rebuild the main stand at Tynecastle, with the requisite corporate facilities, then revenues will increase substantially, while the fantastic atmosphere at Gorgie will still be retained. Once you start to play in front of full houses, the demand for tickets picks up substantially. You can see what happened at Celtic: prior to the arrival of Fergus McCann, they were playing in front of relatively small crowds. Before [Kevin] Keegan came to Newcastle, the players were running out to crowds of less than 15,000 – now every game is a 52,000 sell out.

'Romanov has also engendered a tremendous amount of publicity for both himself and the club since becoming majority shareholder. If you are a Scottish businessman working in London – which I quite often am – and you say you are from Edinburgh, people will ask if you are a Hearts supporter because of the attention Mr Romanov has created in a short period of time. Perhaps that is just a small indication that the balance of power is slowing shifting to the East . . .'

If there is one slight worry about Vladimir Romanov among Hearts supporters, it concerns how long the multimillionaire will stick around. What would happen if he suddenly decided to head back to Lithuania and subsequently put the club up for sale – would Hearts be back at square one? That, however, does not appear to be an issue for now, at least not according to *The Scotsman*'s Stuart Bathgate. 'The Romanovs are involved in Hearts for the medium-to-long term,' he said. 'The club is part of their overall business strategy, and they are applying modern-management methods to it – something that is a novelty in Scottish football. Having worked really hard for decades to build up his boring businesses – the money-making Birac aluminium plant in Bosnia, for example – Vladimir wants to do something interesting with his money. He loves football, he loves the attention he gets at Tynecastle and he is fascinated by the whole project, so, in a sense, it's a game for him, albeit one that he takes pretty seriously. He maybe overestimates his own footballing knowledge at times, but he's shown himself to be a quick learner.

'Vlad is not going to stay at Hearts for ever – he still regards Lithuania as his home – but I am sure he intends to leave the club in a very healthy state when he eventually decides to head off into the sunset, taking the money he has made with him. When Romanov does eventually decide that he has had enough, Hearts will be much more commercially attractive to possible investors. He has a serious long-term plan – a lot of people in Scottish football do not realise that.

'The only man I can think of who has made a serious profit with his involvement in Scottish football is Fergus McCann. He showed he knew how to turn a business round and that there was a massive untapped audience at Parkhead. Hearts are not on that scale in terms of their latent support, but Romanov knows that Hearts have a lot of scope for expansion. He is aware that there are a lot of Hearts supporters who are quite well off but, at the moment, are not spending anything with the club. Providing the right conditions – hospitality and success on the field – will help attract these people to spend money and invest in the club.

'One concern for me is that I'm not sure if Romanov delegates enough. He does put people he trusts in senior posts, but I think there are times when he is still too hands-on. It's always difficult for a self-made man to adapt to a bigger, more corporate business structure, but he must be aware by now that he has done certain things that have produced an adverse reaction. I'm sure Steven Pressley and other senior players have let him know that more stability is required.'

If one of Vladimir's aims when he took over at Hearts was to attract publicity, then he certainly succeeded, but it appeared that Charlie Mann was being undermined by some of Romanov's comments and actions at times. Unsurprisingly, the public-relations executive disagrees and claims he is a good fit for both Romanov and journalists. 'I know how the industry works,' said Mann. 'I know where people get information from, and I often hear about things after a journalist has told me something – that is not to say I have not had an inkling about it. The timing of when I find out about a certain development may be slightly later than other people, but there is nothing that has really surprised me yet. My job is to deliver advice to Vladimir Romanov, whether that advice is taken or not is a different story.'

It has often been claimed that Romanov knows more English than he actually lets on, sometimes answering English questions immediately in Russian without the need for translation. However, Charlie Mann disputes that his 'boss' is trying to pull the wool over our eyes: 'I was surprised when I saw him speak briefly in English at the civic reception the day after Hearts won the Scottish Cup. He said, "Hearts fans, I love you, I love

Edinburgh, I love Scotland." I don't think he knows many more English words! My conversations with him have always been through a translator – I have never exchanged two sentences in English with him since I started working for him, even if we have been alone in the boardroom or in a car.

'He is getting used to our culture and trying to learn English, while we have to get used to his approach and his style. It is not a style that is common here, but it is common in continental Europe – just because it is different does not make it wrong. We in Britain are not used to being told brutally honest facts about our abilities, our standards and our style of operating. He has come in and he has been honest. He has asked questions and delivers what he believes is a true assessment of the situation. Some of us may not like it, but he has a different style of management. He's totally driven to succeed.

'I believe I have to stand my ground with him, and I think he appreciates that and respects that. I do not think it will be such a roller-coaster in subsequent seasons, but it will still be very interesting. Romanov still has a lot to accomplish at Hearts, both on the domestic and European stage. I am still hugely interested in the project and am delighted to be involved in it. Vladimir Romanov is adamant he is at Hearts for the long term, and I hope I am too.'

Vladimir Romanov is still in the embryonic stage of his involvement with Hearts. Hopefully, his grand plans for the future will ensure that the club is regularly competing with and beating the Old Firm, enabling the Jam Tarts to dine annually at Europe's top table. The incredible foresight of Elias Furst ensured that he made an indelible mark on the history of the club, but if that can be eclipsed over the next few years by the man leading the second Russsian revolution at Tynecastle, the supporters of Heart of Midlothian Football Club are in for one heck of a ride.

TEN

THE SEASON THAT WAS

Roller-coaster (n.)

1. A steep, sharply curving elevated railway with small open passenger cars that is operated at high speeds as a ride, especially in an amusement park.
2. An action, event or experience marked by abrupt, extreme changes in circumstance, quality or behaviour.

Or this definition when relating to life at Hearts under Vladimir Romanov:

Hearts roller-coaster (n.)

1. A thrilling ride that tempts you to get on but does not tell you when it is safe to get off . . .
2. An emotional experience full of ups and downs, marked by extreme changes in circumstances . . . and managers!

A football roller-coaster affects different people in different ways. Supporters are in it for the long haul; they take what is thrown at them and accept that emotional peaks and troughs are commonplace. Players are more short-to-medium term, also experiencing the wave of emotions but able to climb off if the going gets too tough (during the transfer window, of course). As for managers . . . those at Hearts need not even bother fastening their seatbelts!

Everything appeared rosy in the Tynecastle garden in the first few months of the 2005–06 season. What came next didn't just jolt the roller-coaster, it practically derailed it for a spell.

George Burley's departure as Hearts head coach was one of the most talked-about events of the season, and the hypothetical question of whether the boys in maroon would have won the league if he had stayed at Tynecastle remains the subject of discussion in pubs and clubs throughout the football world . . .

'We will never know what would have happened had George Burley been in charge for the whole season,' said John McGlynn. 'A lot of people will say his departure cost us the title, a lot will say it didn't. There's no doubt it was a major disruption, but how much it affected the players is extremely hard to say. The players loved working under George, so there's no doubt there was a reaction – but to go out and beat Dunfermline on the day they were told their manager had gone was a show of incredible mental strength. They found out the news that the manager they loved was no longer at the club at 11.30 a.m. when they arrived for their pre-match meal at Dalmahoy. To then start the game against the Pars so well was amazing – they deserve the utmost credit for that.

'I think there would have been a big question mark about some of our players from various countries being able to handle the Scottish winter. Would we have been able to continue playing that style of football when the weather was rotten? Would the players' fitness have come into consideration during the winter – especially those who had not had a full pre-season with us? Every team has a sticky patch, no matter who they are – no doubt we would have had the same at some point of the season. How would we have got through that? There are so many questions that remain unanswered . . .

'Despite all the turmoil behind the scenes and all the upheaval, I think we proved in 2005–06 that we are now a force to be reckoned with, and, in my opinion, the years ahead have real promise as far as Hearts are concerned.'

Hearts' failure to win away from home between 17 September (when Burley was still in charge) and 14 January was another reason why the Jambos failed to hold on to their early season lead. 'To go nearly four months without an away win is simply not championship form,' said Doug Smith. 'If you look back over the season, the 3–2 defeat against Celtic on 1 January, having led 2–0 at half-time, was clearly a major blow. We may have had a bit of luck at times against Gretna in the cup final, but we certainly did not get any breaks at Tynecastle that day. A Hearts win would have taken us to within one point of Celtic, but, instead, the deficit became seven points, and it was simply not possible to claw that back. In saying that, Celtic really came on to their game in the second half of the season, and it would have been extremely difficult to overcome them.

'We won the Scottish Cup. We finished second in the SPL. If you were doing a school report comparing performance, the 2005–06 season was a big improvement from 2004–05, and everyone at the club must be congratulated for that. You can only improve upon the previous season – the task now is to better the achievements of 2005–06.'

Hearts captain Steven Pressley took on the mantle of the 'Old Castle Rock' during the season – he was both mentally and physically strong on and off the pitch, despite all the unrest, and led his team to one of their best-ever campaigns. Burley's exit was a low point of the season for Elvis, and it remains a source of contention for the skipper. 'I could not say that if George Burley had stayed we would have won the SPL title,' he said. 'That would be disrespectful to Celtic. Make no mistake, winning the league is no easy task, and I think they deserve enormous credit. They showed great consistency throughout the season and ultimately deserved to win the title.

'In saying that, I think it would have been a far more competitive end to the season between Celtic and Hearts if George had remained in charge. They won the league, I am not taking that away from them, but I do not believe they would have won it by such a significant margin.'

Hearts had just lost their first league game of the season when Phil Anderton was sacked by Vladimir Romanov at the start of November but were still very much in contention at the SPL summit. Speaking to Paul Kiddie in May 2006, the former chief executive was of the opinion that the league title was there for the taking, had Burley remained in charge. 'I believe if George had been given the authority to bring in the players he thought would have been beneficial to the club, then Hearts could well have challenged Celtic. It would have been interesting to see what would have happened. I think Hearts would have been disappointed if they had not been second, but that is not to belittle the achievement of splitting the Old Firm. The squad did remarkably well to keep focused on the league despite all that happened, but George's departure must have had some kind of impact.

'It was a terrific achievement finishing second, and the players who did so deserve enormous credit, particularly the likes of Steven Pressley, Paul Hartley and Craig Gordon. However, you have to ask "what might have been", had they not lost to Hibs at Easter Road shortly after Burley left, and had they not dropped two points at Tannadice in February 2006 amid all the speculation about who was picking the team. Celtic were in transition and Rangers were coming towards the end of the McLeish era – only time will tell if 2005–06 was the season that Hearts let a good chance to win the league slip away . . .'

A mixed bag of opinions, then, regarding whether Hearts would have won the league if Burley had remained in charge for the entire season. A slightly different view, however, was put forward by one of Vladimir Romanov's trusted lieutenants, Liutauras Varanavičius. He believed even more success might have been possible, had Burley taken over the reins earlier than 30 June 2005. 'If I could change one thing about season 2005–06, I would have appointed George Burley earlier than we did. We needed more time to prepare the squad and more time to bring new players to the club before the start of the season to get them fully fit. That became a major problem approaching the end of the year.

'The performance of the team deteriorated – I don't think it was due to the coaching – as many of the players were brought in too late and were unable to get a full pre-season behind them. This ceased to become an issue when we signed new players in January, but the damage had already been done . . .'

He may have been in charge for only 114 days, but it was still plenty of time for George Burley to make a huge impression. His 75 per cent win rate is unlikely ever to be beaten by a permanent manager of Hearts, and even though he was only in the hot seat for a very short spell, the style of football witnessed by supporters will live long in the memory, according to Gary Mackay. 'Throughout the summer of 2005, following the departure of Robbo, I always believed Vladimir Romanov would appoint a non-British head coach,' he said. 'I was shocked but pleasantly surprised when George Burley was given the job – it pleased me that Vladimir Romanov had put his faith in a Scot with a knowledge of British and European football in both his playing and managerial career. I travelled to Rugby Park on the first day of the season full of optimism, eager to witness a George Burley Hearts team playing in a competitive environment.

'Despite a resounding 4–2 win at Kilmarnock on the opening day of the season, being a pessimistic Hearts supporter, I refused to get too carried away – it is very difficult to maintain that sort of high-tempo performance on a weekly basis. It was the first day of the season and the past has proved that random results can take place on the opening weekend.

'It didn't take me long to be convinced, though – a 4–0 hammering of Hibs at Tynecastle in week two assured me that George Burley was not only the right man for the job, but he could be the first manager since Jim Jefferies to bring silverware back to Gorgie!

'As the weeks and early months unfolded, the results and performances were 100 per cent better than I could ever have anticipated prior to the start of the season. The 1–1 draw against Celtic at Parkhead also gave me a huge shot in the arm. I felt, on the back of that performance, that if Hearts could stay in touch at the top of the table until January, then George's expertise in buying quality football players – combined with the excellent high-tempo football being played – could tip the scales Hearts' way in our bid to win the title for the first time since 1960.'

The fact that the Hearts players were able to take the field on 22 October 2005 and beat Dunfermline 2–0 – despite the incredible events that morning – showed everyone that the team spirit and belief that would be required throughout the turbulent season were very much in place. However, it's understood that Vladimir Romanov did not take too kindly to messages of support for George Burley that were written on T-shirts displayed by Rudi Skácel at the end of the match and by Paul Hartley as he was substituted in the 90th minute, but Gary Mackay fully understands why the players reacted the way they did. 'Watching Paul and Rudi display their T-shirts at the end of the game takes me back to the day when Alex MacDonald was relieved of his duties at Tynecastle,' said Gary. 'John Robertson and I told the press of our bewilderment, and this resulted in a very public carpeting by Wallace Mercer in what is now the Executive Club at Tynecastle. Players react like this because we don't like change – we all want stability. These players wanted stability even more so as they were sitting at the top of the SPL, and I felt for them.

'It wouldn't have mattered who came in after George Burley – the training methods preferred by George were always going to be well nigh impossible for Graham Rix to replicate. Change was always going to disrupt things for the players, as no two coaches will ever have the same philosophy and get the same results and performances from their squad.

'I wish Vladimir Romanov hadn't sacked Burley, but we have to remember that the football club is bigger than one person. I spoke to Vladimir and Roman in the Gorgie Suite after the game against Dunfermline and told them that. They have reignited a fire in the stomach of a hugely passionate support. I know some supporters reacted very negatively when George left and Graham Rix arrived, but a look at the bigger picture will show a far brighter and more optimistic future than could ever have been imagined under the leadership of a former chief executive.

'Of course, there are times when I have felt aggrieved at certain decisions made by the present hierarchy at Tynecastle, but I am convinced that every decision taken by Vladimir

Romanov is in the best interests of the football club. I may be blinkered after he saved us from ruin, but in my eyes he can have as long as he wants, and do what he wants, to achieve his goal of bringing success to Hearts on a regular basis – anything is better than the uncertain future we faced only a few years ago.

'There may be ups and downs at Tynecastle, but one thing is guaranteed: supporting Heart of Midlothian Football Club is never boring or mundane. We are currently in a period of change designed to stabilise our club for many years to come. This will ensure that Steven Pressley, Paul Hartley, Craig Gordon and Robbie Neilson get to talk solely about football at press conferences and don't have to concern themselves with issues affecting the club off the pitch.

'These four players were part of a squad that performed to a level in 2005–06 that will be deservedly lauded for years to come. They coped with all the pressure and the continued press speculation to ultimately achieve success – and that is what football is all about. They made me and every other fan proud to support Heart of Midlothian Football Club.'

The 2005–06 season proved to be a successful one on the pitch, but there was similar good news off the field. A record number of 'Sold Out' signs were seen at Tynecastle as Hearts' average attendance for league matches reached 16,768 – the 17th-highest since the war and the best since season 1964–65. The boys in maroon are once again 'the talk o' the toon', although the media coverage has not always been positive. 'The press have certainly been kept busy since the arrival of Vladimir Romanov, but I feel some of the Glasgow-based newspapers have not given Hearts the credit we deserve,' said Hearts supporter Ian Dickson from Penicuik. 'I cannot rationalise why a press corps who have bemoaned the lack of competition for the Old Firm for years want to ridicule us at every opportunity. It has not been lost on me that the chief agitators – Andy Walker, Davie Provan, Murdo McLeod, Charlie Nicholas and Gerry McNee – all have Celtic at heart. Others have criticised but not to the venomous extent of this bunch. They can continue to provide negative copy and say disparaging things if they want, but if Hearts manage to obtain the kind of success that Mr Romanov is planning for, then I will gladly watch as they remove egg from their faces.'

Despite the regular negative comments from some journalists through in the West, there are others who have the best interests of Hearts in mind because they are supporters of the club. The 2005–06 season at Tynecastle ensured season-ticket holder Ewan Murray, Scottish football correspondent for *The Guardian*, did not get a moment's peace. 'I reckon I have probably filed just as much copy concerning Hearts in those 12 months as that concerning Rangers and Celtic combined, such has been the level of interest in events at Tynecastle,' he said. 'I speak to my newsdesk in London on a daily basis during the football season, and there is no doubt that Hearts' profile has increased dramatically since Vladimir Romanov got involved – every day during the course of that conversation they will ask me, without fail, what is happening at Hearts!

'Before coming to Scotland, I would suggest that not too many people in British business knew who Vladimir Romanov was. Now nearly everyone knows. Further examination by them would reveal his association with Ūkio Bankas. That route was not possible prior to his arrival at Tynecastle.

'There is now an appetite for Hearts south of the border. The SPL badly needed another club to challenge Rangers and Celtic – whether it was Hearts, Hibs or Aberdeen. That is why I think it was so important that Hearts managed to hold off Rangers to finish second and split the Old Firm. That really showed everyone they were able to compete properly for the whole season.

'The whole Hearts story is fascinating for people in England who only usually hear about the two big Glasgow teams. A lot of what Vladimir Romanov did was controversial and newsworthy, and the fashion in which a lot of things were done was pretty spectacular – some of his methods were certainly unorthodox, and that grabbed attention. But the club provided added intrigue to what was previously, and correctly, regarded as a stagnant competition.'

The decision by the SFA to bring 'shadow directors' under its jurisdiction means Vladimir Romanov will have to be slightly more careful what he says in future, particularly towards match officials and players at other clubs. Expressing a delight that one of his least favourite players – Neil Lennon, for example – picks up a booking will now find Romanov dragged before the beaks, as will opinions that refereeing incompetence cost Hearts the chance of winning matches. However, it is unlikely that this will cause Romanov to lose any sleep, according to Murray: 'I do not think anyone will ever succeed in trying to "muzzle" Vladimir Romanov. He loves the attention and loves being in the spotlight. His PR people in Scotland must have nightmares at times because of some of the things he says, but he is well aware what the SFA can do, and he is also well aware of what he can and cannot say.

'In saying that, perhaps he is keen to experience being in front of an SFA committee – I can just imagine him listening to lectures from people who run Highland League clubs. Romanov would almost certainly ridicule the association and, many would argue, with good reason.'

He may appear naive at times when making some of his more unusual comments, but Vladimir Romanov knows exactly what he is doing and what he is saying, according to Stuart Bathgate from *The Scotsman*: 'Romanov is a pretty astute guy. He can learn quite quickly – and he's not mad! He can be impetuous at times, and self-indulgent on occasions, but he is also exceedingly methodical: witness the huge dossier he has on more than 5,000 Brazilian players that was shown on the BBC documentary *Romanov: King of Hearts* in June 2006.

'He has come from an entirely different background, a harder and more dangerous background, than anyone associated with Scottish football. The era in Scotland of former miners being players and managers, guys who know the realities of life and who know what happens on the pitch, has gone. Jock Stein was the last, as far as I know. Everyone else in Scottish football has had fairly limited experiences of life compared to Romanov, and that has to help him as he plans for future success with Hearts.'

There are many ways to measure the increased interest in Hearts since the arrival of Vladimir Romanov, not least the pre-match press conference at Riccarton. Previously, the manager would speak to the assembled newspaper journalists before embarking on a series of interviews with the radio stations present and then doing one-to-one chats with the television reporters. These days, the press conference is simply split in two – newspapers and broadcasters (with all microphones having to be placed on the table) – due to the numbers of journalists that now attend.

'I genuinely don't think anyone could have anticipated what was about to happen at Tynecastle at the start of the 2005–06 season, but Hearts is now a brand and a name that is established and one people talk about,' said Andy Gillies from BBC Radio Five Live. 'If I go down south – whether to work or to visit relatives or friends – and talk about Hearts, they all know what is going on at Tynecastle because of all this national exposure. That would not have happened before. I cannot recall a season when we have covered a club outside the Old Firm in such depth and, indeed, in which a club outwith Rangers and Celtic has caught the imagination of the nation in the way Hearts have.

'There is a bit of a joke in the London offices that Roddy Forsyth and myself have a permanent seat at Tynecastle, because we always seem to be there. We probably covered just about every Hearts game in season 2005–06 – absolutely unheard of in the past.'

BBC Radio Five Live has an interest in Hearts for a few reasons, but mainly because a non-Old Firm team is making the top league more interesting again in Scotland. With Chelsea dominating the Premiership to such a great extent in England recently, the fact that Hearts are reversing that process north of the border is both a great irony and a great tale.

'I think the most interesting thing is it took the English media a bit of time to catch up with what was going on at Hearts,' said Gillies. 'I can remember at one point, early in the season when the unbeaten run was gathering momentum, somebody in the London office said to me they wished they had paid more attention when I told them Vladimir Romanov was taking over.

'From the moment George Burley was sacked, the whole Hearts thing just took off – it became a different animal, one that had to be monitored at all times. On many occasions, we sat with our mouths wide open at press conferences or stood outside the training ground almost in disbelief at what was going on. Those are the things that maintain the profile of the club and keep people interested.

'Sometimes it is very hard to sell a story to the network, simply because they are based in London and do not have much access to the Scottish press or sense of the impact that is being made. Now, every Hearts story grabs the attention – that was certainly not the case prior to Vladimir Romanov's arrival.'

Nearly 17,000 fans crammed into Tynecastle every second week but thousands more followed Hearts' progress from afar, mainly via the official Hearts website and the *Hearts World* online commentary service, ensuring that they were kept right up to date with events at their favourite football club. Even from his home in Perth, Australia, Barry Wood was able to feel an immense sense of pride at the end of one of the most remarkable seasons in the club's history. 'I feel the two things that stood out the most were the team effort and how the players stuck together in the face of constant adversity and upheaval,' he said. 'It is testament to the professionalism of the whole squad that they represented the club with pride and gave everything they had every week. It's easy now to look back and think "What if?", but I believe that Burley could have delivered the league title. However, we can look back on a very successful season for the club: Tynecastle sold out every week, enterprising play on the park, Champions League football secured for the first time and only our second trophy in 50 years.

'I am sure Heart of Midlothian would still exist without Vladimir Romanov, but I doubt very much if we would have been celebrating at the end of the 2005–06 season or would have had as much of the media spotlight!

'Vladimir Romanov is striving for success and is willing to do whatever it takes to get it. For too long Scottish football has lacked someone with character, and now he seems to be putting the cat amongst the pigeons and rubbing a few people up the wrong way. He might find himself in a spot of bother now and again, but if we continue to make progress on the park, there will be very few complaints from Hearts fans. Who knows what the future holds for us, but one thing is for sure: it will never be boring following the Jam Tarts – even from the other side of the world . . .'

Another supporter usually unable to get to many Hearts games – this time because of his workload – is Ken Stott. However, once the team got their league campaign off to a flying start at the end of July 2005, he did everything in his power to ensure Saturday was marked 'day off'. 'It was quite a good season for me, as I managed to get to around 12 matches at Tynecastle,' said Stott. 'It normally costs in the region of £75 a game for my season ticket in the John Robertson Lounge, as most of the time my work schedule doesn't permit weekend trips home! I'm not able to go to every match, but I wouldn't relinquish the season ticket for anything.

'It was an incredible season, unlikely ever to be replicated. Every day I'd reach for the paper with a mixture of foreboding and excitement – wondering "What's happened now?" It was tremendous when I was out and about in London: people would constantly ask me, "Isn't that the team you support?" and I would proudly say, "Yes!"

'Playing Rebus – a Hibs supporter – is a bit ironic really, but it's good fun. I've always been tempted to wear a Hearts top underneath my costume! I've had to wear a green-and-white Hibs badge for a couple of scenes, and it would be nice knowing I'm also wearing something maroon and white – I would just have to make sure I wasn't caught!

'It's impossible to predict what's going to happen next at Hearts – it's like trying to dream up a city like Venice without knowing it exists! Who would have thought our club would be taken over by a multimillionaire former Russian submariner? Who would have thought that John Robertson, Hearts' all-time top goalscorer and hero to thousands, would be sacked and replaced by George Burley, who wouldn't even last four months before he, too, was emptied despite winning nine games in a row? Who would have thought that Graham Rix, a really strange choice, would be employed then sacked after four months to be replaced by a Lithuanian coach who wasn't considered good enough for the job initially? All this while money is pumped into the club like never before, 20 players are signed – 11 in one month – and second spot is secured, as is the Scottish Cup for only the third time in 50 years. You just could not make it up – and that is only scratching the surface of the whole story! The past was appalling: we were looking forward to oblivion, so anything is better than that. We finished second and won the cup in Romanov's first full season in charge – that's not bad for starters!'

One of the many highlights of the season for supporters was the chance to witness the players parade the Scottish Cup through the streets of Edinburgh and then show off the silverware at Tynecastle. Radio Forth's Scott Wilson was, as usual, the man with the mic inside the stadium and said that day capped off a season he would never forget: 'It started with a pre-season tour with what seemed like a fraction of a team, a new manager and an owner who wasn't afraid of publicity. It ended with a place in the Champions League qualifiers, a Scottish Cup win and the chance to parade silverware around Tynecastle. In between times . . . well, you couldn't make it up!

'Highlights of 2005–06 for me include the opening home match against Hibs. I had waited years for us to use pyrotechnics at Tynecastle, and it was one of the best match introductions ever. You could just envisage the journos using headlines such as "Hearts Damp Squib", had the players not lived up to the hype, but boy how they did! A 4–0 thrashing of our greatest rivals . . . and it could have been more.

'I'm sure everyone will flag up the Scottish Cup semi-final win as their favourite match of the season, and it's hard to argue with that – Hearts were simply majestic that day. While I'm not a man to bear a grudge, it was extremely pleasurable to see thousands of empty seats in the Hibs end. They had argued vehemently for the game to be played in Glasgow when common sense would have dictated that it was played at Murrayfield. The journey home that day was great, despite "well-known" Hibee mates [Grant Stott] having their phones turned off!

'The "meet the players" night at Dalmahoy for sponsors was also thoroughly enjoyable – almost the entire squad showed up. They were all in fine form and happy to take the mick out of themselves and one another. I asked Rudi Skácel a question which he answered by saying, "How would I know? I'm just a refugee!" Takis's insistence on getting home to "practise for a Scottish baby" was also memorable, while Andy Webster's honesty when asked about his contract situation was commendable.

'The match against Aberdeen when we qualified for the Champions League was emotional stuff. I walked out of the tunnel, having privately spoken with the players, and was well prepared for what I wanted to say on the pitch, but the sight and sound of every fan singing "The Hearts Song" brought a lump to my throat and a tear to my eye. I have waited years to play the Champions League theme at Tynecastle, and that night an ambition was realised!'

To finish the season on such a high note by winning the Scottish Cup was simply the cherry on top of a special year. Keeper Craig Gordon was one of the heroes that day, saving Derek Townsley's spot-kick in the penalty shoot-out. It made a change for the Scotland international to go home from a cup final with a smile on his face, after he had experienced disappointment eight years previously. 'While Jim and Billy were busy in the dressing-room at Parkhead in 1998, giving the half-time team talk,' said John McGlynn, 'I was out on the pitch with the Under-16 squad for a penalty shoot-out against the Rangers youngsters. It was great to be involved in some way on such a huge day for the club, but we missed seeing Colin Cameron score the early penalty, as we were making our way into the stadium via a fire exit. The Under-16s lost 4–2 on penalties, and it's ironic that our goalkeeper that afternoon was none other than Craig Gordon – who'd have thought that eight years later he would be involved in another shoot-out at a Scottish Cup final?

'As a Hearts supporter, winning the cup with his team was a huge achievement for Craig – he's been able to live the dream. He has always talked about winning a medal with Hearts, so for him to achieve that at such a young age after coming all the way through our youth system is great. Goalkeepers don't normally peak until their late 20s or early 30s, so for him to have made such an impact already, both domestically and internationally, is fabulous.

'He's been associated with the club since he was 12, and I have had the pleasure of working with him for many years, but I have to admit it took a while for him to grow to the size he is now. When Craig was younger, there were concerns about his height, that maybe he wasn't going to make it, but we always had faith in him. I was first involved with Craig at Under-15 level, and there was no mistaking the talent he had as a goalkeeper. However, he could not kick the ball very far and was very frail. I was always concerned about the time it took for him to grow properly, but I felt his raw ability allowed him longer to fill out. I can remember telling him to do more work in the gym in a bid to get a reaction from his body and maybe that paid off.

'Thankfully, Craig eventually started to mature, his body developed a bit more and he started to shoot up. In my opinion, he has developed into the best goalkeeper in Britain and one of the best in Europe. I'm convinced he has a very successful future ahead of him. Hopefully, he will stay at Hearts for as long as possible.'

Craig Gordon's progress was undoubtedly one of the highlights of the season, something that was acknowledged when he was named as the Scottish Football Writers' Association Player of the Year. The young keeper's progress was also monitored from afar by his former mentor Gilles Rousset, who was as pleased as anyone to see his former 'boot boy' win the cup and emulate his achievements in 1998. 'When Craig joined the ground staff, I could see he had potential,' said the Frenchman. 'He was good technically, although he wasn't the strongest – he was very slim and very light. Thankfully, he developed into a big, strong lad and working with Antti Niemi, Roddy McKenzie and myself certainly helped improve his technique. I'm delighted he's now doing so well for Hearts and Scotland, as he is a very nice young man. I have to say that, because he did a great job looking after my kit and my boots when he was a youngster!'

Steven Pressley spent a few days after the final celebrating his first trophy win as captain of Hearts, but, like the true professional he is, it didn't take long before he was focusing on the next task. 'We had a fantastic season, but now the challenge is to sustain this success each year while continually improving,' said the skipper. 'The Old Firm, over the last ten or fifteen years, have dominated the Scottish game. It's up to us to show we can now compete with Celtic and Rangers and bring silverware back to Tynecastle on a regular basis. With Mr Romanov's investment, I believe we can mount a serious challenge to them while continuing to progress as a club.

'From a personal perspective, I can always do better, and I can always learn. In recent years, I have learned a lot about dealing with and manipulating situations, managing people and becoming a better captain. I think the most important thing is to be honest with people. I learned a great deal during the 2005–06 season. I am very proud to be captain of this particular squad. They are the best group of players I have been involved with, and it is an honour to be their skipper.

'I would love to be a manager one day, but I want to play football for as long as I can. I speak to Stephen Frail on a regular basis about coaching. He is an excellent coach, and I like to hear his thoughts, but he is always telling me to play as long as I can. If I am asked by the authors to contribute to another book in three or four years' time, I would hope to do so as Steven Pressley the player and Hearts captain, but, ultimately, I would love to get involved in coaching and subsequently management.'

It's claimed that replicating success can be even harder than achieving it in the first place. Finishing second in the SPL and winning the Scottish Cup did for starters, but Gilles Rousset is confident Vladimir Romanov has put the foundations in place to ensure his old club can go from strength to strength and finally realise their huge potential. 'When I was at Hearts, you could see there were many possibilities for the club,' he said. 'The fans were magnificent and turned out in numbers every week, and the fact that more than 250,000 supporters lined the streets of Edinburgh when we paraded the Scottish Cup told me how big the club could be if they were able to get success on a regular basis.

'You can say what you like about Vladimir Romanov, but it's worth remembering he saved Hearts from oblivion. It's very hard to buy success – many owners have tried but only Roman Abramovich has really been successful because he seems to have an endless amount of cash. Money helps you get success, but that has to be coupled with sensible management at board level. To be successful at a football club, you have to build brick by brick. You don't start to build a house with the roof, you start with the foundations.

'The training ground is now completed, and Hearts have good foundations in place from which to be successful. I know Mr Romanov wants things done quickly and has been frustrated with the time taken to obtain planning permission for the main stand, but sometimes it's not such a bad thing if you have time to do a job properly. That's what happened here at Lyon [where Rousset now works as the club's goalkeeping coach].

'When chairman Jean-Michel Aulas took over in 1987, the club was in the First Division, the league below the Premier Division. It was a sleeping giant with huge potential, a great history and a massive fan base but had suffered from mismanagement over the years. At first, there was not much money available for Mr Aulas to buy players, so he invested all his cash in a youth academy and drew up a ten-year plan. He knew it would be extremely difficult to achieve overnight success, but he was willing to wait a few years while the youngsters came through the ranks into the first team. During that time, he also brought back some old favourites, such as Raymond Domenech and Bernard Lacombe, who were very popular with the fans and were able to help with the youngsters.

'When the first crop of young players were ready, they were gradually introduced into the first team. They gained decent experience, and the best were then sold to raise money to buy more experienced players to help the next batch of kids coming through. It was a very simple method, but it was also very effective because Mr Aulas insisted on being given time to make changes. He has never stopped building for the future since taking over all those years ago. Undersoil heating for the training pitches has just been installed to make sure the squad can train outside all year round, if they wish. He is always trying to improve conditions for the players.

'There is no doubt that Mr Romanov has plenty of cash

available to spend on Hearts, and I'm convinced if it's spent wisely, coupled with a period of stability in the coaching/management department, then they, too, have a great chance of success on a regular basis. I'm already preparing for a Jambo invasion if Lyon are drawn against Hearts in the Champions League in years to come!'

To be able to compete in European football's premier competition, Hearts will need to get the better of at least one of the Old Firm every season. Not the easiest of tasks, but one that Stephane Adam thinks the Tynecastle outfit are certainly capable of: 'Hearts have a very good team, with a number of quality players, but if they want to be successful in the long term and challenge Rangers and Celtic, as well as being successful in Europe, they need to secure the signatures of two or three experienced players who have played at a high level and have experience of success in the Champions League, the UEFA Cup or internationally. Being able to sign guys like Takis Fyssas, a Euro 2004 winner, and Edgaras Jankauskas, a Champions League winner, was a big coup for the club, and I think that shows the extent of Vladimir Romanov's ambition.

'When I played for Metz in 1996, and we beat Olympique Lyonnais in the French League Cup final, Lyon were a reasonable team who attracted an average of 15,000 fans every week. They won silverware once in a while but usually played second fiddle to the likes of Marseille and Paris St-Germain. Things started to get better when they managed to get decent investment from the business community and things took off from there. They are now regular winners of the French top division and annual contenders in the Champions League. I see similarities between them and Hearts.

'A lot of people laughed when Vladimir Romanov said he wanted to win the Champions League with Hearts. Is there something wrong with showing ambition and aiming very high? Edinburgh is a big city, and Hearts have a massive support – just look how many people turned out to watch the teams of 1998 and 2006 parade the Scottish Cup through the streets of the capital. If the investment is right – not only in terms of finance but in terms of policy as well – and there is stability, then anything is possible.

'If Mr Romanov can successfully rebuild the main stand and continue financing the project, as well as giving Valdas Ivanauskas and Eduard Malofeev time to implement their thoughts on the team, then I see no reason why Hearts cannot emulate what Lyon have recently done in France and not only challenge the "big two" in their domestic league but also get success in Europe.'

Tynecastle has hosted some of European football's biggest names: Standard Liège and Benfica played European Cup ties in Gorgie in 1958 and 1960, respectively, while Inter Milan were the opposition in the Fairs Cup in 1961. The atmosphere at Tynecastle on a European night is second to none in Scotland – as Locomotive Leipzig, Bayern Munich and Slavia Prague will testify – and former club chairman George Foulkes is hopeful that it won't be long before Hearts can welcome Europe's crème de la crème back to their famous old ground: 'If we can get the capacity of Tynecastle up to 25,000 by redeveloping the main stand to include a decent corporate-hospitality section, while at the same time making it compliant with UEFA regulations, then I look forward to European football returning to our spiritual home. In the longer term, if the team continues to be successful, then it might be right for the club to think about moving to an all-purpose stadium to handle the support. But, in the short term, I think rebuilding the main stand is the right idea. I would not object to sharing a really good stadium with Hibs in the medium-to-long term, and I don't think Hearts supporters would mind either, as long as it provided the right venue for the team to play in and resulted in success on the park.

'I think Vladimir Romanov is genuine with regards to the resources he is putting into the club – he is determined to be successful. The club will continue when Romanov is no longer around. When that happens, I think there will be people willing to invest in Hearts, and we will not have the same problems trying to find investors as we had before Vladimir arrived in Scotland.'

George Foulkes never did give up his season-ticket seat in the Wheatfield Stand. A good decision in hindsight, following his departure from the boardroom, and he can now be found in section D, row 8, seat 15 every second weekend. 'I enjoyed my 18 months as chairman, even with all the turmoil, the browbeating from Robinson and all the difficulties,' he said. 'It was great being there, and I really got on well with all the staff and players and was getting to know them very well, Steven Pressley in particular. I also had great respect for the fans. I miss that, but I do not miss the turmoil of what was happening. There were literally nights when I didn't sleep because I was thinking through all the club's problems in my head and trying to come up with solutions.

'I must admit to mixed feelings: I'm glad to be away from the pressures, but I miss being involved in the boardroom. I arrived and had to try and help stop the move from Tynecastle to Murrayfield. When I left, there was the problem of dealing with Vladimir Romanov wanting to have total control. It was never dull!

'During my spell as chairman, I also got to meet some wonderful characters, including Sir Bobby Robson, who I met at the funeral of Johnny Haynes. He genuinely impressed me, and he seemed very keen to come to Hearts. Phil was in the process of talking to him, but, in the end, I don't think

Vladimir wanted Sir Bobby Robson because he is such a big name in media terms, and that appointment might have taken some of the spotlight off Romanov.

'There are not too many things that I regret during my time as chairman, with the exception of a couple of things I said. First, a comment I made: "I brought him [Vladimir Romanov] in, and I very much regret that now." I don't, in fact. That was a mistake to say that – I went over the top. The truth is, I helped bring him in. There was no alternative – I wish there had been, but there wasn't – and it's a pity it hasn't worked out as positively as I had hoped. Second, I regret questioning Romanov's credibility following the decision to get rid of George Burley.

'I can get quite emotional about Hearts. In a way, Vladimir is both a hero and a megalomaniac. He did save the club, but he was the only show in town and came in at a time when we were in difficulty. On the other hand, his management style is such that he does like to control everything. Now, I may have expressed my feelings rather too graphically in the past, and I certainly regret that, but I spoke to Vladimir at the Politician of the Year awards in November 2005 and we agreed not to make any more new comments about each other. I also saw Roman the day after the cup final at the City Chambers reception. I congratulated him, and he was very friendly towards me. I could, though, have gone on to say that they might have won the league as well, but I didn't. They must wonder, though – if they have any sense – what might have been, had they kept Burley . . .

'Romanov's investment, on the whole, has been good for Hearts. It's put the club on the map in the UK and beyond, and it's set us on a course that, although rocky, is the right one. There will still be problems – Chris Robinson is still lurking in the background – but I think we are set for an interesting and hopefully very successful future.'

The Romanov revolution began with a bang, courtesy of Vladimir's dramatic stage-managed entrance at the EGM to halt the sale of Tynecastle in January 2005, and there have been very few indications that life at Hearts will ever return to normal as long as he is associated with the club. Much of what he has brought to Gorgie has been positive – the signings of big-name players, such as Edgaras Jankauskas and Takis Fyssas, wouldn't have been possible without funding from Romanov – and the club's achievements in his first full season cannot, and will not, be forgotten. Unfortunately, there have been a few negatives as well, including his apparent insistence on interfering in team matters, which severely undermines the coaching staff and prevents much-needed stability. It's also pleasing to see 'Football Officialdom' being challenged for the first time since Fergus McCann dared to take on the establishment, although Vlad still has a fair way to go if his long-term plan of taking over the reins at the SFA is to come to fruition!

Romanov claims he'll be around for a while yet; he's set targets for both himself and the club, and is unlikely to depart until those have come to fruition. Far be it from me to suggest that a period of prolonged stability at Tynecastle would help him achieve his footballing aims and ambitions . . .

It's only just the beginning of what is shaping up to be a dramatic ride for everyone associated with Heart of Midlothian Football Club. Fasten your seatbelts and welcome aboard the Romanov roller-coaster – there's no turning back now.

EPILOGUE

ONE NIGHT IN ATHENS

HEARTS SUPPORTERS SPENT THE SUMMER MONTHS OF 2006 continuing to bask in the achievements of the season gone by, while looking forward to their first taste of Champions League football. The historic moment – the first-ever Champions League draw to include the name of Heart of Midlothian – arrived on 23 June: Hearts would begin their campaign in the second qualifying round of European football's premier competition against either Široki Brijeg from Bosnia or Belarussian side Shakhtyor Soligorsk.

Seven days after the draw in Nyon, Switzerland, Valdas Ivanauskas was confirmed as the 25th permanent boss in Hearts' history – exactly a year to the day after George Burley had been appointed. Speculation had linked former Rangers midfielder and Dynamo Kiev coach Alexei Mikhailichenko with a move to Tynecastle, and his representatives in Russia were adamant that a verbal agreement had been reached with their client; however, Ivanauskas was given the nod with John McGlynn chosen as his assistant. Both men would report directly to Eduard Malofeev, the club's new sporting director.

'Valdas is at the transitional stage between finishing his playing career and becoming an experienced coach,' said Vladimir Romanov. 'He's still got a lot to learn, but he's got the German school behind him – that sense of discipline and order. For example, you'll never see the players turning up late for training. If they're 30 seconds late, he slaps a fine on them. He's got a good basis and learns quickly.'

It was announced that Murrayfield Stadium would host Hearts' home European fixtures for 2006–07, and the venue was used for a pre-season friendly against Osasuna to give those players who had not experienced playing at the home of Scottish rugby a chance to test out the pitch and the facilities. Hearts beat the Spaniards 2–0, courtesy of goals from Ibrahim Tall and Andrius Velička – one of four Lithuanian trialists from FBK Kaunas who came on as substitutes. On the same night, Široki Brijeg beat Shakhtyor Soligorsk 1–0 in Bosnia to win the tie 2–0 on aggregate and set up a meeting with Hearts.

Murrayfield then played host to the first competitive action of the 2006–07 season on Wednesday, 26 July, three days before the start of the new SPL campaign, and history was made as Hearts played their inaugural match in the Champions League in front of 28,486 supporters. An own goal from Branimir Anić eight minutes into the second half sent the Jambos on their way, before Ibrahim Tall had the honour of becoming the first Hearts player to score in the competition as he doubled the home side's advantage from close range after 79 minutes. Roman Bednář capitalised on an error in the Bosnian defence six minutes from time to add a third and ensure that the trip to Široki Brijeg the following week was not going to be as dangerous as it might have been.

'To get our inaugural Champions League campaign off to such a flying start was fantastic for everyone associated with the football club,' said Gary Mackay. 'It was great to reward supporters with a decent result, and the fans should be applauded for their patience that night, as they refused to become frustrated, despite the goalless scoreline at half-time. I have never been a fan of using Murrayfield for football. The shape and sheer size of the stadium is not conducive to producing a good atmosphere or replicating the noise at Tynecastle on a European night, so to record a 3–0 victory – not conceding an away goal – was very satisfying.'

Planes, trains and automobiles were utilised as around 300 Hearts fans made their way to Bosnia – some direct from Edinburgh to Mostar on the official team charter and others via Croatia and other countries in Eastern Europe. The Hearts support inside the Pecara Stadium was boosted by the arrival of around 150 Bosnian workers from Vladimir Romanov's Birac aluminium plant in Zvornik in the north-east of the country – all of whom were given white T-shirts to wear with 'HEARTS' emblazoned on the front.

The hard work had been done in the first leg at Murrayfield, ensuring the match in Bosnia was virtually a formality. A goalless draw away from home secured the team's safe passage into the final qualifying round of the Champions League.

'The fact Hearts travelled to Bosnia with a 3–0 lead over Široki Brijeg ensured the atmosphere in the small Pecara Stadium was never going to be anywhere near as intimidating as that in the 25,000-capacity Bijeli Brijeg Stadium when we played Velež Mostar in 1988,' said Gary Mackay. 'It might have been interesting if Široki Brijeg had scored an early goal in the second leg, but Hearts always looked very comfortable in that environment, despite being nowhere near their best. The hard work had been done at Murrayfield, and it was the result, not the performance, that mattered that night.'

Once again, UEFA headquarters in Nyon, Switzerland, was

the venue for the draw that would decide which team stood between Hearts and a possible £6 million jackpot. AC Milan, Liverpool, Ajax and Arsenal were all possible opponents for Valdas Ivanauskas and his squad, but the Jambos were paired with AEK Athens. Hearts were potentially just 180 minutes away from securing a place in the lucrative group stage of the competition. They just had to do what no other Scottish team had done before in European competition: get the better of the team from the Greek capital . . .

The dream for all entrants in the 2006–07 Champions League was to play at the magnificent 75,000-capacity Olympic Stadium in Athens on 23 May 2007. Hearts made it to the venue that would host European football's showpiece game, but, unfortunately, they were nine months too early.

Playing against Europe's top teams with a full complement of players is hard enough, but to try and compete with AEK Athens with ten men at Murrayfield and nine men in Greece was akin to trying to reach the summit of the Acropolis, 156 metres above sea level, while wearing flip flops. 'Although it was wonderful to take part in the Champions League for the first time in our history, it's easy, with hindsight, to ponder what might have been without all the injuries and suspensions,' said Gary Mackay. 'There is nothing that could have been done regarding the injury situation, but I fear that ill-discipline cost us dearly in the tie. If Bruno Aguiar had already been warned about throwing the ball away, as the referee from the first leg at Murrayfield has suggested, then he should have known better. Who knows, we may have travelled to Greece with a one-goal advantage, instead of a one-goal deficit, if Bruno had heeded the warning from the match official.

'Julien Brellier's dismissal after just half an hour of the second leg, when Hearts were arguably on top in the match, was extremely frustrating – it resulted in Paul Hartley dropping deeper and our attacking threat from midfield was immediately lost. Any glimmer of hope that Hearts had was then extinguished in the second half when Neil McCann lunged at one of their midfielders and joined Julien in the dressing-room before the rest of their teammates.

'However, there are many positives we can take from the tie that augur well for the future, including Jamie Mole's performance in Athens on his European debut. If we had been at full strength in both legs against AEK, then I am convinced we would not have been far away from qualifying for the lucrative group stages of the Champions League. I am also sure both players and officials will have learned valuable lessons that will only be beneficial the next time we qualify.'

Disputes about refereeing decisions in both legs will rage on, but, ultimately, Hearts were not quite good enough for European football's premier competition in 2006. The opportunity to compete against some of Europe's big guns in Edinburgh and travel to other wonderful stadia across the Continent was denied. However, those fans who travelled to Athens and Bosnia have had a taste of life on the road in one of the world's premier sporting tournaments, and it has whetted the appetite.

Yes, defeat to AEK in the final qualifying round of the Champions League was hard to take, especially as the team was so close to securing a place in the group stage of the competition. However, things need to be put into perspective. Less than two years previously, Hearts – according to a former chief executive – were faced with the prospect of having to sell Tynecastle to raise finance to pay off the club's debt. A switch to Murrayfield was on the cards, despite many predicting the move to the home of Scottish rugby would, ultimately, sound the death knell for the club. But the arrival of Vladimir

Romanov has heralded the dawn of a new era for Heart of Midlothian Football Club.

Although slightly unorthodox at times (to say the least), Romanov promised to split the Old Firm and bring silverware back to Gorgie – he delivered both in his first full season as owner. More importantly, in the eyes of many fans, he ensured that the team would continue to play at Tynecastle. Some of his methods may be frowned upon, some may be laughed at and some may be applauded, but he's doing it his way and the alternative doesn't bear thinking about.

Romanov claimed in October 2005, shortly after taking complete control of Hearts, that within three years he wanted the club to be in a position in which 'to come back without the [Champions League] trophy would be shameful'. There were guffaws aplenty when the club's maverick owner came out with that remark, but perhaps he was simply dreaming with his eyes open. As successful American businessman and philanthropist Nido Qubein once said, 'When a goal matters enough to a person, that person will find a way to accomplish what at first seemed impossible.'

The defeat at the hands of AEK in the Olympic Stadium in Athens proved that Hearts still have a long way to go before being considered one of European football's powers, but with Vladimir Romanov at the helm at Tynecastle, it would be folly to write off any ambitious plans he has for the future, however crazy they initially appear to be. Who knows, perhaps the next time the Jambos are involved in the Champions League they'll be taking part in European football's showpiece game, not just a dress rehearsal . . .

Anything is possible, if you believe.

APPENDIX ONE

THE DIARY OF AN INCREDIBLE SEASON

JUNE 2005
30th – George Burley is appointed the new manager of Hearts.

JULY 2005
10th – Hearts draw 0–0 with St Pat's in George Burley's first match in charge.

18th – Hearts announce the appointment of Julija Gončaruk as a new non-executive director, and Chris Robinson resigns from his post on the Tynecastle board.

20th – Hearts draw 1–1 with Middlesbrough at Tynecastle with supporters admitted free of charge for this pre-season friendly.

22nd – Steven Pressley eventually signs his new two-year contract after appearing as a trialist in friendly matches against East Fife, Stirling Albion and Middlesbrough.

30th – Hearts kick off the new season with a 4–2 win at Kilmarnock.

AUGUST 2005

7th – Hearts beat Hibs 4–0 at Tynecastle in the first Edinburgh derby of the season.

11th – Midfielder Paul Hartley agrees a new three-year contract extension with Hearts.

20th – Hearts maintain their 100 per cent record and go three points clear at the top of the SPL with a 2–0 victory over Aberdeen at Tynecastle.

SEPTEMBER 2005

2nd – In an interview with Radio Forth, George Burley says he would quit the club if Vladimir Romanov ever tried to interfere with team selection.

9th – George Burley and Rudi Skácel are named Bank of Scotland SPL Manager and Player of the Month, respectively, after Hearts' unbeaten start to the season.

21st – Hearts suffer their first defeat of the season as a much-changed line-up loses 1–0 at Livingston in the third round of the CIS Cup. Teenage striker Jamie Mole is handed his debut, starting up front on his own at Almondvale.

24th – Hearts make it eight wins in a row after a 1–0 win over Rangers at Tynecastle.

OCTOBER 2005

2nd – Hearts drop their first SPL points of the season in a 2–2 draw at Falkirk – Craig Gordon is sent off.

3rd – George Burley and Andy Webster are named Bank of Scotland SPL Manager and Player of the Month, respectively, as Hearts maintain their unbeaten start to the league season.

15th – SPL leaders Hearts remain unbeaten following a 1–1 draw with Celtic at Parkhead in what turns out to be George Burley's last match in charge of the club.

20th – George Burley turns down the chance to sign former Germany international striker Fredi Bobič.

21st – Vladimir Romanov agrees to purchase the SMG and HBOS shareholdings to become Hearts' majority shareholder, increasing his stake in the club to 55.5 per cent.

22nd – George Burley is sensationally sacked due to 'irreconcilable differences' with Vladimir Romanov, despite guiding the team to an unbeaten start to the SPL season.

27th – Former Chelsea boss Claudio Ranieri flies to Edinburgh for talks about a possible move to Hearts. Discussions also take place with Sir Bobby Robson, who is in the capital for the funeral of former England captain Johnny Haynes.

29th – Hearts lose their first SPL match of the season, going down 2–0 to Edinburgh rivals Hibernian at Easter Road.

30th – Celtic take over as SPL leaders with a 4–2 victory over Dundee United at Tannadice.

31st – Chief executive Phil Anderton is sacked by Vladimir Romanov. Chairman George Foulkes resigns in protest. Vladimir's son Roman takes over as chairman and chief executive, the latter on a temporary basis.

NOVEMBER 2005

7th – Vladimir Romanov gets closer to securing the 75 per cent he needs to take Hearts into private ownership by agreeing to buy the stakes in the club held by Robert McGrail and former chairman Leslie Deans.

8th – Graham Rix is appointed as the new head coach of Hearts. Vladimir Romanov turns to Rix despite speculation linking the club with Sir Bobby Robson, Claudio Ranieri and Ottmar Hitzfeld.

25th – Former Rangers secretary Campbell Ogilvie joins Hearts as general secretary and operations director.

28th – Hearts announce a pre-tax loss of £2,728,000 in the year ended 31 July. Turnover for the year was up by £1.26 million thanks largely to the team having reached the group stages of the UEFA Cup. However, operating charges increased by a greater amount.

DECEMBER 2005

2nd – It is confirmed that Vladimir Romanov now owns 80.01 per cent of shares, giving him the ability to delist the company from the London Stock Exchange.

17th – Graham Rix is confident that he will be given time to transform the fortunes of the one-time SPL leaders, despite a 1–0 defeat at the hands of Rangers at Ibrox.

20th – The SFA delays making a decision on whether Graham Rix is a 'fit and proper person' to hold the position of head coach of Hearts. The General Purposes Committee adjourns the meeting 'pending the submission of further information by the club'.

26th – Hearts record their biggest win in almost five years with a 5–0 hammering of Falkirk at Tynecastle.

30th – Young striker Calum Elliot signs a new three-and-a-half-year deal, keeping him under contract at Tynecastle until the summer of 2008.

JANUARY 2006

1st – Hearts' title hopes suffer a major setback as they are beaten 3–2 by Celtic at Tynecastle, despite leading 2–0 at half-time.

4th – Calum Elliot is rewarded for his recent good form as he is named the Bank of Scotland Young Player of the Month for December.

7th – Hearts beat Kilmarnock 2–1 at Tynecastle in the third round of the Tennent's Scottish Cup.

17th – Former Hearts chairman Wallace Mercer dies from cancer at the age of 59.

21st – Winger Neil McCann suffers knee-ligament damage at Kilmarnock in his first game since rejoining Hearts.

28th – Hearts record their second victory of the season against Hibs with a comfortable 4–1 win at Tynecastle.

30th – A club spokesman confirms that Hearts have been offered the chance to sign Middlesbrough striker Jimmy Floyd Hasselbaink by an agent, but they have no interest in signing the player.

31st – Hearts set a new club record transfer fee by splashing out £850,000 for Bosnian winger Mirsad Bešlija, just one of seven acquisitions on deadline day. In total, 11 new players joined the club throughout the month.

FEBRUARY 2006

1st – Paul Hartley picks up an automatic one-match suspension from the SFA disciplinary committee for an off-the-ball kick at Celtic's Ross Wallace during the stormy clash at Tynecastle on New Year's Day. The offence was referred to the video review panel after being missed by match referee Iain Brines. In addition, the twelve disciplinary points Hartley collects for the red card means he goes through the eighteen-point threshold and earns a further two-game suspension.

4th – Hearts beat Aberdeen 3–0 at Tynecastle in the fourth round of the Tennent's Scottish Cup – Rudi Skácel and Takis Fyssas both missed the match, with 'flu symptoms' given as the official reason for their non-appearance.

7th – Graham Rix calls a morning meeting to inform his players that the team selection for that night's match at Dundee United is 'out of his hands' – six changes are being made to the starting line-up with Andy Webster relegated to the bench following a dispute over his future. Graham Rix refuses to comment publicly on press speculation that he had no input and did not pick the side for the midweek match.

8th – Vladimir Romanov agrees to a meeting requested by the Hearts players, following rumours that the Lithuanian selected the team for the 1–1 draw with Dundee United at Tannadice.

10th – Graham Rix says he 'fully expects to pick the team' for Saturday's SPL match against Aberdeen.

11th – Hearts and Graham Rix say they have resolved the row over claims that Vladimir Romanov meddled in team selection against Dundee United. A players' delegation, led by captain Steven Pressley, met the Lithuanian after the 2–1 home defeat by Aberdeen.

13th – Former Hibs boss Jim Duffy is appointed as the new director of football at Hearts.

15th – Hearts non-executive director – and president of the Lithuanian Football Association – Liutauras Varanavičius resigns from the Tynecastle board due to a conflict of interests after Lithuania are drawn in the same Euro 2008 qualifying group as Scotland.

25th – Hearts beat Partick 2–1 at Tynecastle to secure a place in the semi-finals of the Tennent's Scottish Cup.

27th – Hearts are drawn against Hibs in the last four of the Scottish Cup, and calls are immediately made to stage the match at Murrayfield.

MARCH 2006

6th – The SFA confirm that the Tennent's Scottish Cup semi-final between Hearts and Hibs will go ahead at Hampden Park, not at Murrayfield, on Sunday, 2 April.

17th – Hearts chairman Roman Romanov confirms that the position of head coach Graham Rix will be reviewed at the end of the season.

22nd – Graham Rix is sacked after just 18 games in charge,

while Jim Duffy also loses his job as director of football. Valdas Ivanauskas is appointed as head coach on an interim basis until the end of the season.

26th – Scotland international Craig Gordon signs a contract extension with Hearts, keeping him with the club until the summer of 2009.

APRIL 2006

2nd – Hearts reach the final of the Scottish Cup after beating Edinburgh rivals Hibernian 4–0 at Hampden. Midfielder Paul Hartley scores a hat-trick at the national stadium.

4th – Hearts confirm that former Scotland coach Berti Vogts has applied to be the next manager of the club.

6th – Celtic beat Hearts 1–0 at Parkhead to secure the SPL title.

16th – Craig Gordon is named as the Scottish Football Writers' Association Player of the Year.

22nd – Hearts – minus Skácel, Jankauskas, Brellier and Webster – are beaten 2–0 by Hibs at Easter Road.

25th – Steven Pressley urges the Hearts hierarchy not to allow 'football politics' to wreck the club's hopes of clinching the remaining Champions League spot. The team captain speaks out after several players are 'rested' for the Edinburgh derby. Hearts' lead over Rangers is reduced to four points, following defeat at Easter Road.

26th – Vladimir Romanov says the club has no option but to put defender Andy Webster on the transfer list. Hearts' majority shareholder says the player's agent has been trying to engineer a move away from Tynecastle for the defender.

MAY 2006

1st – Physio Oliver Finlay is suspended indefinitely by Hearts for allegedly questioning the interventions of Lithuanian therapists at the club's Riccarton training base.

3rd – Hearts clinch second place in the SPL and a spot in the Champions League qualifiers with a 1–0 victory over Aberdeen at Tynecastle. It's the first time the club has qualified for the European Cup since October 1960 and the first time since 1994–95 that the Old Firm have failed to finish in the top two places in the Premier League.

4th – Paul Hartley is named as the Bank of Scotland Player of the Month for April.

13th – Hearts win the Scottish Cup for the seventh time in their history, following a nail-biting penalty shoot-out victory over Second Division champions Gretna at Hampden.

17th – Paul Hartley is named as the Bank of Scotland Player of the Season.

JUNE 2006

21st – Calum Elliot signs a new five-year deal that will keep him at Tynecastle until 2011.

23rd – The first-ever UEFA Champions League draw featuring Heart of Midlothian takes place in Nyon, Switzerland. Hearts will face either Belarussian side Shakhtyor Soligorsk or Široki Brijeg from Bosnia and Herzegovina in the second qualifying round.

30th – Valdas Ivanauskas is confirmed as the 25th head coach/manager of Hearts, exactly a year to the day after George Burley took charge, while Eduard Malofeev is confirmed as the club's new sporting director.

JULY 2006

19th – Hearts will face Bosnian opposition in their inaugural Champions League tie. Široki Brijeg beat FC Shakhtyor Soligorsk 1–0 to clinch their first-qualifying-round tie 2–0 on aggregate. Meanwhile, the Jambos beat Osasuna 2–0 at Murrayfield in a Champions League warm-up match.

25th – Christophe Berra and Jamie Mole both sign new five-year deals with Hearts.

26th – Hearts beat Široki Brijeg 3–0 at Murrayfield in their first-ever match in the Champions League. Ibrahim Tall becomes the first Hearts player to score for the club in the competition.

28th – Greek side AEK Athens will provide the opposition for either Hearts or Široki Brijeg following the draw for the third qualifying round of the Champions League.

29th – Czech international midfielder Rudi Skácel leaves Hearts and joins his former boss George Burley at Southampton in a deal worth £1.6 million to the Gorgie club.

AUGUST 2006

1st – Lee Wallace is the latest Hearts youngster to put pen to paper on a five-year deal at Tynecastle.

2nd – A 0–0 draw against Široki Brijeg in Bosnia and Herzegovina secures Hearts' progression to the third qualifying round of the Champions League.

9th – Two late goals from AEK Athens at Murrayfield deny Hearts a famous European victory as the Jambos lose the first leg 2–1. Bruno Aguiar is shown the red card midway through the second half.

23rd – Hearts' inaugural Champions League campaign comes to an end at the hands of AEK Athens. Julien Brellier and Neil McCann are sent off as the Jambos lose 3–0 in the Greek capital, going out 5–1 on aggregate.

TENNENT'S SCOTTISH CUP 2005–06: THE COMPLETE RECORD

FIRST ROUND
Saturday, 19 November 2005
  Partick Thistle 1, Albion Rovers 1
  Preston Athletic 2, Gretna 6
Saturday, 26 November 2005
  Stirling Albion 2, Elgin City 1
  Cowdenbeath 0, Greenock Morton 3
  Spartans 1, Berwick Rangers 0
  Dumbarton 4, Forres Mechanics 1
Monday, 28 November 2005
  Alloa Athletic 9, Selkirk 0
  Stenhousemuir 3, East Stirlingshire 2

FIRST-ROUND REPLAY
Tuesday, 22 November 2005
  Albion Rovers 1, Partick Thistle 3

SECOND ROUND

Saturday, 10 December 2005

Gretna 6, Cove Rangers 1

Arbroath 1, Dumbarton 0

Ayr United 3, Greenock Morton 2

Queen's Park 2, Raith Rovers 0

Lossiemouth 0, Spartans 5

East Fife 0, Peterhead 3

Threave Rovers 0, Forfar Athletic 4

Stenhousemuir 1, Partick Thistle 4

Stirling Albion 1, Inverurie Loco Works 0

Alloa Athletic 1, Montrose 0

THIRD ROUND

Saturday, 7 January 2006

Alloa Athletic 1, Livingston 1

Spartans 3, Queen's Park 2

Queen of the South 1, Hamilton Academical 1

Heart of Midlothian 2, Kilmarnock 1

Dundee United 2, Aberdeen 3

Ross County 5, Forfar Athletic 0

Falkirk 2, Brechin City 1

Inverness Caledonian Thistle 1, Ayr United 1

St Mirren 3, Motherwell 0

Hibernian 6, Arbroath 0

Rangers 5, Peterhead 0

St Johnstone 0, Gretna 1

Stirling Albion 0, Partick Thistle 1

Dunfermline Athletic 3, Airdrie United 4

Sunday, 8 January 2006

Clyde 2, Celtic 1

Dundee 2, Stranraer 0

THIRD-ROUND REPLAYS

Wednesday, 11 January 2006
  Livingston 1, Alloa Athletic 2
Monday, 16 January 2006
  Ayr United 0, Inverness Caledonian Thistle 2
Tuesday, 17 January 2006
  Hamilton Academical 1, Queen of the South 0 (aet)

FOURTH ROUND

Saturday, 4 February 2006
  Inverness Caledonian Thistle 2, Partick Thistle 2
  Hamilton Academical 0, Alloa Athletic 0
  Heart of Midlothian 3, Aberdeen 0
  Airdrie United 1, Dundee 1
  Falkirk 1, Ross County 1
  Rangers 0, Hibernian 3
  Clyde 0, Gretna 0
Sunday, 5 February 2006
  Spartans 0, St Mirren 0

FOURTH-ROUND REPLAYS

Tuesday, 7 February 2006
  Alloa Athletic 0, Hamilton Academical 3
Tuesday, 14 February 2006
  Dundee 2, Airdrie United 0
  Gretna 4, Clyde 0
  Ross County 0, Falkirk 1
  St Mirren 3, Spartans 0
Wednesday, 15 February 2006
  Partick Thistle 1, Inverness Caledonian Thistle 1 (aet; Partick
  Thistle won 4–2 on penalty kicks)

FIFTH ROUND
Saturday, 25 February 2006
  Gretna 1, St Mirren 0
  Hamilton Academical 0, Dundee 0
  Falkirk 1, Hibernian 5
  Heart of Midlothian 2, Partick Thistle 1

FIFTH-ROUND REPLAY
Thursday, 9 March 2006
  Dundee 3, Hamilton Academical 2 (aet)

SEMI-FINALS
Saturday, 1 April 2006
  Gretna 3, Dundee 0
Sunday, 2 April 2006
  Hibernian 0, Heart of Midlothian 4

FINAL
Saturday, 13 May 2006
  Heart of Midlothian 1, Gretna 1 (aet; Heart of Midlothian won 4–2 on penalty kicks)

APPENDIX THREE

HEARTS STATS 2005–06
Courtesy of www.londonhearts.com

FINAL SPL TABLE

	P	HW	HD	HL	HGF	HGA	AW	AD	AL	AGF	AGA	Points	GD
Celtic	38	14	4	1	41	15	14	3	2	52	22	91	+56
Hearts	38	15	2	2	43	9	7	6	6	28	22	74	+40
Rangers	38	13	4	2	38	11	8	6	5	29	26	73	+30
Hibernian	38	11	1	7	39	24	6	4	9	22	32	56	+5
Kilmarnock	38	11	3	5	39	29	4	7	8	24	35	55	-1
Aberdeen	38	8	9	3	30	17	5	6	7	16	23	54	+6
Inverness Caledonian Thistle	38	5	6	7	21	21	10	7	3	30	7	58	+13
Motherwell	38	7	5	7	35	31	6	5	8	20	30	49	-6
Dundee United	38	5	8	6	22	28	2	4	13	19	38	33	-25
Falkirk	38	2	6	11	14	30	6	3	10	21	34	33	-29
Dunfermline Athletic	38	3	5	11	17	39	5	4	10	16	29	33	-35
Livingston	38	3	4	12	15	33	1	2	16	10	46	18	-54

PLAYERS MAKING THEIR COMPETITIVE DEBUTS FOR HEARTS

Player	Date	Comp	Venue	Team	Score
Roman Bednář	30 Jul 2005	SPL	A	Kilmarnock	4–2
Edgaras Jankauskas	30 Jul 2005	SPL	A	Kilmarnock	4–2
Rudi Skácel	30 Jul 2005	SPL	A	Kilmarnock	4–2
Julien Brellier	07 Aug 2005	SPL	H	Hibernian	4–0
Takis Fyssas	14 Aug 2005	SPL	A	Dundee United	3–0
Michal Pospíšil	14 Aug 2005	SPL	A	Dundee United	3–0
Samuel Camazzola	17 Sep 2005	SPL	A	Inverness Caledonian Thistle	1–0
Jamie Mole	21 Sep 2005	LC	A	Livingston	0–1
Steve Banks	02 Oct 2005	SPL	A	Falkirk	2–2
Nerijus Barasa	14 Jan 2006	SPL	A	Dunfermline Athletic	4–1
Lee Johnson	14 Jan 2006	SPL	A	Dunfermline Athletic	4–1
Mirsad Bešlija	04 Feb 2006	SC	H	Aberdeen	3–0
José Gonçalves	04 Feb 2006	SC	H	Aberdeen	3–0
Juho Mäkelä	04 Feb 2006	SC	H	Aberdeen	3–0
Martin Petráš	07 Feb 2006	SPL	A	Dundee United	1–1
Luděk Stracený	07 Feb 2006	SPL	A	Dundee United	1–1
Bruno Aguiar	11 Feb 2006	SPL	H	Aberdeen	1–2
Chris Hackett	05 Mar 2006	SPL	A	Livingston	3–2
Ibrahim Tall	15 Apr 2006	SPL	H	Kilmarnock	2–0

FIRST-TEAM APPEARANCES

Player	Rank	SPL					Scottish Cup					League Cup					Total				
		G	St	Sb	Ud	Off	G	St	Sb	Ud	Off	G	St	Sb	Ud	Off	G	St	Sb	Ud	Off
Craig Gordon	1=	36	36	1			5	5				2	2				43	43	1		0
Robbie Neilson	1=	37	36	2	1	1	5	5				1	1				43	42	2	1	1
Paul Hartley	3=	34	34			4	4	4				2	1	1			40	39	1		4
Rudi Skácel	3=	35	33	2	2	8	4	4			1	1		1	1		40	37	3	3	9
Andy Webster	5=	30	30	2			4	4				2	2				36	36	2		0
Takis Fyssas	5=	32	32			3	4	3	1	1							36	35	1	1	3
Steven Pressley	7	29	29			1	5	5				1	1			1	35	35		0	2
Julien Brellier	8=	30	28	4	2	11	4	3	1	1	1						34	31	5	3	12
Calum Elliot	8=	28	17	15	11	6	4	4			4	2		2	2		34	21	17	13	10
Deividas Česnauskis	10	25	15	20	10	8	4	4			2	2	2			1	31	21	20	10	11
Edgaras Jankauskas	11	25	24	1	1	12	4	4			1	1	1			1	30	29	1	1	14
Saulius Mikoliūnas	12=	23	16	14	7	12	4	1	3	3	1	1		2	1		28	17	19	11	13
Michal Pospíšil	12=	23	13	13	10	10	4	1	3	3		1	1			1	28	15	16	13	11
Roman Bednář	14	23	19	4	4	9	2	1	1	1	1						25	20	5	5	10
Jamie McAllister	15	16	8	17	7	3	2	1	2	2		2	1				20	10	19	9	3
Christophe Berra	16=	12	10	21	2		2		4	2		2	1	1	1	1	16	11	26	5	5
Lee Wallace	16=	13	2	27	11		1		1	1		2	2				16	4	28	12	
Stephen Simmons	18	11	1	19	10	1						2	2				13	3	19	10	1

Player	Rank	SPL					Scottish Cup					League Cup					Total				
		G	St	Sb	Ud	Off	G	St	Sb	Ud	Off	G	St	Sb	Ud	Off	G	St	Sb	Ud	Off
Bruno Aguiar	19	10	10	4		2	2	2	1		1						12	12	5	0	3
Samuel Camazzola	20	8	5	10	3	3			1			1	1			1	9	6	11	3	4
Mirsad Bešlija	21=	5	2	3	3	1	1	1			1						6	3	3	3	2
Neil MacFarlane	21=	5	1	6	4				1			1	1			1	6	2	7	4	1
José Gonçalves	23=	3	3	2		1	2	2			1						5	5	2	0	2
Ibrahim Tall	23=	4	3	13	1	1	1	1									5	4	13	1	1
Martin Petráš	23=	5	4	6	1	2											5	4	6	1	2
Lee Johnson	23=	4	1	7	3	1	1	1									5	2	7	3	1
Nerijus Barasa	27	4	1	4	3	3											4	1	4	3	3
Steve Banks	28=	3	2	31	1	1			5					2			3	2	38	1	1
Luděk Stracený	28=	3	1	1	1	2											3	1	1	1	2
Juho Mäkelä	28=	2	2	2	2	2	1	1	1	1	1						3	3	3	3	3
Chris Hackett	31	2	1	1	1	1											2	1	1	1	1
Gary Tierney	32=			2	2							1	1				1	1	2	2	0
Jamie Mole	32=			1	1							1	1			1	1	1	1	1	1
Neil McCann	32=	1	1			1											1	1		0	1
H. Thórarinsson	32=	1	1	2	1	1											1	1	2	1	1

FIRST-TEAM GOALSCORERS

Player	Rank	League			Scot Cup			CIS Cup			Total		
		H	A	Tot	H	A	Tot	H	A	Tot	H	A	Tot
Rudi Skácel	1=	9	7	16		1	1				9	8	17
Paul Hartley	1=	8	6	14		3	3				8	9	17
Edgaras Jankauskas	3	6	2	8	1	1	2		2	2	7	5	12
Michal Pospíšil	4	5	2	7	1		1				6	2	8
Roman Bednář	5=	3	4	7							3	4	7
Steven Pressley	5=	1	4	5	2		2				3	4	7
Calum Elliot	7	5		5	1		1				6		6
Saulius Mikoliūnas	8	2	1	3							2	1	3
Stephen Simmons	9=	1		1							1		1
Andy Webster	9=		1	1								1	1
Bruno Aguiar	9=		1	1								1	1
Christophe Berra	9=	1		1							1		1
Juho Mäkelä	9=	1		1							1		1
Deividas Česnauskis	9=				1		1				1		1
Jamie McAllister	9=				1		1				1		1

264

PLAYERS SCORING THEIR FIRST COMPETITIVE GOAL FOR HEARTS

Player	Game No	Date	Comp	Venue	Team	Score
Roman Bednář	1	30 Jul 2005	SPL	A	Kilmarnock	4–2
Rudi Skácel	1	30 Jul 2005	SPL	A	Kilmarnock	4–2
Michal Pospíšil	2	20 Aug 2005	SPL	H	Aberdeen	2–0
Edgaras Jankauskas	4	23 Aug 2005	LC	A	Queens Park	2–0
Calum Elliot	19	26 Dec 2005	SPL	H	Falkirk	5–0
Bruno Aguiar	3	05 Mar 2006	SPL	A	Livingston	3–2
Juho Mäkelä	2	08 Apr 2006	SPL	H	Dunfermline Athletic	4–0
Christophe Berra	33	15 Apr 2006	SPL	H	Kilmarnock	2–0

THE SEASON IN FULL

Date	Comp	Venue	Team	Score	Att	Scorers
30 Jul 2005	SPL	A	Kilmarnock	4–2	7,487	Skácel 13; Bednář 46; Mikoliūnas 61; Hartley (pen) 89
						Naismith 12; Greer 74
07 Aug 2005	SPL	H	Hibernian	4–0	16,459	Skácel 13; Hartley (pen) 58; Simmons 71; Mikoliūnas 83
14 Aug 2005	SPL	A	Dundee United	3–0	11,654	Pressley 6; Bednář 12; Skácel 91

265

Date	Comp	H/A	Opponent	Score	Attendance	Scorers
20 Aug 2005	SPL	H	Aberdeen	2–0	16,139	Skácel 20; Pospíšil 85
23 Aug 2005	LC (2)	A	Queen's Park	2–0	2,429	Jankauskas 15; Jankauskas 44
27 Aug 2005	SPL	H	Motherwell	2–1	16,213	Skácel 40; Jankauskas 70 Foran (pen) 76
11 Sep 2005	SPL	A	Livingston	4–1	8,405	Skácel 11; Webster 27; Hartley 34; Hartley (pen) 63 Dalglish 44
17 Sep 2005	SPL	A	Inverness CT	1–0	6,704	Skácel 28
21 Sep 2005	LC (3)	A	Livingston	0–1	3,805	Pereira 54
24 Sep 2005	SPL	H	Rangers	1–0	17,379	Bednář 14
02 Oct 2005	SPL	A	Falkirk	2–2	6,342	Pressley 75; Pressley 91 Duffy (pen) 27; Pressley (og) 68
15 Oct 2005	SPL	A	Celtic	1–1	60,100	Skácel 16 Beattie 13
22 Oct 2005	SPL	H	Dunfermline Athletic	2–0	16,574	Skácel 21; Pospíšil 24
26 Oct 2005	SPL	H	Kilmarnock	1–0	16,536	Jankauskas 34
29 Oct 2005	SPL	A	Hibernian	0–2	17,180	Beuzelin 78; O'Connor 81
05 Nov 2005	SPL	H	Dundee United	3–0	16,617	Hartley 4; Skácel 28; Pospíšil 57
20 Nov 2005	SPL	A	Aberdeen	1–1	14,901	Skácel 64 Smith 13
26 Nov 2005	SPL	A	Motherwell	1–1	8,131	Hartley (pen) 90 McLean 41

Date	Comp	H/A	Opposition	Score	Attendance	Scorers
03 Dec 2005	SPL	H	Livingston	2–1	16,583	Skácel 8; Skácel 15 / Walker 63
10 Dec 2005	SPL	H	Inverness CT	0–0	16,373	
17 Dec 2005	SPL	A	Rangers	0–1	49,723	Lovenkrands 35
26 Dec 2005	SPL	H	Falkirk	5–0	16,538	Hartley 20; Skácel 25; Elliot 41; Pospíšil 73; Elliot 92
01 Jan 2006	SPL	H	Celtic	2–3	17,358	Jankauskas 6; Pressley 8 / Pearson 55; McManus 87; McManus 91
07 Jan 2006	SC (3)	H	Kilmarnock	2–1	12,831	Pressley 24; McAllister 75 / Nish 86
14 Jan 2006	SPL	A	Dunfermline Athletic	4–1	8,277	Pressley 28; Pospíšil 54; Pospíšil 67; Skácel 81 / Burchill 58
21 Jan 2006	SPL	A	Kilmarnock	0–1	8,811	Invincible 46
28 Jan 2006	SPL	H	Hibernian	4–1	17,371	Hartley 27; Skácel 41; Hartley (pen) 44; Elliot 50 / O'Connor 58
04 Feb 2006	SC (4)	H	Aberdeen	3–0	17,353	Pospíšil 21; Elliot 34; Pressley (pen) 45
07 Feb 2006	SPL	A	Dundee United	1–1	10,584	Hartley (pen) 83 / Brebner 34
11 Feb 2006	SPL	H	Aberdeen	1–2	16,895	Elliot 9 / Pressley (og) 69; Clark 87
18 Feb 2006	SPL	H	Motherwell	3–0	16,976	Jankauskas 4; Jankauskas 14; Elliot 78
25 Feb 2006	SC (qf)	H	Partick Thistle	2–1	16,365	Jankauskas 6; Česnauskis 63 / Roberts 75

Date	Comp	Venue	Opponent	Score	Attendance	Scorers
05 Mar 2006	SPL	A	Livingston	3–2	5,058	Aguiar 17; Jankauskas 72; Bednář 87 / Brittain 59; Mackay 77
11 Mar 2006	SPL	A	Inverness Caledonian Thistle	0–0	5,027	
19 Mar 2006	SPL	H	Rangers	1–1	17,040	Jankauskas 10 / Buffel 65
25 Mar 2006	SPL	A	Falkirk	2–1	5,966	Hartley 22; Jankauskas 81 / Gow 45
02 Apr 2006	SC (sf)	N	Hibernian	4–0	43,180	Hartley 28; Hartley 59; Jankauskas 81; Hartley (pen) 88
05 Apr 2006	SPL	A	Celtic	0–1	59,699	Hartson 4
08 Apr 2006	SPL	H	Dunfermline Athletic	4–0	16,973	Pospíšil 7; Bednář 14; Mikoliūnas 25; Mäkelä 83
15 Apr 2006	SPL	H	Kilmarnock	2–0	16,497	Hartley 70; Berra 87
22 Apr 2006	SPL	A	Hibernian	1–2	16,654	Bednář 45 / Riordan 14; Benjelloun 78
30 Apr 2006	SPL	H	Celtic	3–0	16,795	McManus (og) 7; Hartley 9; Bednář 63
03 May 2006	SPL	H	Aberdeen	1–0	17,327	Hartley (pen) 52
07 May 2006	SPL	A	Rangers	0–2	49,792	Boyd 36; Boyd 74
13 May 2006	SC (f)	N	Gretna	1–1	51,232	Skácel 39 (Hearts win 4–2 on penalties) / McGuffie 76

YELLOW AND RED CARDS

Player	Sent-Off	Booked
Julien Brellier	1	14
Paul Hartley*	1	7
Steven Pressley	1	7
Edgaras Jankauskas	1	5
Takis Fyssas	1	5
Roman Bednář	1	4
Saulius Mikoliūnas	1	1
Craig Gordon	1	1
Rudi Skácel		11
Calum Elliot		7
Robbie Neilson		4
Bruno Aguiar		3
Deividas Česnauskis		3
Luděk Stracený		2
Nerijus Barasa		2
Martin Petráš		2
Samuel Camazzola		2
Michal Pospíšil		2
Juho Mäkelä		1
José Gonçalves		1

*Hartley also given a retrospective red card for violent conduct versus Celtic on 1 January.

REFEREES

Referee	Games	W	D	L	Hearts		Opponents	
					Sent-Off	Booked	Sent-Off	Booked
Stuart Dougal	6	5	0	1	0	10	4	13
Alan Freeland	5	5	0	0	0	10	0	19
Craig Thomson	5	3	2	0	1	7	0	12
Douglas McDonald	5	2	2	1	2	13	1	14
Charlie Richmond	4	3	0	1	0	6	1	10
Mike McCurry	4	3	0	1	1	5	1	6
Iain Brines	4	0	2	2	2	14	0	11
Kenny Clark	2	2	0	0	0	3	1	2
Eddie Smith	2	2	0	0	0	0	0	4
John Underhill	2	1	0	1	1	5	0	0
Calum Murray	2	1	1	0	1	1	0	4
Kevin Toner	1	0	1	0	0	2	0	1
Craig MacKay	1	1	0	0	0	2	0	1
Steve Conroy	1	0	0	1	0	4	0	2
Ian Fyfe	1	0	0	1	0	2	0	3